ELEGIAC PAEAN

PRADEEP BERRY

Elegiac Paean by Pradeep Berry

This book is written to provide information and motivation to readers. Its purpose is not to render any type of psychological, legal, or professional advice of any kind. The content is the sole opinion and expression of the author, and not necessarily that of the publisher.

Copyright © 2021 by Pradeep Berry

All rights reserved. No part of this book may be reproduced, transmitted, or distributed in any form by any means, including, but not limited to, recording, photocopying, or taking screenshots of parts of the book, without prior written permission from the author or the publisher. Brief quotations for noncommercial purposes, such as book reviews, permitted by Fair Use of the U.S. Copyright Law, are allowed without written permissions, as long as such quotations do not cause damage to the book's commercial value.

ISBN: 978-1-951670-46-7 (Paperback)
ISBN: 978-1-951670-47-4 (Digital)

Printed in the United States of America.

Contents

Author's Note vii
Preface xi
An Introduction to Connie: My Connie, My Light 1
True Love and Great Destiny 3
Our True and Pure Love But Love 6
My Heartfelt Tributes to Connie 7
Knowledge Theory vs. Pragmatism 13
The Medical Negligence 18
Life and Death Episode Message 23
The Story of Sati Savitri 41
A True Story About Faith and Greed 42
My Loss and Pain for Connie 44
Another Painful Chapter for Connie and Pradeep 47
Remarkable Quotes for a Remarkable Woman 52
More Quotes by Chanakya 54
My Uncle's Advice 72
Beginning of Our Love 74
Connie was My Destiny 85
Some Nice Quotes for Our Daily Life 87
Gandhi Ji—His Messages and His Teachings 89
Nelson Mandela 90
Swami Vivekananda 91
Education and Career of Connie 93
My Connie: The Blessed Lady 98
Connie's Passion for Reading 100

Reading Passion and Her Polymath	102
Connie's Love for Music and Arts	105
Her Exposure to World Travel	107
Connie—Her Charm and Beauty	111
Connie's Character and Thinking	113
The Wanting to Feel Connie's Presence	115
Making Good Use of Time	117
Yearning for Connie's in One Form or Another	121
Connie is Still With Me	125
Her Home was Her Life	130
Cleanliness and Housekeeping were in Her Blood	132
Her Love for the Best Cuisines	136
Great Deeds and Ethical Values of Connie	138
Our Love Destiny Would Continue—But With Unhappiness	142
Connie and Her Devotion to My Professional Help in Many Places	144
Sympathy and Empathy—But Pain	149
Cruises—Part of Her World Travel	151
Connie's Character	154
The Truth Always Wins	157
Realization and Enlightenment of Pain After Connie's Demise	164
Grief-stricken Reactions	169
Seeing Connie Everywhere	174
My Emotions and India	178
My Present Life—Pain After Connie	181
Connie's Efficiency in Everything	186
Connie was My Destiny—Like a True Episode on the TV Program-Wanted	188

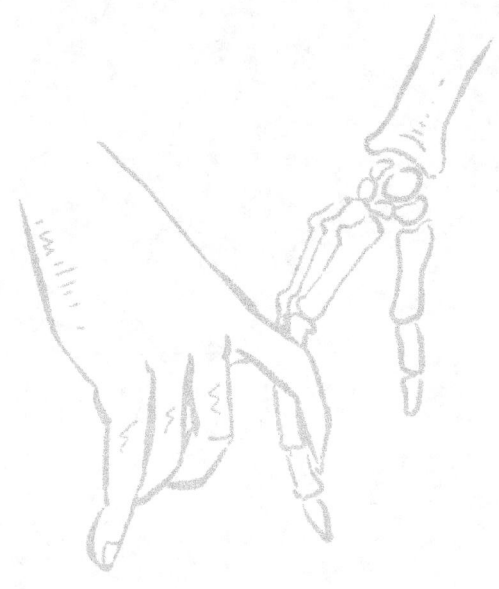

Never seek happiness outside yourself.
Life isn't about what happens to us; it's about we perceive what happens to us.
Master your past in the present or the past will master your future.

— *Life: A Book of Eastern Wisdom*

Author's Note

Writing has always been one of the exceptional skills that I have needed from the sixth grade to the present day. As time progresses, high school, undergraduate, postgraduate, and, importantly, in my professional career, writing is indispensable. In addition, as I advanced my career, I developed a greater interest in writing and discovered that reading was the thing I enjoyed most. I must mention that my beautiful, educated, precious, priceless, and most loving wife of over 41 years, Constance A. Berry, "CONNIE," always encouraged me to read and write in subjects other than my professional reports, newspapers, and research on different aspects of my career. I recall many incidents when Connie took me to different parts of the world, and interacting with people from different cultures was one of the most positive things for us. Many people asked me to write books, and I considered doing so but did not act on those thoughts. Finally, Connie told me, "Pradeep, I wish you were a professor and a writer." Those words are still in my brain, in my heart, and close to Connie. I could never have imagined that my first book would be for my wife- After thinking and thinking of many titles, I invented a great title- MY CONNIE. This is to honor her and to show our love. On February 28, 2015, I decided to write my first book of our immortal love, and this book is my life, my happiness, my sorrows, my power, my biggest strength, my companion, and my new life. There are many happy and sad chapters of our lives in this book. It is easy to understand that happiness and unhappiness are part of life, but much more difficult to bear the reality. This is like the difference between what we study in schools and the practical world—Experience. Our love was and even now remains immortal, MY CONNIE.

I must thank many people, without whom it would have been difficult for me to handle the most tragic time of my life on February 28th, 2015.

On the family side: To start, when Connie and I first visited India in July 1979, after close to four years of our marriage, it was my first trip back to India after moving to the US. Today, I cannot believe that I came to the USA with seven dollars and only thinking of going back as it was no land for me and I was homesick. I was well-educated and regretting that I had ever left my home country. I had no plan to marry and meant to go back to India at the earliest possible time. I still today can't tell if it is reality or a dream. I came to the USA with so much reluctance and only seven dollars in my pocket, and now I was flying back to New Delhi with Connie, and we both were excited. I was feeling on the flight, and on arrival, if I genuinely have come to India, and it is also true that I am married to a highly educated and intellectual American girl. There were over 100 immediate and extended family members were waiting to receive us at the Delhi Airport. I do not recall how we all went straight to my elder biological brother Arun Berry's house. For days morning till night, family members and friends came to visit, all day and all night, for close to 18 hours. It was very common for every family member to stop by with no phone call or invitation, drop by, and all the food and beverages were to be served. It is impressive, I used to think, but today, August 16, 2016, when I am writing, it is extremely painful to me that I was writing something in July 1979. After so many years, Connie, who was the darling of my immediate family and extended family, is no more. I am the same Pradeep who came alone and was happy for 40 years, and now again, I am alone. Is this is a movie or reality? I wonder, and since I see Connie sleeping next to me and immediately remember the truth, I get distraught. My family would drop by, sometimes at 6 in the morning, sometimes at 10:30 in the night.

My family had judged in no time that Connie, an American, was educated, self-made, polite, intellectual, and top of that, she was my wife. She was the second daughter-in-law of my Berry family and maternal family. I would not hesitate to say that Connie was the family star after our marriage until her demise.

I am very grateful to my biological brother Mr. Arun Berry, his wife Shobha, and their two sons Ashiem and Ashish, Ashish's wife Mona, and their two daughters- (my grandnieces) Krishna (10) and Radhika (5). My Grandnieces Krishna and Radhika cheered me during my depressing time. I went to India three times to see my family after Connie's demise. Dr. P.N. Behl, a world-renowned dermatologist, and his English wife, Mrs. Marjorie Behl, and his family were there for me during those grief-stricken times. Dr. Behl was more than a father to me. His mother was my Berry grandfather's sister. It is an important point I just thought, that I was the second person after Dr. Behl, who had a foreign wife in our whole extended family. I recall that when I was 8 years old, the marriage of Dr. Behl and Mrs. Marjorie Behl was a novelty, and he was a very prominent person with an English wife in our history.

ELEGIAC PAEAN

Until August 16, 2016, that I never thought I would go. Further, Dr. Behl was a shining star in India, and his influence on me as a child and teenager until I met Connie was a significant influence on my career. But Connie exceeded with much more—over 100,000% to help my advanced career and world travel. In our whole extended family in India, and my real aunt's extended family in the USA, I am humbly and politely extremely grateful to Connie all my life that Connie made me shine in the USA as Dr. Behl was shining in India. By no means do I mean to insult and demoralize anyone. Many of my family in India and the USA are stars and have done very well, and perhaps in their views they have done better than me; however, I have to honor Connie and say that because of her, I feel that I progressed well in the American culture and I know more than any family members in India and In the USA. Money, success is separate thing. But the travel and adventures in life and depth analysis of her intellectual planning and finding out the different traveling and exploring the places, reading, writing, reading over seventy thousand books, watching absolutely the best movies, Broadway shows, attending the Symphony and all the world experience Connie and Pradeep are much ahead–(God forgive me for writing)—more than my great Dr. Behl, as he was too devoted in his medical and dermatology and academic side. In that way, he was much ahead of all of us, including me. It's a comparison between academic and passion for work and work, whereas ours was working. Our academic and advanced careers, writing, and literary reading texts were terrific, but it was important not to miss traveling and exploring the world. One cannot do everything; many variables have to be in the playground.

My immediate family has asked me to move back to India; however, I can't as my mind and soul is in my home where we spent 42 wonderful years, just Connie and me.

Connie's loss has been deeply felt everywhere.

To end my notes, no matter what I write or say, there is no way I can ever forget MY CONNIE. She was very special- priceless and one who made my life and my destiny. She will always remain in my heart and soul as long as I am alive. Connie, I am very grateful to you for all the help in my career and your devotion as a faithful wife and a friend in everything in my life. I have lost the most important part of my life- a true partner at this junction, and you left me too early. I can't say goodbye to you as you are always with me in my heart and body, ever shining everywhere.

Loving husband forever.
PRADEEP K. BERRY
August 16, 2016

Preface

MY CONNIE is the first book I have written in memory of my loving and precious wife, my true friend, and my whole world, with whom I spent over 41 years. My purpose was to write this book to give my tributes to my wife and let readers decide, think, and evaluate: Are we truly living in a good society? I want readers to make a special note to "never depend upon anyone." Friends and relatives are good and nice while you are wealthy and healthy. TEST YOUR RELATIVES AND FRIENDS WHEN YOU ARE IN TROUBLE FINANCIALLY OR SICK. Very few will come or care. Invite them for happy occasions and super functions, and they will be there. An important saying goes, "When you cry, you cry alone; when you laugh, they will laugh with you." My message based upon my experience is that everyone cares for themselves and their families, once they are married and have their children and grandchildren." This is true even between real brothers and sisters, but relations between siblings are not as hard and cruel as a person with an evil spouse. Always choose one or two friends or relatives who you know that they would stand by when you are in trouble of any sort. We are living in a Dark Age of the world. Please never live in a company of unfaithful people. It is the most painful and unbearable thing I have gone through, her sickness and finally dying in front of me- the last four breaths, and she was gone. I was shaking and lost the power to think. I saw her face and her side where she took four breaths. I was hoping that what I saw was true but possible that her good karmas and my love and devotion would be heard by all the supreme lords or even one, and her last four breaths would be reversed, and she would start breathing. I have seen many miracles and true happenings where a dead person suddenly starts moving on the bed or even in the casket. I was with her body for over six hours, touching her feet, kissing her on her forehead, asking for forgiveness, touching her shining feet, and taking blessings from her feet, a compelling tribute in the Indian and ancient culture. Blessings from the feet of a lifeless person. Many variables and things were coping and upsetting. I failed. And I was reminded that I had to do her cremation and place her ashes next to her parents in her plot. I must write that none of my relatives were present, none of my father's sister's children and grandchildren. I never wanted them to know, even as none of them ever called or visited Connie when she was sick, and they knew well that Connie was sick. Why should I call them? Just to get a large crowd showing how many people were there during her cremation. Connie and I attended all of their happy occasions and four deaths, going to the cremation and the temples for prayers of four days. Connie's only wealthy biological brother and wife was the most pathetic and shameful act—only evil people can do such things. Connie truly loved the one real elder brother but due to his being a puppet and henpecked qualities given to him by his very smooth and clever spouse, who was jealous and, in my opinion, evil. Regardless, one must be a free man. That brother had no guts to come at the time of her death, and he found out 14 hours before from the hospital staff, and he was watching Connie on the face time that Connie was going to die. But he did not come even through today, August 2, 2016. Not even a single member of his family and children and grandchildren whom Connie loved and loved gave them plenty of money and presents for Christmas, birthdays, any functions. They are wealthy. Those grown-up children and their spouses never gave anything to her, their one and only loving aunt. They did not come. Face Time, and this brother stated, which are in the medical records, "Name withheld is on the death bed and prefers you to make a decision." In my opinion, it was a conspiracy and falsification of medical records. Had I not gone out from the Cardiac Unit for 60 minutes for shower and work, it would not have happened. The dismissed doctors came in my absence, and that is how the brother called on FaceTime, and he stated, "Connie, you want to be cremated, and you want your ashes to be put in your plot next to your Mom and Dad." He did this around 1 PM on February 27, 2015, and Connie died at 1:10 AM morning of 28th February. I was in the hospital with Connie's caretaker and one couple—a friend of mine who my brother in India informed that Connie had died and please go to the hospital as Pradeep is alone and lonely. He came around 11:30 on the 27th of February 2015 and was surprised that Connie was alive. At 9 PM, two nurses came when Connie was dying, and they put an oxygen mask on her and gave her a morphine injection, and Connie was fine. He also went to his house to bring his wife to be there. Connie looked better, and I asked the nurse if I could use the restroom, as I needed to empty my bladder since 2 PM. They allowed me. I was positive that Connie would be fine. God had given her a new life, but Connie died at 1:10 AM in February 2015. I have seen many painful things in my life, tragedies, death, and birth. Knowing that we all have to leave this earth and world and keep going. Although I have written thousands of articles and extensive detailed management reports and policies in my professional career, CONNIE was a born reader. Her influence on me was to read not only the different types of newspapers, such as the *Wall Street Journal, New York Times*, and the *Chicago Tribune*, but my business books and articles were enough to read. I don't have time to read anything other than the business sections and articles on the different topics. I wasn't fond of fiction. Later, she suggested that I should read other true stories and books. So we were readers; however, I could never read different newspapers and magazines, health journals, and many novels. So serious, and I said, where do I have time. She said you could read whenever you find the time.

Connie was a born reader, and her influence on me to read was a boon to start reading more diverse books. I was extremely busy with work and travel, writing detailed information about the collateral, and writing reports. I was an excellent reader and a writer. At the same time, I planned to write books on academic topics, do research, and write a biography of a few people. However, many reasons cropped up not to write. The most important and happiest was my wife and best friend of over 41 years, Connie Berry. We both were very close from the moment we met. During our working years, I traveled due to my professional leverage and merger and crisis management as a senior manager to evaluate large loans to our borrowers in the USA and Canada and a few in Europe. I used to take Connie with me whenever she could due to her profession teaching Spanish, Social Studies, English, Mathematics, and French. She was everything for me, and I was everything for her. During my travels, we were connected over the phone four times a day and night. When time permitted, she would travel with me and explore the city or town where I was working. She was the most innovative adventurer I will ever see in my life. I left my high-paid professional career on September 1, 2005. Still, I did a few projects in the West Indies in December 2005 and Joliet, IL in July 2006. I did some marketing strategies projects at home as I decided not to travel for work but ourselves all over the USA and the world, including Hawaii and Sanibel, Captiva, and Marco Island from the second week of January until the first week of March since 2005 and 2014 to escape winter. Most of our travel before and after 2005 was different excellent cruises. I wanted to spend every minute of my life with Connie Darling, and she was Constance Berry, whose husband was the most critical part of her life, and that was Pradeep Berry, the writer of this book, MY CONNIE. It is a result of the most painful death of my love. The idea of writing a tribute to my passion has long been in my mind, and I would say that since 2005, the thoughts were involved, but no writing was in place. My laptop and my troubled mind started to write this love story on March 16, 2015. There was no going back, but the idea was to move forwards to write a book, and in a few weeks, I started writing daily. That is MY CONNIE. A true story of my life and the death of my mind. Devotion and intelligent people who are not interested in their own lives are becoming increasingly popular and challenging. I hope my readers are not offended.

Pradeep Berry

1

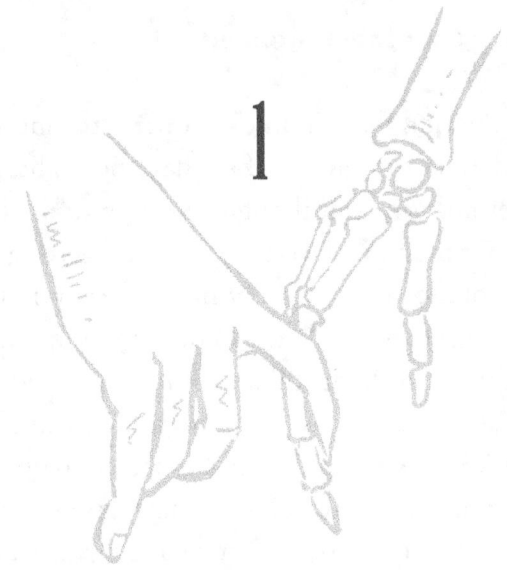

An Introduction to Connie: My Connie, My Light

"MY CONNIE"—Truly, an extremely rare, priceless, precious destiny and a special gift of GOD to me—we were "TWO BODIES WITH ONE SOUL." Before starting this biography of our true love, I have to give my highest tributes to MY CONNIE and how she became an immortal love for me, a love that will, perhaps, be immortal for us both. I write this book to share my passion and give Connie maximum credit for this love, destiny, and evergreen lifelong love. With valuable messages about the nature of love, this book creates the love, hope, and faith we shared. Imagining this destiny and love is the only comfort I have left. I had never realized how life could be changed by love, and through my devotion to fulfilling Connie's desires, I am sure God would fulfill my wish and hers. Perhaps it is a challenging test of life, an exam we had to face to pass again with a Gold Medal in our next love. In this book, I examine how destiny and love and have shaped the course of my life.

Hauntingly Disturbing Pain Every Moment

It is imperative to mention that Connie's demise is the most painful and shaking pain and is in my mind every movement of my day and night. Even before sleeping, dreams, and when I get up, pain and thoughts wander in my brain. I feel as if I am dreaming, but I think so much to face my life while getting up. And Categories, I can emphasize that Connie's love is in my mind every minute of the day, maybe except when I am sleeping. However, the moment I am up, my pain is extreme. In addition to thinking about her, I am still avoiding reality and don't want to believe that Connie Darling has left me, and I go through the painful and upsetting mind, body, and soul. I don't know what to do and how to cope up. I start looking at her pictures and videos and her computer, chair, walker, and whatnot. I can't think if I am getting peace of mind or more pain. But then I try to compromise by praying her pictures and touching her chair, computer, and walker. That gives me some peace mixed with pain, and the lights in her study room are a small solace. It still looks as I am on a business trip and will be with her on Friday. I was dreaming that she was no more, which took my pain to the extreme. That time I was totally in a world of thoughts, specifically, how intelligent, intercultural, and intellectual she was. I have never met or met any wife like that. I have compared many of my family and friends, but I can't find anyone like her. I then suffer from extreme unbearable pain.

I go in-depth thoughts and become stop whatever I am doing for a short time and some time for a long time. I then had to force myself to concentrate on what I was doing or was planning to do. This much distraction is due to love but love we had for each other. After that, I want to be alone and be isolated. I read one quote" "Life asked Death, why people love Me, But Hate You? Death Responded, Because You Are A Beautiful Life, And I'm A Painful Truth." Yes, it is the most painful, anger, unexpected, unbelievable, and why God didn't grant one thing only didn't fulfill my prayers. Is God is so cruel to his followers and doesn't listen to me? Friend's prayers? These things are still rattling in my mind and only painful, precisely when you love someone so much.

2

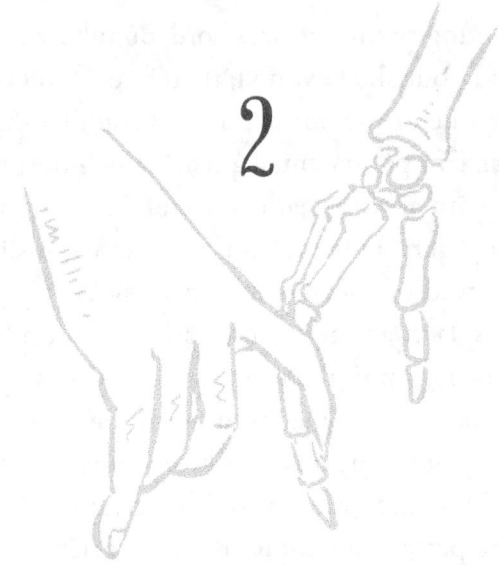

True Love and Great Destiny

True and pure love of anyone- whether that person is your significant other, mother, father, or whomsoever- is a double-edged sword that brings pain and joy. If, on the one hand, you were never gifted with that love, you would not feel as much pain when the loved one passes; however, if you have been blessed with deep love, the downside is that the pain is that much deeper after they are gone. According to Khalil Gibran, the Lebanese author, life, and death are "even as the river and the sea are one." Gibran also writes that "like seeds dreaming beneath the snow, your heart dreams of spring." He says to trust in your dreams, for in them is hidden the gate to eternity. I also turn to the holy words of Lord Krishna, as recorded in the *Gita*, a Hindu religious text that is used in courts of law. In this book, when Arjun was grieving over the death of his son Abhimanyu, Lord Krishna told him, "Why grieve? What son? Whose son? It was a mortal relationship, and with death, mortal relationships break for good." "Soul has already taken a new birth." "Do your duty by killing your enemy brothers who betrayed you and killed your son. Otherwise, they will kill you and your four brothers." This episode is one of the most popular and influential Indian histories, as recounted in Mahabharata's Sanskrit epic history. The story of the Mahabharata can be found in texts, films, and internet searches. Further, many American and Indian stage actors have played this episode on the stage worldwide.

Speaking of the fleeting nature of life, Lord Buddha wrote that "Our body is given by our parents and nourished by food; therefore, it will be destroyed one day." This quote comes from one of the books on Lord Buddha that I read in school. A passage in India, "Sadanaam parmatama ka hai," which means "God always exists, but there is no relation with anyone before birth and after death," speaks to the fact that our existence is temporary. However, it is not always possible to realize this pain we experience when a loved one leaves us, vanishing despite this knowledge. The knowledge provides no solace, and it is excruciating to lose a loved one. The degree of pain we each feel depends upon the love or the closeness of our relation, and we may feel more pain for the loss of some loved ones than we do for other friends and acquaintances. It depends upon the depth of love that we think, and with that love, we may hope that it will become easier to cope with our loss, although that may not be true. Instead, as time passes, sometimes the pain gets worse and withdraws our former desires to travel, dine out, and do other great things that we did with our lost ones and leaves us wanting to live an elementary life.

"Thinking of you much at this difficult time. What we know is not much. What we do not know is immense"- Pierre Simon Laplace, Mathematician, Statistician, Physicist, and Astronomer

"One or the Other"
One or the other must leave.
One or the other must stay.
One or the other must grieve
This is forever the way.
This is the vow that is sworn
Faithful till death do us part
Braving what has to be borne
Hiding the ache in the heart
One whomsoever adored, first will be summoned away
This is the will of the Lord.
One or the other must stay.
By- Edgar Guest. Complied by Gabriel Y F

Yes, these are great words and philosophies about the loss of loved ones and may not hold universal truth—or be true for everyone; however, it doesn't provide me with any comfort, solace, or peace of mind. The loss I feel has vanished all of the comforts I once took in spiritual and religious learning and left me with unbearable pain that will last my lifetime as I withdraw from the world we explored together. Our relationship was extremely strong, built on true love, attachment, and devotion to one another. The death of one half becomes a living death for the other half.

3

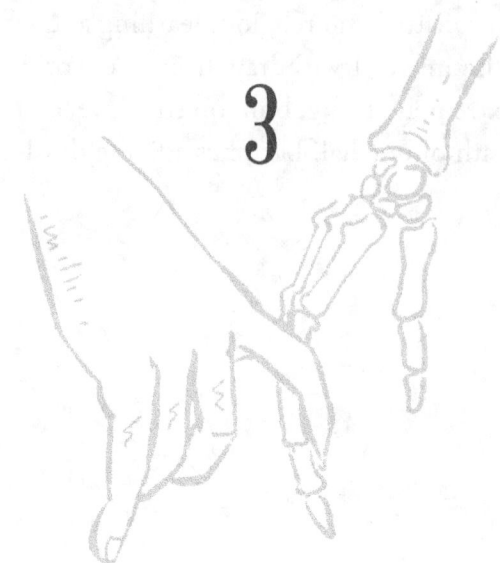

Our True and Pure Love But Love

Now I will about my most precious love and the friendship I had for my darling wife of over 39 and half years, Mrs. Constance Ann Berry, Connie, née Constance A. Fuller. We both not only loved but worshipped one other for our pure and true love. I can say with great pride that we were true "Two Bodies and One Soul." Our love was a special gift granted by the supreme lord. That kind of love is, in my opinion, extremely rare and results from a unique destiny. I am reminded of a book I read, and I don't remember the name, "It wonderful song cum poem of love." The pain of losing that love is rattling me to the bone, while at the same time, I cannot believe the absolute happiness and the world are over for my other half.

4

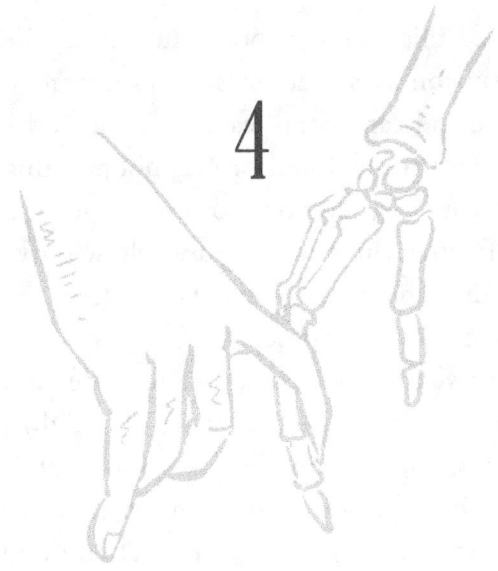

My Heartfelt Tributes to Connie

The Painful and Sad Chapter of My Life

The sad chapter of my life and the trauma I went through began when Darling Connie fell from her bed at home on February 20, 2015, and was taken to a check-up at the hospital. Although her results were normal, the hospital kept her for two days for observation. Connie was to be discharged on the 22nd of February, 2015. However, this never came to pass, and she died on February 28, 2015. The 28th was the date when we were to travel back home from the trip we had planned to Sanibel Island, where we had been going for the last ten years to be away from the cold and snow of late winter in Evanston. We canceled the trip in November 2014 after the negative report from Mayo Clinic that placed her on palliative care, meaning that her cancer had spread in her airways and there was no specific cure. Connie was so considerate; she said, "I hope you're not disappointed that we can't go." She stated, "If you want to go, you can go." I replied, "No way, I would never go without you anywhere. I cannot even think about that and would be with you—no matter how much cold or snow I have to suffer." I was taking complete care of her with great happiness. The message, "Do your duty- Life is a duty, and you must perform your duty with happiness," came to my mind. "If you cannot perform your duty, sit outside the church, temple, or road and ask for alma (money). I believed this message about duty all my life, but it pained me to think of staying in Evanston as my duty, as it was not my duty but necessary for my wife. It was my love and care from heart and soul, and I rejected this message of my childhood for the first time. I may or may not pass this message of duty onto others, particularly the young generation; however, it became a hurtful message for Connie. I asked myself: What duty, which duty, whose duty, why duty, why is this word DUTY is in the dictionary? Duty may be bothersome, but not when love is involved; then it becomes a true purpose.

My purpose was to save my beloved Connie from demise, but I lost that battle, which bothers me. I ask God: "Why, Why, and Why did I lose that battle."I was serving her like we serve God, and why didn't God see that devotion, knowing that it was loved with a passion. We both had the most important thing: we were one loving couple and extremely happy with each other and hoping that the supreme lord would watch our true love and would grant us our one wish and not separate us. Again, we were begging the supreme lord to extend our love and Connie's life. We know God is always watching our love and sincere devotion and ask for any forgiveness. There was a time when Connie acted as a mother for me as well as my wife. When Connie was sick, especially from April 2013, my devotion, love, and pain were beyond reach, and I asked God one thing only. "My supreme lord, please grant Connie a long life, take some of my karma, and give it to Connie by curing and extending her life. Evaluating our deeds, we realized that we both did good deeds, and perhaps our few mistakes were mitigated by good ones. In balance, it seemed that the good was enough to ask God for Connie's health and life in return. I begged as a mother asked for her child. Lord says, "I would help you, MY CHILD," as seen in the churches. What happened to that CHILD? The answer is obvious for us all.

I have excellent knowledge of spirituality, death, and birth. These are things over which we have no control, especially death. Despite this, I was not ready for Connie's demise. She had told me her family had a history of long life and good genes, living up to 92 to 95. She was very positive, had tremendous good health throughout our marriage. She was intelligent and active. She said she would live a long time as she had been swimming regularly for years, golfing, walking, doing all the household work, cooking, shopping, teaching, and driving. In addition, she spent hours reading, was well versed in computer technology, served as the president of our building association for 25 years, had knowledge of building laws, watched all the best movies, traveled extensively, pursued higher education, and lived a healthy life. She was conscientious about our diets. I, too, also believed and knew she would be given that inheritance of long life. However, I was unsure about my longevity, as my birth mother died at age 26 after leaving my elder brother and me at age eleven months and two months. My younger aunty-my mother's sister- was forced to marry my father to avoid bringing a stepmother into our family. She was married to my father for five years and died at the age of 25, two hours after giving birth to my sister. After her loss, my father married his third wife from another family- our stepmother, who separated us from my father and had two boys by him. She is still alive at age 88, but my father died before her at age 80, on November 14, 2003. My paternal grandparents died at 81. My maternal grandmother died at age 56, and my maternal grandfather at 93. However, I was pretty convinced with Connie's positive approach; we would live to 90.

I mentioned my childhood pain as Connie is not with me, and that brought back the pain of my childhood to some degree, but Connie's loss is more painful than the childhood pain. Perhaps, as part of my tributes to Connie, I am writing about this chapter of my life. Otherwise, I would not have noted too much pain in my life and my brother's life when we were young in India. As described above, after the loss of our two mothers, our father was controlled by my stepmother. It is hard to believe, but it happened to us, and both grandparents raised us. After the demise of my parental grandparents, my father and stepmother, two of my uncles' wives also started mistreating us. They started asking me in particular to do so much household work. They would set me to counting thousands and thousands of enormous delivery boxes from 50 to 80 trucks and then tell me to open and count the inventory every morning at 4 AM. After that, I would eat breakfast, make lunch for my uncle when he was in the hospital, study, and go to school. I went to college and finished my Chartered Accountancy- a high-powered post-graduate degree. I would take dinner to my elder uncle in the hospital during this time, studying and sleeping there like a nurse. These paternal aunties would give us food, but after a while, we felt that they were obliging us rather than caring for us, although the family business met all our living expenses.

This situation greatly bothered my father's elder brother. But he was at a loss on how to help us; to fight with four to one was a losing battle. After his marriage, my aunts asked my elder brother to take his separate kitchen apart from the rest of the family, although he and his wife lived in our family mansion. I started eating with him, as my brother asked me not to eat with our aunts and uncles anymore. It was a little shock to my aunties when they realized they had done something wrong and felt guilty for their behavior towards us. My brother insisted that I not eat with them as their actions hurt him. My aunties told me they did not separate me from the family, but I did what my brother told me. Although the electricity and water bill was paid from the business expenses and we stayed in one of our big mansions with no cost to us, the family did not show us generosity. Later, these aunties tried to insist that we pay for our electricity and water bill, but my father's elder brother intervened and insisted that there was no way he would allow us to pay anything.

I want to tell a true story about witnessing my grandfather's grief for the death of his son, my uncle, who was only 32 years old. When my Grandfather Berry came to the cremation and saw my Grandfather Mehra, he realized that he had not understood the pain of Grandfather Mehra for the loss of my mothers, his two daughters. Grandfather Berry broke down and apologized sincerely and from his heart, saying that now he knew what it was to lose a child and felt deeply for Grandfather Mehra's losses as well. This touched me deeply as a child, and I sometimes look back at that moment when I think of my Connie. Her loss brings my childhood suffering back to me. All of these forgotten things come back to haunt me. I am still willing to forgive and forget again, but the pain of Connie's loss is killing me. As powerful as that moment was, it is lost in my misery for Connie. Four months later, Prime Minister Pandit Nehru died of the shock of the conflict with China over the Dalai Lama in 1963. When he died, I was in my uncle's room, and my grandmother was lying on the floor, weeping. In reality, though, she wept from the shock of Nehru's death, but really from the end of her son. I was also crying for Nehru, who I had met many times and regarded very highly. I truly grieved for him. My grandmother told me, "Pipo, why don't you go and attend Nehru's last rites?" I told her that it would be too difficult for me because of the security that would make getting across the city almost impossible. She told me that I should go to see if it would heal me.

I realized that I wanted to go, and immediately I thought that maybe I should wear my Eagle Scout uniform. I also had my Boy Scout bicycle, and I went to get it. Right away, I started pedaling. I crossed all of the roads, crossed police lines, and no one stopped me. They started saluting me because Boy Scouting was very renowned at the time. I was able to get close the Nehru's body, and I saw his funeral. I was both happy and sad, and when I returned home, my grandmother was pleased that I had gone to see Nehru's cremation. It was healing for her to know that even Nehru, a powerful man, could die unexpectedly as her son had. I wanted to give this speech at an Eagle Scout ceremony for my nephew, but I will share it here now, instead.

After that function, Connie told me she would not attend any more tasks for my B family in Chicago. On July 14, 2012, I forced Connie to come with me to graduation for my cousin's daughter in Orland Park despite Connie's determination to avoid that part of the family. Connie was not feeling well because she had just finished her chemotherapy, but she was such a good person that she accompanied me not to go alone. We were both welcomed like a king, and there is no doubt that my cousin and my uncle were delighted to see us. After that, everybody came to us, and they were very nice, but after greeting us, they only blended with other Indians. V.B. took our pictures, but later on, a 100% change came because Indians remain Indians, and they showed us that they did not want to associate with my American wife. V.B. had no choice but to call some American guests, as his daughter went to school with Americans and the kids and their parents had been invited. My cousin played loud music and tried to show off, which looked shallow. We could not socialize over the sound of the music. We wound up sitting with a lovely American couple, trying to talk, but we all began to feel angry that we had been placed off in the corner. Connie was offended and left the party early, leaving me. My uncle was the only one who was bothered that she and I left early, and no one ever called to see if we were OK and ask why we left the party early. To this day, nobody called me to see how I was or ask why I left early. Even my family, born and raised in this country have never thanked me or called me.

During her sickness, I had many job offers for senior positions, but I refused these. For the last forty years, I have wondered why, and I think the reason is that I wanted to leave the painful atmosphere of my family home. Now I am convinced that it was my destiny to have Connie as my wife. I am happy that I forgot my Indian career and would take Connie as my destiny over wealth and a great job in all my future lives.

Only I can feel my loss, no matter what family, friends, and outsiders are trying to tell me, no matter what they say in sympathy, or to provide me comfort and take me out of my loss. It does not affect me, on my loss, and the sorrow of my daily existence. I only want one thing- Connie. Later, I will discuss the trauma we went through, the pain and suffering of her illness, and the events of her last eight days in the hospital. I can never forget those events, nor can I forgive her doctors. There was more positive than negative in my life due to our love, and I am writing about my experience of grief. I do not want to offend anyone. I know many people have gone through the same loss, but I am concentrating on my pain. My friends and relatives know my trauma and discomfort but cannot understand what I have gone through, and I am still going through today, on March 27, 2016. I am not ready to follow anyone's advice or to try to forget the past. I want to bear this loss alone, grieve alone, cope alone, and find some temporary ray of light, although darkness will always be in my heart and soul. I am trying to stay healthy, keeping myself busy working on legal cases and housework. I feel that the cleanliness of our home is essential, as Connie was a perfectionist and always kept a spotless home. I have written a separate section about the importance of her housekeeping.

I am working all the time to get justice for Connie's early demise, which, in my opinion, was the result of her doctors' negligence. Everyone tells me what I will gain if I get justice (which may take years or not happen because doctors are politically powerful); what will I gain? Connie cannot come back. I don't want to listen to that. I have lost my one love. I know that people die suddenly, but I am angry that God did not listen to my prayers and devotion. The one thing I wanted was for Connie to get better, no matter how much I had to sacrifice or how much hardship I had to bear.

I lost that battle, and I feel angry with my Lord- why did God not see our devotion to each other and give her an extended life so that our ends would be together? I am not a cruel person, but it has taken my happiness away and left me with pain and withdrawal from the world. I no longer do the things I did with Connie. Now, my life is limited to traveling to India to visit my brother. I don't have much of social life. I make business calls and run errands. Some people I speak to analyze our love, but some do not. I am not asking for any sympathy, but I do respect what people tell me. I get happiness from my brother, his family, my grandnieces in India, and some good friends in the USA, but darkness follows every moment in my heart and soul.

5

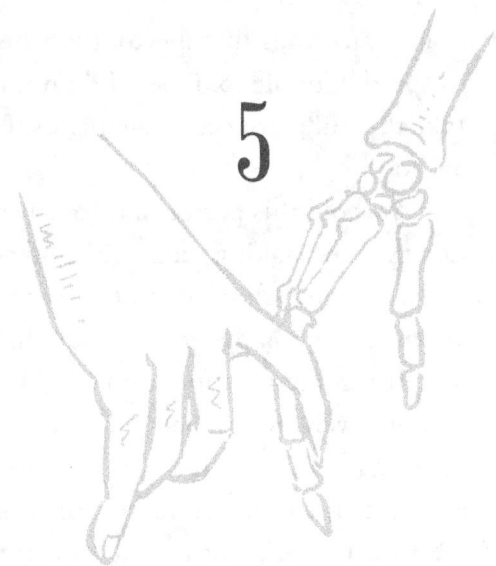

Knowledge Theory vs. Pragmatism

At some point, we must come to the following realization of death: everyone has to die- Man is born alone and will die alone. Does death become destiny or destiny become death? Everyone has their faith in this dynamic puzzle, and some try to cope with the imminence of dying early in life, while some choose not to think of it depending upon their LOVE. When we lose a loved one, we all believe that if the perceived cause of death would not have happened, perhaps death could have been avoided. Few examples, if he or she would not have traveled, had not driven, had not gone out in the night or attended a wild party with heavy drinking and driving, had not ridden in a car without a seat belt, hadn't gone boating in the night, perhaps death could have been avoided. Yes, we all realize that death will come, but we are filled with regret when it does. That is the first reaction of someone to death. However, our old sculptor and knowledge, Vedanta says, "Death or Its Destiny." This comes from our ancient beliefs that I learned when I was 16 years old.

Was it destiny that Connie's death was coming, or was it due to negligence? Some people commit suicide, some shoot others and then kill themselves. Alcohol and accidents, car and motorcycle accidents all take lives. Connie and I always remember an incident that happened 35 years ago. After a party, I drove on the Edens Expressway with Connie around midnight while coming back from Oak

Park, IL. We both saw a big man in his 40s speeding on his motorcycle. Connie and I were surprised by his speed. Connie told me, "I do not understand how some people are so daring and take their life into their own hands. Look at him- he might be going over 100 miles an hour."

Connie and I discussed how bold this person was to drive at such a high speed. Connie said, "I am surprised that he is taking such a risk and without a helmet." She mentioned that she worried about him slipping on the wet road, as it was raining, and that we should pray that nothing happened. We saw him coming towards us a few minutes later, going south in the northbound lane. He crashed into the wall and died on impact. Cell phones were not available in 1983, so we went to look for a phone booth, but before we had gone far, three police cars arrived on the scene. Would you call this his destiny or the result of his lack of common sense?

Connie always told me to drive defensively and with total concentration and avoid driving at night, especially when we went to parties and functions. She was always careful to make sure that we just had one small drink. I had the habit of drinking three or four scotch and sodas, whereas Connie never liked me drinking that much. She would only have one drink and had reasonable control over her habits. I don't know how she put up with me then, and I ask her forgiveness for my childish habits. Although I didn't see it at the time, now I know I was wrong. I regret it and think about her love, care, and concern for me from the first time we met. I even think of that time, that place, and our expressions and happiness. I see that moment in my thoughts and have noticed that place many times and stay there for hours thinking. The place is there today- the windows and stairs and neighborhood and street are still as they were, except for minor changes on the side roads. The street names and roads are still the same, and the place where I lived when we met is there. We walked together on those streets for safety. She had to put up with my childish habits, although it made her angry. I realized her advice was right and wanted to cut back on drinking. God helped me one day in 1989, and I decided I would try not to drink the next day, which was a Saturday when I would not have to go to the office. I had a wonderful meal and a lovely sleep. Since then, I have never touched even wine or beer. My relatives and friends were shocked and begged me not to be a saint and have just one drink, but I decided not to. When we were flying first class, I was tempted to have a few drinks, but I did not start alcohol again. That was my final decision that I have lived with until today, August 16, 2016. When we used to drink, I had the habit of continuing to buy wherever there were great sales. Connie asked me why I would stock up on liquor, which takes up space in our home. Once I quit, Connie was amazed until her death by my determination.

My brother and friends were also amazed. Why drive in the dark when you can drive in the sunshine? It has been over 15 years since we found out that the motorcyclist in the horrible crash was not drunk, but driving and speeding for fun took his life. Connie and I discussed that accident with many of our friends, and they all agreed that he must have been stupid and brainless. Our Vedanta would say it was his fault and that if he did not speed, he would not have died. After Connie's demise, even if someone gives me millions of dollars, I will not drive on the highway for more than a few miles.

Our life was most beautiful from our marriage throughout the 41 years we had together. Every moment of those years is on my fingertips and running in my head all day like a movie, and it is painful. I must write that our love was so unique that her death crushed me forever. This is because of our passion. I cannot help repeating many parts of our love. Now her death moves around in my mind all the time, and I openly write and admit that I'm not particularly eager to deal with anyone, nor do I want to be social as every moment, Connie comes into my brain, my mind, and my soul. I always keep her pictures with me throughout her life, in my pocket, jacket, and phone, and I wear some of her unisex chains and watches. I do not want to give away many of her things, nor do I want to sell them no matter what someone offers me in cash. Our love and sadness during her last few months from 2013-2014 were worse and worse, and February 2015 was like a death for me when my Connie died. I cannot ever forget our 41 years of marriage, and I can say that every moment is like a photographic memory for me. Six years ago, Connie and I attended many parties, and I loved driving at night, drinking, dancing, and going all over the city.

In India, and perhaps in other old civilizations, people believe that when death has to occur, it takes the person to that place where death is to occur. To some degree, I believe this because I have seen many instances of this in my life. I would give a few examples to demonstrate.

The story involves a friend of my Uncle Belh and his wife, my English aunty. Their marriage is more proof that love is blind. My uncle, Dr. P.N. Belh, was a world-renowned dermatologist who studied and practiced in the UK and US before eventually returning to live in India permanently with my aunt. He traveled the world for conferences and to serve as a visiting professor and numerous institutions. My auntie's parents would visit her and my uncle in India frequently.

In the early 1920s, a young Indian Muslim boy, Rashid, left India for the UK as six. Eventually, he was befriended by my aunt's parents, who raised him like a son. Rashid remained a bachelor his whole life and lived with her family. In time, Rashid became the Surgeon General of the UK, where he met a young PN Belh at a hospital and decided to give the young student a chance. In this way, Uncle Belh got a medical internship from Rashid, and they became friends.

In 1971, after the death of Mrs. Behl's father, my aunt, her mother, and Rashid came to India for a six-month visit. This was Rashid's return to India after eighty years of living abroad in the UK. At the end of their stay in Delhi, my aunt's mother and Rashid planned to leave to return to the UK on a Sunday night; however, Rashid chose to stay two extra days for work. My aunt's mother, Violet, flew back alone, but she got a call that Rashid had passed early Monday morning upon her arrival at home. His body was immediately buried, according to Muslim tradition. Violet returned to Delhi and tried to take Rashid's body back to the UK for interment, but to no avail. My aunt's mother traveled between the UK and India for the next several years to visit her daughter and family. Many years after Rashid's death in 1976, my aunt called me to say that her mother was coming to see Constance and me in the US. A day later, my aunt and uncle called again to say that Violet had passed away in Delhi. She was cremated and buried next to Rashid in Delhi. Was it her destiny to die in India much as her adopted son had, or did this just come to pass by chance?

Another story in my family was the tragic death of my cousin, Dr. Behl's son Anil. We were very close growing up, and he was a gem of a person. I taught him Hindi when we were young, and we became great friends, as close as brothers. I was like a father of sorts to his little sister, Vinita. He was studying his M.D. and was dating a girl, Neera, who was like a sister to me. Anil was crazy for Neera, and they were very close. Anil went to England for four months with his family, and while there, Mrs. Behl had a car accident and was very seriously injured. Dr. Rashid and Violet called Dr. Behl and told him to come to see Marge many times, but he did not go because he was devoted to his work. At that time, Anil Behl was away from Neera for two years, and I used to talk to her every day to see if I had any news about Anil. Finally, Dr. Behl called Mrs. Behl and Anil and threatened to disown him if he did not return to Delhi. Anil started studying his M.D. in Gwalior and was again away from Neera. Neera sacrificed for all these years, and finally, they got married.

I was already in the States at this point and had not been here long when I got a call from my family telling me that Anil was killed in a car crash. I sent a telegram to Dr. and Mrs. Behl and Neera, who had Natasha's one-year-old daughter. When I went to India, Anil was gone, but seeing Dr. Behl for the first time brought us new life because we had been mourning his passing. Later, Dr. Behl adopted an orphan,

Shushil, and they loved him very much. He had no profession as an adult, so Dr. Behl set him up as a businessman, and then, later on, Shushil got married, and Vinita was very friendly to him. Later on, they had to work through difficulties, but they resolved those with my help, and now everything is ok. At her wedding in August 2003, which Connie and I were able to attend, Natasha included the memory of her father and grandfather, and she gave tributes to them and me and Connie.

At the same time that some people's deaths seem predestined, other people fall asleep and never wake up in the morning. People get heart attacks while driving, in the house, in the ambulance, and die. Some get saved. Who or what should we believe and why? Do we justify the reason for a loved one's death for our solace as God's decision? Or do we blame a series of events and decisions for explaining why the person went to that place of death? Would they be alive if they had not gone there? I think no one knows this answer, and if someone says he knows, perhaps, he is justifying death to himself and others. However, even those who believe that life and death are in the hands of God and fate will still question whether a loved one might have lived on if particular events had never come to pass.

6

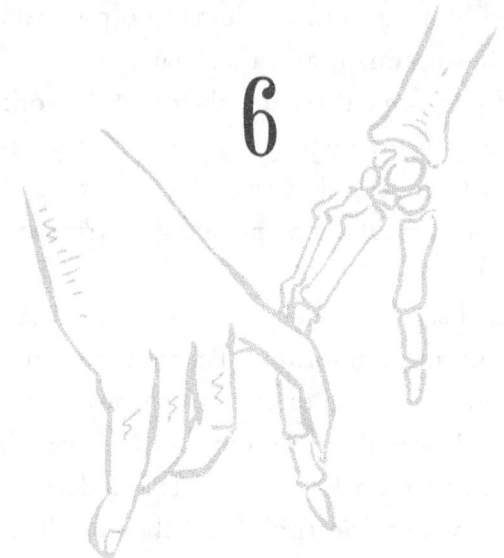

The Medical Negligence

How do we explain death as God's choice or destiny if there was apparent negligence by the medical doctors? In our case, I argued for two years that Connie's doctors caused the problem and needed to let other specialists examine her case. When doctors are overconfident, they think they know best and ignore the intuition of their patients and families. Connie's doctors discouraged us from going to Mayo Clinic for a second opinion, asking us what the doctors at Mayo would do that the doctors here in Chicago were not already doing to diagnose her illness. How can we justify this kind of hubris from doctors? We trust doctors to save our lives, placing them next to God. Doctors have the power to play with our lives, and even those with good intentions may promote a new drug or play into the plans of pharmaceutical companies to make money. In this equation, some people gain, some lose, some live, and some die. A good physician will always refer a patient to a specialist when asked or when realizing that he or she cannot handle the case or may have misjudged an initial diagnosis. An overconfident doctor who feels that he can handle every issue is dangerous. Rather than admitting that they need help, these doctors fear embarrassment. To bolster their egos, they may risk a patient's life.

I may be naïve, but I believe that three or four instances of this sort of medical negligence cost me the last ten or twenty years of life I expected to share with my

Connie. It would have been easy for the medical profession to avoid her early death as some wrong treatments were given to Connie by overconfident doctors pursuing the wrong diagnosis. She went from pursuing a route back to health to palliative care after Mayo Clinic detected what her two doctors had missed. God did not want her to retreat to palliative care but instead wanted her to continue to fight on. Otherwise, a third doctor who took over her case after Mayo Clinic would not have given us hope; he would have told us that her end was near. Instead, he was full of hope and ready to pursue a new treatment plan. He was prepared to correct the mistakes of past doctors but was never given a chance to help her heal as the hospital's terrible mistake finally cost Connie her life.

I started looking at the medical documents about a month ago, especially from February 20-28, 2015. The night of the 27th, at 1:10 AM, my Connie left for Heaven, but I immediately went to Hell. Many people from different parts of the world have told me for the last 42 years that Heaven and Hell are right in our lives. No special heaven or hell is waiting after death. But most people say that the beloved is in heaven, in peace. I never used to discuss this subject; however, I have seen people suffering and living in hell, whether they are ill, disabled, suffering from tragedy, or going from wealth to poverty. Some people go from a lavish lifestyle to begging for alms, lose a high-powered job and are unable to find work, or find themselves working for minimum wage. I have seen this happen to many people. Is that hell? Then where is the natural place for Hell? What happens to the soul and body, and where does the soul go? In India, the body has to be cremated, and in many countries, the dead are cremated and interred in the ground. Connie never did anything terrible, but she was in hell. Yes, she got sick and later became highly ill due to the negligence of her doctors. I went to every doctor's appointment with Connie, and she was not given proper care. In my opinion, there were many errors, and some of her medical records were falsified. I was in the hospital with her 24 hours a day for 8 days. On the 22nd of February, at 6 P.M., Connie was fine, and at 6:15 P.M., she had a salad. At 6:30 P.M., she had a cardiac arrest. That was the most dangerous thing, and CPR was not performed for one hour. That was the beginning of the end, her death warrant. You could see that the nurses and doctors did not want to perform CPR until I aggressively demanded it. This delay was the beginning of her death.

On the 27th of February, I was gone for less than two hours, and, in my opinion, the doctor we had dismissed as her doctor had no business to come into her room. He caused her tubes to be taken out without my permission, and he had no business even being in the room. I believe that he chose to let Connie die to protect himself from the ramifications of his neglect rather than admit he had botched her treatment. Upon my return, the doctors and nurses did not acknowledge that I had power of attorney, and while I was forced into hostile arguments with them, they were eight people against one. They told me that they did not care for my wishes, as they had to respect her wishes. It was all made up, as Connie was crippled and unable to speak or write anything due to the tubes in her mouth and her hands. I could not fight them, and I stayed and talked to Connie after her tubes were out, and she desired to live and come home. So much went on, and no one was helping Connie. In my opinion, the doctors falsified the reports and the document where Constance signed her DNR order. That document is not in her medical records, and even today, August 16, 2016, the hospital has never been able to produce the document.

Mr. (Name withheld),

Thanks for your kind message, and you must have received the medical records and discussed the entire story. I want to add that I forgot that Constance fell from the home bedroom on the 20th Morning, the day she was to have chemotherapy. An ambulance was called for precaution, and they took her to North shore health care in Evanston. She was kept for a night for urinary tract infections and was to be released the next day as her tests were okay. I saw the DNR code, and Constance and I told Dr. X and Dr. Y on the call to change to complete code DR to save her from any cardiac arrest or problems. Both Dr. X and Dr. Y came to the room in front of the nurses and me and assured us that they had changed the code and Constance would be saved by all means, and that was what Constance and I wanted. We were assured that Constance was to be released on Monday, 22 or 23 February 2015. She ate some salad around 6.25 pm in front of her caretaker and me and a nurse. So on, she felt some breathing problems and got a cardiac arrest. I called the nurse, and other staff came and requested Doctors to perform CPR, but doctors refused as DNR wasn't changed. I shouted like a tiger to do the CPR. My tiger-like voice and shouting scared them, and they did the CPR, but 8- 9 minutes were wasted, and most likely, that was the first step for her death. They were clear that the. Tubes would be out on March 2nd, Tuesday, 2015. I had to make the decision to take her home on the after the tubes with palliative care or take her to the holy family hospital after they make a small hole in the neck and later rehabilitation. A hole would be closed after she is absolutely fine.

They were sure it would work but did I have to go through all that. I told them yes and would take a great gamble, and Constance told me by my writing notes and body language, and I was prepared to take her to the Holy family hospital. The second reason for her death was again Dr. XB, who had given the case to Dr. MN, was no longer her Doctor had no business hanging around that room and area. In my opinion, finally, he achieved what he wanted- death. He had no business to persuade palliative care and the same nurses who were telling me that I had to make a decision by March 2nd and the same with the palliative care doctors assuring me that they would respect what I wanted. Constance and I wanted anything to avoid demise. XB wanted death, and therefore, I was gone for 2 hours to North Brook on Friday 27th February 2015.XB and his cronies told me when I got back at 1.30 PM that they were going to take out the tubes against my will and against Constance's wishes which I have where she marked that I should decide as she wants to live her home. XB did not listen and said that Constance told him to take the tube out. Lies but lies. She hated XB after MCR gave us a negative and palliative care report.

We both had been blaming XB and never wanted to see his face. Tubes were taken without our will around 3 PM, and Constance talked to me till 4.30 PM. Still, the palliative care doctor came to tell me that Constance may not survive as we promised that we would shift her to the palliative care unit, and after a few days, "Mr. Berry, you can take her home with our team, and she might live 1 to even 10 years as she is doing well." However, no care was given after 4.30 PM Friday. Weekend fun. Everyone was gone, and no one came till I was yelling, screaming, shouting, and I have 32 minutes videos and six minutes videos from my Wireless phone. One can see Constance was suffering, and I was shouting, and nurses were walking around, but no one came. After I made fifty phone calls from my Wireless phone and later hospital, Constance died at 12.50.

I was holding my urine for 9 hours. It was only at 9 PM when two Indian nurses came and put on the oxygen mask. Morphine injection extended Constance's life from 9 PM when hospice and palliative care nurse came at 7 PM and didn't do anything and declared dying at 9 PM. Still, Indian nurses extended Constance's life close to four hours and at 12. 35 minutes after holding 9 hours of urine went to the bathroom, and when I came with confidence that Constance would live and God listened to my prayers, but God didn't give me what I wanted as Constance died atv12. 50 after I saw her taking her last breathing. What a trauma I went through, and this whole thing is stronger than the medical records, and I would like to be a prosecutor to speak in the court and judge. I am ready to give my testimony in front of XB and other Doctors and nurses. I have to get the malpractice case active and do whatever I can, even seeing the attorney-general or the president of the USA. I would not have the guts to write to you and in the courts. If I weren't genuine, I would not have the nerve or guts to do anything unless I am right.

Thanks.
Pradeep Berry

7

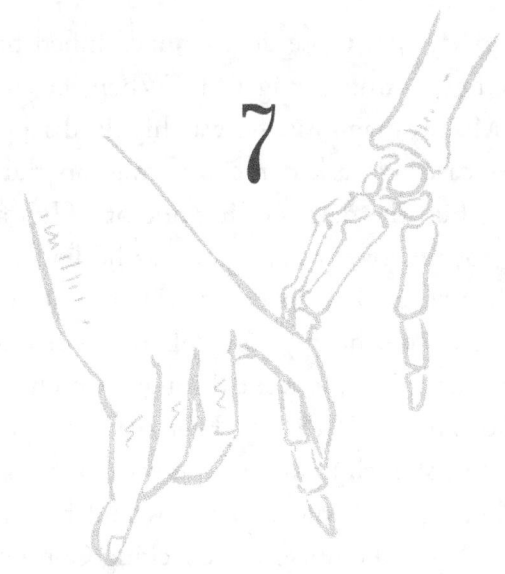

Life and Death Episode Message

I write about this episode in the hope that others may be enlightened from reading about our tragedy. I hope that it may save lives for others to read our saga. Don't trust your doctor blindly, and if needed, get a second opinion. In four days, MCR was able to diagnose Connie's condition, which her hospital (HH) should have detected long before had they conducted the same tests that MCR ran. Connie and I were both still optimistic that she would have many years left in this life. In my opinion, her two doctors at HH ruined her case with two years of negligence that finally resulted in her death. What difference did her death make to those doctors? Although they do not seek all options to heal their patients, they are still working, which is the noble cause of good doctors. As patients, we trust our doctors almost as we trust God when we are ill. Do Connie's doctors think of this bond of trust? In my opinion, they do not. They should have been open to referring her case for a second opinion. Still, their egos and overconfidence kept them from referring to her case even when I specifically requested a second opinion. Connie and I were both convinced that those doctors ruined her life, ultimately causing her early demise. After going to MCR, Connie told me many times that the doctors at HH first ruined her life, now they were taking her life. She told me this many times, which was the most painful thing for me to hear. As long as I live, I will suffer that pain and regret.

Connie was right to say that those doctors had ruined her life and eventually took what should have been a much longer life. When the specialist at HH agreed to take her case after MCR's diagnosis, he was highly disappointed with how his colleagues handled her case. He asked me who was on the team for her earlier treatments, and we gave him the names of her doctors. He was angry that her case had not been handed to him two years before, as he had worked cases like hers as his specialty for thirty years. The specialist ordered more tests and put her on a three-month course of chemotherapy, with plans to run different tests after the chemotherapy was complete. Connie went through two chemotherapy treatments in December 2014 and January 2015. On February 20th, while getting ready to go for her third treatment, she fell at home. She was taken in an ambulance to the hospital, HH, for a checkup and told that she would be ready for discharge the following day, the 21st. While the nurse was checking Connie, I saw that her chart read DNR. Connie, and I told her doctors that this was no longer her wish. The doctors assured us that they would immediately change her chart to ensure she received all possible life-sustaining care should something happen.

On February 22nd, while waiting to be discharged, Connie was feeling OK but not very hungry. She ate a little salad and five minutes later began to feel short of breath. She suffered a cardiac arrest. Nurses and doctors arrived immediately but refused to perform CPR as the code on her chart had not been changed from DNR to DR. I lost my temper and was like a tiger fighting for Connie, telling them that two on-call doctors witnessed her desire to change the DNR code and threatening to take it to court if they did not perform CPR immediately. Eight minutes elapsed between Connie's cardiac arrest and the start of CPR, eight long minutes that ultimately cost Connie her life. Had the doctors at HH done their duty and changed to code per Connie's will, and had the nurses and doctors present on the 22nd performed CPR immediately, I believe that Connie would still be with me today and for many years in the future.

Connie was put on a ventilator after her cardiac arrest. The tubes were to be removed on March 2nd, 2015, and I had to decide the next step. Although she could not speak with the breathing tubes in her mouth, Connie and I communicated through body language and noted that I wrote to ask her questions and get her answers. I would write things down, and she would respond "yes" or "no." In this way, I was sure that I knew her wishes and could be her advocate while the ventilator silenced her. Tragically, the doctors went behind my back when I left the hospital briefly to attend to the family business. A nurse was with Connie and assured me that she was getting better and I could step out for a short time.

While I was gone, several doctors, including her former doctor who had ruined her case and who we had dismissed in October 2014, came into her room. In my opinion, her former primary doctor came to her room from the part of the hospital where he worked to take advantage of my absence and to save his name, his fame, his position, and the annual honor of being named the top head and neck oncologist. I was distraught and angry to find him there, and I asked him why he had come to Connie's room while I was away. I told him that he had not been her doctor since October and referred the case to a breast and lung oncologist colleague. He did not answer me directly but argued that he had come earlier when I was not in the room along with two other doctors and nurses. He told me that they had to respect Mrs. Berry's wishes, so they had called me back to her room so that they could respect her wishes. I argued with them, telling them that they had all come late that afternoon when I was gone for an hour. That was an extremely dirty, daring, and unethical thing for them to have done. He had persuaded his medical team to be his 'yes' people, conspiring with him. Now that I had returned to the room, he had his team of doctors and nurses back anything he said because of his high position. I bluntly told them, all with anger, that they were unethical, amoral doctors who should be ashamed that they broke the oath they took after getting their MDs. Shame on them and shame to their oath. I told them that they all deserved to be punished and that their medical licenses should be revoked forever because they betrayed Connie and me.

Although on a ventilator, I told them that Connie communicated through her body language and notes and told me her wishes. I have those notes with me in my temple of gods, Connie, and some of my departed beloved souls. Mrs. Berry had stated her desire that Pradeep, as her husband, would make the decision and that she was willing to try a tracheostomy. She was ready for that, and so was I. I told this to many nurses, the Director of Social Services, and her palliative care doctors. I know the Director of Social Services, and if the need arose, I would request that an honorable judge ask her why she was against the procedure Connie and I decided on. She wanted things done her way and kept an eye on me, watching my movements and the time I spent sleeping in Connie's room. She told me bluntly, like a military order, "Mr. Berry, I do not want to see you in the cardiac unit after 8 P.M. or 8:30 at the latest." She threatened to tell the whole staff that I was to be gone at 8:30 P.M. sharp.

I asked many times why she would do such a thing. Who was she to dictate such terms when the other staff and nurses were so encouraging to me, telling me, "Mr. Berry, it is so great that you are with your wife at this time of crisis," even offering to let me sleep in an empty room. I thought that was nice, but I told them no thanks, as I wanted to be with my wife. I stayed next to her, sitting in a chair or lying down in two chairs, taking a 15-minute nap, or sleeping for an hour or two here and there. I was pretty sure that this director had bad intentions and that some conspiracy was driving her actions. Why else would she have tried to restrict me but not the other spouses? I was angry and blasted her to stop dictating her terms to me, as I did not care who she was. I told her she was not my mother or my relative and that if she tried to threaten me again, I would report her to the hospital chairman. If she tried to do tricky things to my wife, I would make sure she was arrested for threatening me. She replied that she was worried about my health and the lack of sleep in a soft voice. I told her to forget all this and tell me what was in her mind, what was her motive? I did not listen to her dictates and stayed with Connie. On the night of the 26th, a nurse told me, "Mr. Berry, we wish we had a dedicated husband like you, as we have not found any husband like you although we have dated a few playboys who betrayed us for physical relations. They treated us like prostitutes after buying us dinner and drinks. We are looking for nice men who would love us and be honest, never cheating on us." I was getting pretty upset and was surprised that these beautiful, attractive nurses and student trainees were so open about their struggle to find a good man. Many men would sincerely love to marry them for their beauty, education, and ambition. But I was shocked and started thinking about how men and women cheat on each other as marriage is a life-long commitment of honesty and friendship.

I always respected Woman for her outstanding qualities of tolerance and work as the engine of the family. A man without a good wife is zero, in my opinion. My love for Connie and her love for me was the greatest thing I have ever experienced or felt. Her every part of her mind and body was Truth and sh soft skin and body that holding her hands and a kiss on the cheek or mouth was so wonderful, and her hands while cooking food or making tea were shining. Her serving me coffee was the best in the world. I was doing the same for her, serving her excellent tea and cooking anything she wanted. I was willing to do whatever to make her the happiest person. I cry when I think of how she used to pack my suits and ties, iron, shirts and tie, and other undergarments so that I would look handsome and intelligent, and she would take pride that Pradeep is her man. I was her man, and she was my Connie.

On September 1, 2005, I was confused about whether or not to go to India for two weeks. I was not sure if I wanted to go or stay. I came home at 3 P.M. Connie asked me why I didn't see my family, as I had already planned to go and purchase the tickets. I said, "I cannot leave you, as you will be alone for two weeks." She said, "Pradeep, I can come with you, but last-minute tickets are costly, and we will have separate seats. I don't think it is fair to spend double or triple the money for a two-week trip, as after your return, we are going on a Norwegian cruise and then Hawaii. I think that would be too much travel for me, and I would not be able to do your packing for the cruise as we are going with the top alumni and professors of the University of Michigan. I think if you want, you should go and come back in one week, and we will talk on the phone every day." I agreed and found I had no good undergarments. Connie surprised me and told me that she had already gone shopping that morning while at work and bought me new undergarments, socks, and new shirts. I was in tears and told her, "No, I want to wear them when I am with you. I can buy new ones in India." She had purchased two dozen pairs of special underwear in my size, which were difficult to get due to some ban on importing clothing. I used only a few and saved them for years. I wore them all except for a new packet that is still unopened in my drawer. It is worth a million dollars today, as it reflects her love for me in doing my shopping.

The shirts and ties she bought me are sitting in my drawers, as I was saving them to use with her on trips to different climates. Lastly, she bought me four silk shirts to wear to a particular function. She wanted me to wear that shirt, which is very expensive, designer-made, 100% silk, and over 100 dollars. Connie started getting sick and hoping that I would wear the shirt to please her. I regret that I was saving it as it was an expensive present and now that polo shirt is still sitting in my drawer. I see those often and feel regret that I never wore them. Connie never saw me wearing those things. They are sitting in the closet along with cardigans she bought me from Carson's and two expensive jackets that cost $350 each are sitting with their labels on, along with many other lovely clothes.

Connie died suddenly due to those shameless doctors. She desires to wear them in March, even going anywhere- stopping for cake at Benson's Bakery after a doctor's appointment or getting something from Harry and David's, or getting her cheese and chocolates and her favorite frozen yogurt with her favorite chocolate from Whole Foods. She would have one every night- one bar is still in my freezer waiting for Connie, but Connie is gone. I thought I could eat that bar of ice cream, but my hands started shaking, and I did not want to eat it. My love for Connie has made me think of that frozen yogurt bar that she was to eat on the night of February 20, 2015, but she was tired and told me that she would eat it on the 21st. I have written that she fell on the night of the 20th, and she never made it back home, as she died on February 28, 2015. That frozen yogurt. All her medical team promised me that they would honor the wishes of Connie and me. I had told them that our caretaker and I would be there in the hospital 24/7 and that if the need arose, I would book a room in a hotel to take showers or for the caretaker to sleep a few hours. I told them I would be with Connie 24/7, and I did not care if I shaved, showered, or whatnot. I would have my few clothes that I needed, and maybe loose pants to sleep in the chair. I could never think of leaving my wife due to my extreme love for her. The whole hospital staff in the cardiac unit knew and was talking all the time about my love for my wife and my dedication and devotion. They supported me, saying, "You never know, your love and devotion may be rewarded, and please try everything to see Mrs. Berry gets better. Please go for the tracheostomy if you want; we have seen many patients recover from that with rehabilitation and medicine. I was determined to take this course, and so was Connie. But on February 27th, 2015, late in the afternoon, as I have stated, in my opinion, the doctors and nurses began their conspiracy. Later, when I got the medical records- anyone can read these and say yes, it is all falsified. I called her caretaker in April 2015, and she got mad and told me, "Pradeep, these are falsified reports as I was there, and this is false." I would testify in court that it is all made up, as she was the witness right there with me and her name is on the medical records. This betrayal and conspiracy- God help me; I am doing my best to see that these inhuman medical doctors be punished.

Today is July 11, 2016, and our marriage anniversary was on the 10th of July. I prayed and prayed and went to donate money to a school for the blind in Delhi and spent two hours with the administrator, some of the staff, and a student. My brother Arun and nephew Ashiem were with me as they drove in Delhi and knew the roads. This is the first time in my life I have ever seen a school for blind students, and they are very bright- studying from their MBA, JD, government jobs, and going to top colleges and high schools. It was the happiest and most painful experience in my life, and I donated cash in memory of my beloved wife, Constance Berry, and they gave me a receipt. This will bring peace to my mind, and I am sure my Darling wife Connie was watching me do that noble cause. This is how I will spend my life until death, and we will meet in our next life. Connie and Pradeep will be together in the next life. We had to make tough choices, including shifting her to the hospital in Mount Prospect for three weeks and then rehabilitation for a month so she could return home that was one choice and the second choice was that once the tubes were out on March 2nd, 2015, we could take her to the palliative care unit for three days before going home, where the palliative care doctors and nurses would come to the house to take care of Connie. Mrs. Berry would be fine and live another 5 or 10 or 15 years as her response had been good and that was her desire she wanted to go home, and she decided that if she had to die, she wanted to die in her own home in the lap of her loving husband, Pradeep. That was precisely what Connie told me.

The doctors took advantage of my absence and told me that Constance told them to take the tubes out and let her die. There was no way this could have happened if I had not left the room for that short time. I would never, ever have allowed her former doctor to enter the room. He had no business to come as he had ruined her case and removed her from her care in October 2014. He should never have come to that location that Friday. Connie wasn't even able to talk- we communicated through notes and body language. She told me to make these decisions for her and do what I thought was best for her. As her power of attorney, I decided to do everything possible to save her.

Again, I became a tiger and blasted the doctors and nurses. My battle for Connie was eight against one. It was my first loss, and all of the palliative care they had promised us was not performed. In spite of my aggressive actions and the phone calls I made, Connie died at 1:10 A.M. on February 28th, 2015. I have videos that some nurses made for me, one of 32 minutes and another of 10 minutes showing how I am fighting to call the doctors, palliative care, and anybody to give her oxygen and treatment, but no one came. The hospital telephones can be seen ringing, saying yes, Mr. Berry, we are sending the nurse- but no one came. At 7 P.M., a nurse finally came but did nothing until 9 P.M., when they declared her dead.

Immediately, two nurses came and put the oxygen mask on her and gave her morphine injections, and Connie recovered. I had been holding my bladder since 3 P.M. one friend of mine showed up as my brother from India had called him to say that Connie had died and I was alone. He came at 11 P.M., and I was surprised, and he, too, was surprised to find Connie alive. He stayed and said it indeed looks like negligence. We were at peace because Connie seemed fine then. He told me to let him bring his wife to the hospital, but I said no because it was getting late. He insisted. I asked the nurses if I could go to the bathroom, and I waited 9 hours. They said yes. I was a king when I talked to one lady while coming back to Connie's room. She told me nothing would happen to my wife as our devotion to each other was marvelous and rare. I was thrilled, but I was not indeed a king. The moment I entered the room, I saw my friend by the computer with the vitals and his wife next to Connie's bed asking me, "Pradeep, Pradeep come, Connie is going, she is going."

I was shaken and broken and looked at Connie, telling her, "Connie, Connie, please do not leave me. Please, Connie, do not give up," asking the nurses to do something, please do something. Her vitals went from 60 to 50 to 40 to 30 and finally at 10 when I saw her last four breaths. Darling Connie died next to me. I was absolutely gone and wept and wept and fell apart. My friends, along with Connie's caregiver, gave me great support. On top of her death, this episode was all the more upsetting once I got her medical records. I ask myself, where is humanity? Why is there so much deceit in the medical profession? Perhaps that is why there is so much darkness in the noble medical profession.

Despite this setback, I was still optimistic that my Connie would live. A great thought came to me: never deprive someone of hope when hope may be all they have left. I thought that miracles happen every day. These messages brought us great comfort. I began to ask God to make Connie normal again by a miracle, which was when Jesus brought Lazarus back to life. That prayer was heard, so why couldn't my prayer save my lovely wife? At the same time, I thought of Savitri and Satyavan, a miracle in India one hundred years ago. Through Savitri's devotion to God, her husband's life was returned to him. Thinking of these two miracles made me more robust, and I felt ready to fight anything. It was a struggle for Connie to go to doctor's appointments during her treatment, and even walking too much in the house was difficult as she had to rely on a walker and oxygen. This was not pleasant for us, but being together and seeing each other's faces gave us great happiness.

Ultimately, I saw my Darling's last four breaths and was present for her death. Two nurses and a couple of close friends were with me. I could never have imagined her death or the way that HH and the negligence of her doctors killed her. It was one of the most painful, shocking, and uncalled-for things I have ever witnessed. My mind went blank. Connie's body, her face- I have no words for the pain I felt in my entire being. Could it be true that I would never see her, talk to her, live with her again? I am left alone. I thought of the miracles- was it possible that God might reward me by granting her life again? All those thoughts ran through my mind. As I write on August 20, 2015, every day since her death, these questions and thoughts run through my mind day and night. I relive that painful episode, and it gives me panic attacks.

I stayed with Connie's body for five hours until it was taken to the funeral home for cremation. I will never forget that trauma as long as I live. After two days, I cremated and put her ashes in her plot next to her parents. Doing this was heartbreaking and broke me. I suffer from that pain and have withdrawn from life. The pain and suffering I am left with are incorporated into my mind and my heart. I must mention that after Connie's demise, I asked Florida Harris if she would be willing to work for me, and her job would be to come at night and sleep in my study room while studying for her Master's in nursing. She agreed, and like a sister or family, Florida was very helpful in doing chores and bringing my grocery and food, and we would eat together, or she would make something for me. If I were up, she would eat breakfast with me or would leave me sleeping. It worked for over a month until I got the power to stay myself. At that point, I worked 16-18 hours a day to handle all the legal formalities and write the book. It was too much work for me by myself. I decided that I would never ask my family in Chicago, friends, and anybody to come and help me. I did not even disclose Connie's death until Arun, with anger, informed my sister and other families in July 2015 about Connie's death.

This book has two parts—happiness and sadness. Sadness has taken over happiness. Sadness is hard to define, and no one can understand that pain but for me. I don't know what I can do while waiting to face the rest of my life; however, I would have to be strong to survive Connie's death. For me, the world is lost: I no longer travel, dine out, go to Broadway shows, read, watch TV or movies, I do not meet any friends, nor do I attend any parties or functions. I want to be alone in a sort of "Robinson Crusoe Economy"- where a man lives alone and does everything himself.

In ancient times, many scholars and learned people took sanyas, during which they would surrender the world to get enlightenment, peace and leave a legacy of learning to the world. Around the world, many generations of people learned from these hermits who withdrew from the world to gain knowledge. In my opinion, today we live in a world in which different generations do not share and pass on knowledge in the same way, and the young ignore the knowledge of their elders. The youth of the 21st century has also contributed to significant technological innovations, and the world has gained. I believe in applying both ancient and modern knowledge to keep the balance in my life. Connie was also of this view and never criticized anyone. We both respected the beliefs of others.

Mahatma Gandhi:

I thought of Gandhi, who fought for equal rights during the British Empire. Even though he was a barrister of law, he was not allowed to practice in England. In South Africa, he was thrown from a train by whites, as he was considered dark-skinned under apartheid. That incident shaped him to fight to free India from the British. He was involved in all the Satyagraha, or strikes, and was prisoned many times. One time, Gandhi was in his jail cell, and his fellow inmate told him that he should write a book, which he refused to do. That inmate's constant, persistent pressure led Gandhi to write his book, capturing the world market. That book was an autobiography by Gandhi, My Experiments living with Truth. This book has so much wisdom and many good messages for humanity and nonviolence. Ben Kingsley acted as Gandhi in the Oscar award-winning Gandhi in 1984. One can see his devotion and the sacrifices he made to free India. Pandit Jawaharlal Lal Nehru, the first Prime Minister of India, Maulana Abdul Kalama Azad, and many great leaders were the freedom fighters who supported Gandhi's movement. Gandhi, who is called the Father of the Nation in India, is well respected. I feel upset that his approach to non-violence was not followed for a long time. The world has changed for the past 60 years, and nonviolence looks like it is gone from the dictionary. John F. Kennedy was a great President of the USA, Abraham Lincoln, Roosevelt, and others who did so much for the USA. Dr. Martin Luther King, Jr., Nelson Mandela, and many great leaders did many great things. George King, the father of her Highness Queen Elizabeth of England, who had a speech problem, finally gave an excellent speech during wartime. The film based upon this true story, "The King's Speech," won an Oscar.

These great people were moving around my mind when Connie was in the intensive Cardiac unit of the hospital. I was devastated that the delay of these doctors by nine minutes impacted Connie's lie and later her death. It crushed me, and I was broken and lost my mind and brain. I can never forget her condition and her last breaths of death, and one cannot imagine what I had to go through because of Connie's death. That death, which I saw for the first time in my life and that, of course, of my wife. How could someone even think I was struggling to save her, but she was dying, which ruined my life, happiness, world, and whatnot. I had forgotten all about my hardship during childhood struggle and all the sacrifices and hard work of mine and education, and, of course, Connie's influence in my life.

I was weak in thinking but kept getting my strength from the knowledge that I had to keep my mind, and my brain focused; otherwise, anything could happen to Connie and, of course, to me and then worry about her cremation and her wishes for ashes in her plot, and chapel of peace. I started praying and praying and again started thinking of many leaders and how they could do such great things. Gandhi was able to say to the British Empire: "It is time you left India." This was a powerful tool, and I was ready when Connie was taken to the cardiac unit. She was mentally alert and wanted to speak to me, and I was there 24 hours watching her like my small daughter, and I thought, "She is my wife. God, Can I ask if you can grant me one thing, my Connie? Give my Connie back either as a wife, sister, mother-daughter, or a small born child, but do not take away this second body of mine and take whatever you want from my karmas or anything I am willing to get to her. I want only one thing, and that is Connie.

I am willing to sweep the tables, clean the bathrooms, willing to do any small or big work for humanity, just like we have been doing since we met." Unfortunately, my rhythm was shallow. Diminishing the theory of lower returns, I decided I needed food, clothes, and our beautiful home fully beautifully decorated better than an outside professional by Connie. Connie's death took away all my happiness and desire to go to restaurants and travel anywhere, except for a month to see my brother and his family. Even today, I would do whatever God wanted me to do to get Connie back. I was sure God was listening to my thoughts and perhaps watching me at the bedside of Connie. He would grant me my Connie. Another valid example of love happened during the Mughal Era of India; one of the kings, Babar, came during Babar and Human. When Human-made 11 circles around the bed of his dying son as he lay dying, God granted his wish, and his son's life was granted. I tried that, but due to the bed's position, I was able to do more than 11 but not in circles. God knows that I am trying circles, but in the hospital bed with all the tubes and equipment, etc., could cause more damage if I start moving, and in any case, I would have never been allowed to do that. It was not my home where I could do what I wanted; however, my intentions and theory were the same. I was still very hopeful, and that is how I thought of Savitri and Satyavan and other miracles in the world. I was confident that miracles happen every day; and that God would perform miracles as Connie did so much for her parents, for her students, for humanity, for the universities, for the library, for Mexico and the Mexican people by giving free education, teaching, writing and songs and many research papers for them, as she was a Spanish teacher and had seen many good and bad things happening there and also in every part of the world. She was entirely devoted to humanity and the idea that God wants me to get access to my door alive and take care of my people- that is what she did for everyone. I was the same way to some extent, but she was the engine in my life for everything. This marriage, our house, household work, laundry, shopping, accounting the household budget, writing checks, shopping, ironing, taking sick and the elderly to the grocery store, helping many neighbors- especially one who was 90 years old and Connie took her every week or sometimes twice for her shopping. We were even taking her out 70% of the time for dining out, movies, bringing what she wanted, driving her to her doctor's appointments, cleaning her house, and whatnot. Connie did that for over 12 years. Even when Connie was sick, Connie took care of her. It stopped when that lady moved to go to an assisted living home in her late nineties.

However, all these thoughts and faith were not granted to me by the Supreme Power. Perhaps there is some sin I must atone for, some slackness somewhere from my current life or past life that was still due, even after my childhood tragedies of losing my biological mother and her younger sister, whose devotion and sacrifice was unbelievable and painful, as she too sacrificed her remarkable career and had to my father to take care my elder brother and me. How hard it would have been to my second mother, Kanta Mummy, who was a few years younger than my biological mother, Shanti Mummy. Both our mothers died. Kanta Mummy died when I was 5 and a half, and my brother was 6 and three months. Kanta mummy died two hours after my sister was born. We brothers remember that death very well, including Kanta Mummy's body, my sister of two hours having her thumb in her mouth, and I was playing with her. I knew and saw each and everything but doesn't recall any emotions or being devastated. The true death and tragedy came before and after Connie's death. All her cremation, the interment of her ashes, and her ceremony for two days and after placing the headstone and then visiting her cemetery more or less two to four times each month. This death and shock is mental agony. It is the most excruciating thing in my life and will remain that way as long as I live. I know that for sure.

After losing our two mothers, another tragedy was waiting for us. My father married Uma Mummy, who came from another family. Because of the three of us, my mothers' parents and sisters and brothers wanted Uma Mummy to be part of our family and more or less adopted her as their daughter. I remember Uma Mummy was lovely and, to some degree, loving and had some passion for us and was part of our studies up to fourth or fifth grades. The change came because of all the expenses of the joint family of over 100 members, including my Berry grandfather's four children, grandchildren, his three brothers who had died and their children, and Berry grandmother's family and their children and grandchildren and outsiders, and so many extended family members were all paid by for by my Berry grandfather. Berry's grandfather was very wealthy. Uma mummy was lovely as she knew that she had to be to get access to Berry's grandfather's money, inheritance, and wealth, which was to be divided among Berry's grandfathers' six children. Uma Mummy was lovely until she had her two boys, and then her interest towards her three step-children began to diminish until it was just a tiny part, and she never paid us a nickel or penny till today. All the wealth was distributed after Berry's grandparents were gone when I was 22 and had finished my post-graduation and Chartered Accountancy. I should have started working and achieved the highest position while making a big salary, and perhaps we two brothers would have bought a house.

ELEGIAC PAEAN

I must mention that real estate is costly in India and especially in Delhi. We still have some of our ancestral houses, although some of them have been sold. I could not even think of buying that. I am taking some of them that cost millions of US dollars. Uma Mummy had to work and support herself. If we had not lived in our big house or Berry Grandfather was not there, we would have been with my mothers' family, and they would have to raise us. My mother had seven sisters and two brothers. During those days, having lots of kids was culturally valued by wealthy families. Things have been different in the last fifty years or more. Later, Uma Mummy rejected the three of us and never wanted us to be her children. Our further downfall from wealth took us to more or less very limited to a life of education, Boy Scouting, sports, clothes, and public transportation, and pocket money was very small until we were in high school and college. We only received our necessities. We, two boys, were the first who finished high school and college and post-graduation, and I did another four years of Chartered Accountancy to make our destiny. However, after 1969, after the death of my Berry grandfather, we both were treated with bias.

The third mother then played a chess game and made a big gamble by taking my father to our other big house far away from the big main palace in Old Delhi, in Katra Neel, Chandni chowk. Our house in Katra Neel is now a big tourist attraction. We resided there and were given the food and basics and some small pocket money until my brother finished his post-graduation and got a job. I had one year to finish and four years to complete my Chartered Accountancy, and then my brother started taking care of me as he was told to separate his kitchen from our central kitchen meant for 18 people. However, the house could accommodate over 300 people. But slowly, every other uncle and Berry family member my grandfather supported left, and we were still there. I used to depend upon my brother. Chartered Accountancy is one of the toughest degrees, with 3% passing and working an apprenticeship from 9 to 6 with no salary or stipend, as no scholarship was allowed do this course. After I finished that degree, I was confused about starting my practice, joining the family business, or joining the army as I was C certificate and would have been a Major after three months of training. I refused great job offers from banks, foreign institutions, the US embassy in Delhi, Australia, the United Kingdom, and anywhere in India. It was a confusing battle, and I had no money to travel. I made a great mistake by not looking into my career at that time. Still, I am delighted that all of this happened, and I have forgotten those days as God had other plans for me after suffering from my wealthy family and never receiving my share of the inheritance. I've never even seen a nickel of the millions of dollars my grandfather left to distribute among my family. My father was a henpecked husband and had two boys from his third wife. It was destiny that they were to get my father's entire portion of the inheritance.

According to the Indian Karta Act, grandchildren have the first right to their grandfathers' property, business, gold, and diamonds. My family did not abide by this law. I came to the USA, and my uncles and cousins got all of the billions of dollars inheritance that my grandfather Berry left. When I met Connie, all of that money became valueless to me. I couldn't buy my Connie for all the money on the planet. She was my wife and my Kohinoor diamond. I only wanted her for myself. Now, I am heartbroken, lost, and living an isolated life after losing my precious Connie on February 28th, 2015. That loss is much more painful than any of my childhood suffering. I do not want that inheritance. Let whoever has the darkness of greed take it and let them pay their dues with compound interest in the next life. Connie's loss is the one that has broken me, and I will always suffer.

I would continue to live a simple life of high thinking, with my outings limited to the health club, her cemetery, and, once in a while, just going somewhere by myself. My company is nature: the moon, stars, and sun, and I find happiness in Connie's study room and sleeping with her beautiful pictures in our king-sized bed on my side and praying and her pictures and her beautiful table lamp. I prepare her bedside table with a glass of water and her sandals by the bed each night. I put out her water glasses in her study and the kitchen and looked at her beautiful pictures hanging in the living room in the morning. Our house is a true, great museum of science and art. This is my happiness. I can go to India to see my brother and his family for a few months, but now I am living in the happiest of places, my Connie's house. It is ours, but I call it My Connie's house, her temple, or church. This is the way God wanted me to find happiness. I am not happy without her, and I think of her each second, but I have to follow the law of nature and God's order, as we are all puppets in his hands and have to do whatever he asks of us. So her house is very soothing for my troubled mind. I have no other choice, as I have resources to travel anywhere, but I will not, as Connie's memory would follow me wherever I go, as we both traveled extensively in the US and Europe. We never traveled in the Middle East due to the heat and climate, but I might see Egypt and Dubai gain the courage. Time will make that decision.

India holds no fear for me, as I am with my brother and his family. Connie's room with her pictures and all the big rooms are decorated with Connie, which is comforting as I have my grandnieces and two nephews and my niece by marriage, who is very kind to me. My brother, his wife, his two sons, and two granddaughters-

my grandnieces are 5 and 10 and are fun and take away some of the pain I feel for Connie, but Connie is in every part of my body. I will never touch another woman in my life. Never. I will wait as I am sure I will meet Connie in my next life. I am sure this will happen.

Today, April 25, 2016. I went to Connie's cemetery and cleaned the granite and the grass and a few other things. I generally spend one hour or 45 minutes when I visit her grave. I could easily spend four hours and would even do not mind going daily. That is my love for Connie. I thought what a shame it is to Connie's memory that her only sibling and his four children and their spouses and grandchildren did not ever come to visit her. I was standing close to Connie's beautiful granite stone where I had them inscribe "Constance Ann Berry. Best friend and most precious darling wife of 38 years." Suddenly, I wondered why I did not have them write for 40 years, as there were some errors in my troubled mind. I chose the inscription, the granite, the color, and the design of her headstone, as I was the only person making those decisions as Connie's brother and his family never came to visit her, even until today. I think it is the most shameful thing a sibling can do to treat his sister so. He and his family are all church-going people. If that is what the church teaches, how can they think of going to church? How does their conscience allow them to go to church, and how does it allow such people to enter?

Connie had one college student, Roberto Ciera. I have a great friend in Mexico, Alfonzo Penna Ciera, who I was thinking of calling. He worked under 36 other people and me when I was the senior management consultant in 1998-1999 in Mount Prospect. Alfonzo came from a wealthy family, and I used to bring him home to meet Connie. Connie immediately told me that he is from a wealthy family. Later, he tried to come to the US and wanted me to join him in San Francisco, but I didn't.

Lovely Dogs. They are serious then and faithful to their master without thinking if they are rich. They can judge the character of humans in no time, even from miles away, and stop them from coming near to you. I wish Connie and I had a dog before she put the evil eye on my Connie. A dog would have torn her apart from this evil from the earth, as great Lord Rama was in the creation of God to kill the great scholar, Ravana, king of Sri Lanka, and I might write a note about this in the book. I got on the Internet and read about the Diwali festival in India or Lord Rama and Great Ravana. This true story happened 5000 years ago in India. You would find out the sacrifice of Rama's half-brothers and how they ran the kingdom of Ayodyapuri until Lord Rama returned from his 14 years of exile along with his wife Sita and younger brother Laxman, how the younger half-brother looked after the kingdom without sitting on the throne but by touching Rama's wooden sandals until he came back and took his throne. That is what I am doing, touching Connie's sandals in the morning and night and placing her water glasses in the kitchen and near her computer and the white glass on her side table in the night. That is the most healing thing for me, that and praying to that noble soul's pictures and sleeping with her framed picture. The picture shows how she was sitting on her chair with a walker in front and another walker with her clothing. That place is a church, a cathedral for me.

So on this visit, I was upset that I should ask them to write

CONSTANCE ANN BERRY
BEST FRIEND & MOST PRECIOUS DARLING
WIFE OF 40 YEARS OF PRADEEP BERRY

I was thinking and thinking and moved around and saw several other stones which had the same color and design as other people's families, and they had a beloved son of XYZ—beloved wife and father or husband of XYZ.

Throughout the two years of Connie's illness, she seemed normal in her daily life- reading, writing, working on the computer, keeping our accounts, watching films, discussing things, etc. We were both still happy as being together was nothing but happiness, and we were filled with the hope that Connie would live at least another ten to fifteen years, as she was an avid reader and learned that new medicines and treatments were being released. I read the same and was also optimistic about our prospects.

In ancient Egypt, people mummified their dead bodies to cope with the loss of their loved ones. I think it was right for those people to see the body and feel that their loved ones were still with them. I could never have done that with Connie, who asked to be cremated. I never thought I, her loving husband, would have to oversee her last rites. Why was this my fate? Connie's pictures and our pictures together fill my house. In this way, my life is a combination of happiness for the memory of our life together and sadness for her loss.

While she was ill, my life was dedicated to serving Connie. I brought her tea and juice in the morning after she got up to study with her walker and oxygen. Later, she would make the painful trek to the kitchen for breakfast. Making and serving her the best of breakfast food was my greatest happiness. I felt the same about cooking her dinner, helping her shower, and bringing her a glass of water first thing in the morning and last thing at night. Taking care of her and bringing her to the hospital for appointments and treatments was a mixture of pain and joy. Helping her prepare for these appointments brought both pain and happiness to my heart and soul.

Connie was extremely positive throughout her illness, although inside, she was most unhappy, not knowing if she would ever get better. I used to give her positive feedback based on my faith in God and the miracle of Savitri and Satyavan. I was devoted to Connie and was hoping God would listen to me; however, I lost that battle and was broken and devastated. After her death, I was only sleeping three to four hours a night, and there was lots of work to do. Most important was to have her cremated, put her ashes in her plot next to her parents, and then put the stone on her ashes (as per her wishes and the wishes of others). God helped me do all that, and by my aggressive approach, I was able to get the funeral done in two days. I didn't want my Darling's body sitting in the funeral home for a long time. She was not a charity case, and I told the funeral and cemetery people that money was not a problem. I also told them that I wanted the best--- but best casket and urns and priests at all the services, including the cremation, the memorial in the Chapel of peace, and later at the burial of her ashes in her plot. The same was for the headstone. I was firm; I would not compromise anything for money. I provided lunch for the people who came to pay their respect to Connie. I also hired a professional video maker for two days to cover the ceremonies of Connie Darling- it is not an excellent video. Still, all those sad memories could stay with me to provide me some happiness, and while they may give me pain, they also take some pain away. I watch those videos quite often. I DO NOT KNOW what I think and how it affects me, but it provides something.

I never thought I would have to do myself how much pain and suffering was going on in my heart and soul to see my wife's funeral. She was the one I married, and now I had to arrange her funeral services. I am extremely upset about it. I was not ready to lose her and never again saw that great wife who played the role of best wife, best friend, sister, and mother through different situations in my life. It reminds me what Sahajahhan must have gone through at the loss of his wife, Mumtaaz Mahel. After her death, he built the Taj Mahel in Agra, India; it is an example of love and one of the world's seventh wonders. No outsiders can understand my pain, which is in my heart and soul and always haunts me. If I start talking about this with relatives and friends, they will not understand my pain, and if they say something, I will not listen or follow their advice.

Now I understand what Great Buddha, who was silent for two years after his enlightenment, said upon breaking his silence. Many Gods were worried about his silence and requested that he speak, but he refused. After many requests from all the gods, he broke his silence by saying that "people who understand me know my silence, and if I say something, they would not understand me and think negatively about me. I, therefore, decided to be silent. My message is even if I can change the life of one person out of millions, my purpose is accomplished." How wonderful were those 39 and half years? I pray to God to take away some of my possessions and give my Darling Connie back--- but I am sure we will be husband and wife in our next lives, and this hope gives me strength, and I am willing to struggle whatever way I have to, but I want Connie back in my next life.

8

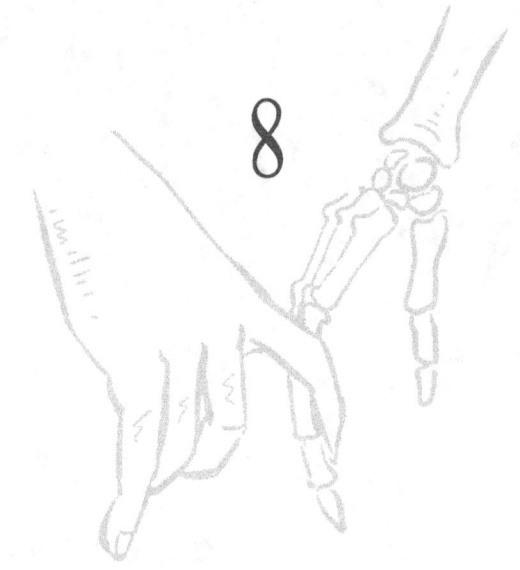

The Story of Sati Savitri

I would encourage readers to read the whole story on the internet or in a complex book.

9

A True Story About Faith and Greed

I would also like to share a true story about faith in religion and greed, I read a long time back.

This is a true story. There was once a wealthy and very generous merchant who never refused alms to anyone. His neighbor was an evil old lady who would curse everybody going for alms. A few years ago, some faithful saints went out asking for alms. The merchant gave them a generous amount of wheat flour, and the saints left happily with their blessings to the merchant. The evil old lady started shouting abuse and curses to both the saints and the merchant. The saints continued, and while they were traveling, a flying eagle dropped a dead rat into their wheat flour. The saints ate the flour and died. People asked their religious leaders, "Who is to be blamed for their deaths, the merchant, the woman, or fate?" The learned religious men replied, "The merchant gave in good faith, so he is above blame. The evil woman is to blame because of her bad tongue and bad intentions. Finally, fate is responsible for their death." I have met some people who could not fulfill their daily needs and others who amass wealth out of greed. I think this story is right- it is the greed for more than killing the sages.

Lord, you are everywhere—omnipresent, omnipotent, and omniscient.

Lord, you are perfect. Your pattern and design of the world are perfect. We accept your orders without question.

The rule of Nish Karma- daily duty: do your duties, deeds, and karmas without identifying the self with it or its reactions. This is self-realization. We are puppets in the hands of God, and we have to perform whatever role he wants us to play.

In the kingdom of God, every event and situation is preordained to happen in its proper time. There is a chain of cause and reaction. But God has allotted a function and duty to everyone, and no man, however great he may be, should interfere with the conscience and lifestyle of another man. Therefore, there is so much discontentment, frustration, and crime in the world.

To practice religion, there are specific rules laid down by the ancient worship

10

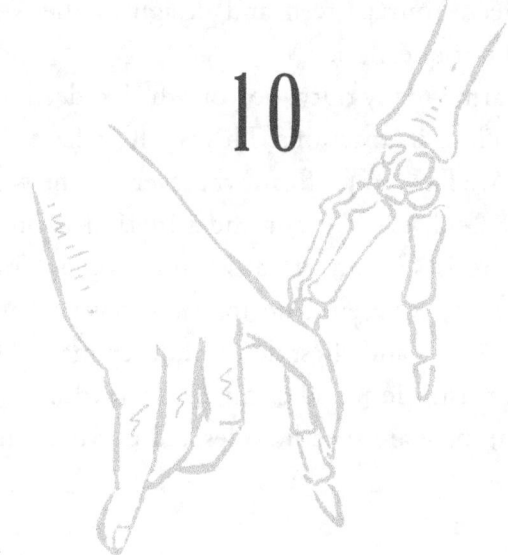

My Loss and Pain for Connie

Compelled Me to repeat the same thing I wrote before. I can say for sure there was no lack in my devotion for Connie throughout our life. However, when Connie was first diagnosed with cancer in 2002 and throughout her illness until her death, the devotion and love for both of us were at their peak. Many of our friends, hospital staff and neighbors, even strangers knew and wished they were blessed with that kind of love and devotion. Further, when Mayo Clinic declared palliative care on November 8, 2014, my devotion and prayers to the Lord to make Connie well again were at their peak. Her body was like a god, and I prayed over that weak body, her walker, her oxygen, her clothes, and any object that was a favorite of Connie's. I was convinced that God would see my devotion and give both of us more strength and that new enlightenment was coming to save her at any cost. I knew miracles happen every day. Our good Karmas or Connie's best Karma would convince God to change the process of palliative care to normal life and choose to give her 10-15 years more to live. That what the only thing I was asking God, and that was what she was asking for as well?

We both shared the good Karmas, which were far greater than any small lousy karma. We began to feel confident that she would have a full long life. We believed in miracles, as we knew of many miracles that had happened. We were sure that she would live another 10-15 good years, as she had already gone through cancer treatments boldly. Connie would tell me, "God helps those who help themselves." God has the power to do anything, to take and to give life. We were not asking God for immortality. We even knew that someday I might be alone with only God for comfort. I wanted my service to God to save Connie. I decided that I would fight her sickness all by myself, without asking for the help of my friends and relatives. I had read true stories of life in the jungle, the suffering of animals and people, and how they were granted new life. When these things were coming into my mind, I was growing stronger and better prepared to handle the stress of Connie's struggle.

My love and devotion to my precious wife increased immeasurably, and I cherished everything about her, down to her daily routine. I gained confidence that God knew how much love I had for Connie. The saying, "If one truly asks God for something with devotion, hard work, and does anything to reach out to him, God is kind to grant that wish," came to my mind. It happened centuries ago during the Mogul era. Hamayun, Babar, and Akbar, the great Mogul kings, asked God for help, and they were granted what they wanted. My devotion, perhaps, exceeded theirs. I know medical science and serious illnesses result in the end, but the saying "nobody goes as long as God is protecting them" also has a truth.

There is a true story. Three ladies told this story we met in 2006 and narrated in front of three top medical doctors. The doctors had told these women that they had only a few months to survive. They told them to say their last prayers as the end was coming. The women went and prayed and waited. They waited and waited, but still, they lived. It so happened that many years later (16 years for one, 19 years for another, and 12 years for the third), these ladies returned to their doctors for a minor illness and asked if they recognized them. These doctors were astonished that their diagnoses had been incorrect. These ladies were childhood friends and neighbors, and my family was in touch with them. I had a few friends who also experienced a similar situation. I had one uncle in India who lived with cancer for 33 years, and a woman I knew survived cancer for 23 years. This gave me new confidence in the ways of Life and Death, and God. Connie and I were so confident that she would survive.

These positive examples made us stronger; however, Connie read the obituary column in the *Chicago Tribune*, and I noticed some died within only a few years of being diagnosed with cancer. These were encouraging and fearful thoughts, be we chose to be positive. I honestly did not want anyone to know how ill she was. First, I was very angry with my friends and relatives who had not reached out to us in several years. I took an oath in 2012 that I would not call them or tell them that Connie was not doing well. I would not be open with those friends who were only interested in paying lip service to our friendship. They never once told us that they were with us and we could count on them. I could read the difference between lip service and sincere friendship. I know everyone has problems, but to my mind and Connie's, we had always gone out of the way no matter what. We still called them to inquire after their well-being, their families, etc. Connie was in touch with their sorrows. Why did we not get that dedication from them?

At that time, I turned to the Supreme Lord and said, "It is our battle; please help us, who have such good karma." I was totally in the hands of God, and so was Connie. And yet, we lost that battle. Later, I had another chance to fight the doctors and medical staff at her cardiac arrest like a tiger to protect Connie. It was ten against one. God helped me fight and be strong like a boxer, a tiger, superman, or the ambassador of God. But I did not win; instead, I lost the most crucial battle of my life. I will never forget this lost battle of love and my future.

11

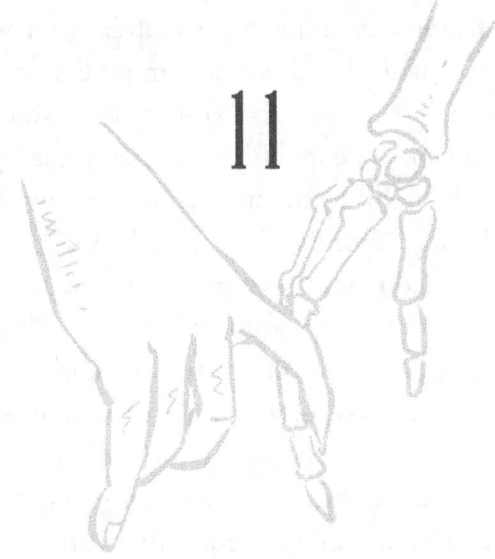

Another Painful Chapter for Connie and Pradeep

Before writing, I want to apologize for mentioning this sensitive issue. Connie's siblings and family did not come for Connie's cremation or any of her funeral services. Connie has only one true sibling, her elder brother, and his family includes his wife, their four grown children, and eight grandchildren. They all go to church every Sunday, but they do not come to Connie's funeral. The entire family lives three hours from Chicago, and even her brother's summer home is a three-hour flight from Florida to Chicago. This is an inexcusable shame. When I informed them about my darling Connie's death, these church-going people made their excuses. Her brother and sister-in-law pleaded his upcoming knee surgery, which I believe could easily have been postponed so that he could attend her funeral. Even Connie's adult nieces and nephews did not come. This showed me that they do not care for their lovely aunt, who truly loved them. But, they had no compassion for their highly educated sister and aunt. It is pathetic and shameless for humanity to act this way. In my strong opinion, the main culprit is his smooth wife, a very power hungry-snob who has crossed the limit of her ego- she is arrogant and convinced that she is much higher class than anybody else. Yes, she would go where there is a benefit, and her husband, Connie's brother, has become most fixed on the

MONEY- they had a fixation on money no matter from where it came. God's law always rules, as their sons-in-law are mooching them enough. Money is like a snake. It never stays in one place. One day you are rich, and suddenly, the money disappears and can put people on edge. I have so many examples in my fifty years' experience. It would be shameful to them and their society if they found out that these church people did not go, nor did they send their kids on the death of his one sister. I would not be surprised that church people would not even allow nor would they associate with them. Why do they go the church? Why? To learn humanity or to make connections, and in my opinion to find some widows or widowers to take them into confidence to leave money for them. God will not forgive them, and they would pay an excruciating high price for me to see this cold love they had for Connie. This same Connie used to buy cards and wrap Christmas gifts for her family, shopping for them even while traveling the world. Connie sews quilts for them and sends the children money for birthdays, Christmas, and other occasions. Over the past 25 years, her nieces and nephews lost their love for their aunt Connie. As small children, they loved her and always wanted us to visit and bring joy into their lives. We used to go to every function they were in concerts, graduations, and holidays. Connie invited her family for Thanksgiving and Easter every year. Connie was exceptionally fond of all of them, and they were her only family. From 1976 until 1998, it was great fun and joy for all of us. Later, things changed—greed is a curse of the land.

    I must mention that the whole of Connie's family has always been very nice to me and would be nice even going forward after her death. I am incredibly grateful to them for all that. I regret and apologize for recounting this lousy episode. One big mistake and years and years of love and my feelings towards them have changed. However, I would never wish anything wrong to them and would like to see them happy and enjoying their life with their kids and grandchildren. Now I am the biggest loser as Darling Connie is no more with me- a terrible loss for me in my life. Perhaps, I am writing this sad family episode to share my loss. I pray to God that one day, I can forget the past and forgive them for their behavior.

    I would say the same for my extended cousins and their large family, including my real uncle and his family. For three years, they never called to ask how I was doing or how Connie was doing. I was mad at them and did not even inform them that she had died. I didn't tell my family of Connie's death until I went to India in May 2015, and even then, I waited until June to tell them my sad news. My elder brother, feeling the persistent pressure of his duty as the head of the family, informed my extended family. Since I returned to the US on July 23, 2015, only three people out of nearly 70 have visited me. As I wrote on August 26th, 2015, the rest of the 30 or more extended family members in Chicago have not called or stopped by. This episode has made me learn more and more about the world and has made me bitter and angry towards my relatives. I, too, am angry with my friends of some 40 years to contact them. It takes years and years to make friends and develop love with family and friends, but in one second or at one incident, the love is gone forever. However, I find peace by writing Connie's biography, which gives me happiness but sadness of 250000% mixed in that too.

Further, I want to share my childhood tragedy. My mother, Respected Shanti Mehra, was born in 1921 in Lahore and Lyallpur, now in Pakistan after India's independence from British rule, which was achieved on August 15, 1947. She was highly educated and wanted to go into civil service during the British Empire. But can we play with destiny? My maternal grandfather was not wealthy, but he was well off. His close friend, Puran Chand (whom I never saw but am still angry at him), convinced that ladies do not go to the UK for jobs and should be married. He suggested the boy of an extremely wealthy merchant in Delhi, India, as a possible husband for my mother.

My mother was devastated and did not want to marry; instead, she wanted a great career. I am still furious and ask why she was forced to marry my father, Mr. Ram Prashad Berry, born in 1921. My paternal grandfather was extremely wealthy. Shanti mummy bore my elder brother Arun and myself before dying tragically young. Arun was 12 months old, and I was only two months of age when Shanti Mummy- beautiful and educated- died. I did not see my mother. My family was at a significant loss and thought that as my father was 27 years old and would remarry, we two boys would get a stepmother who would neglect and ruin us. My maternal grandparents forced my mother's younger sister Miss Kanta Mehra to marry my father to avoid stepmother. Respected Kanta Mehra, who completed her double master's in English and was going for a great career, was too absolutely devastated and did not want to marry. She had no choice but to marry my father. I am distraught with my grandparents and my father for forcing her to marry. We two brothers remember her being a great mother and extremely beautiful and educated. She loved us like her children. But God had other plans. She bore one daughter, my sister, and died after her birth at the young age of 25. Arun was six and a half, and I was five and a half when we lost our second mother. We both remember her death and funeral.

My father, who was now 27 years old, married his third wife, Mrs. Uma Malhotra, age 27, our stepmother. She played the role my family had feared very well by separating both of us from our father and producing her two boys. That was the end of our great inheritance. We were brought up by our two grandparents and our mothers' younger sisters. Sometimes, it bothers me why our paternal grandparents, who owned many properties, houses, and had a fortune, left a trust or some provision to ensure that we get part of the wealth. As it was, we had only a good education- but nothing else—Arun and I made our successful destinies. My paternal grandfather's children had no education, but they did have money, which has been appreciated 100 times. My two half-brothers and other cousins, as well as a living uncle, are grabbing all the money and giving it to their children. I would have never done this greedy act. I am agitated and still cannot believe that anyone in the Berry family would do that. They have no compassion, no shame, no guilt, and no sympathy that we had lost our two mothers and suffered, including my father, who became a puppet in my stepmother's hands did not give us two brothers a penny. I feel my stepmother must have been an insensitive person. But although I must feel something about my father's death on October 14, 2003, I don't know whether or not I feel sorrow for his loss. We two brothers and two half-brothers performed the last rites for our father; however, Arun and I lost our inheritance, and our two half-brothers grabbed our inheritance. My grandparents were both very charitable and helped many people, but my paternal grandfather's children did not do any charity at all. It is hard to believe that our stepmother did this dirty thing, separating us two smart, intelligent boys who had many things to offer from our family. My father, too, became like a stepfather and never gave a penny to both of us or our sister. He changed as a henpecked husband in my stepmother's hands, although he could not forget our two beautiful mothers and used to talk to us when he was alone with us.

Greed is ruining humanity everywhere; however, the world continues to exist as there are good people, and some of them are very compassionate. Connie was the most ethical, honest person, and I was the same as Arun. My great uncle, Dr. P.N. Behl, advising me about this family war over money, told me, "Son, either fight or forget." He told me to give him my power of attorney, and he would get my share, as he was very well connected and had a way to get us our share of the inheritance, but Arun and I did not listen to him. According to Indian law, grandchildren have the first right to their grandparent's property and assets. Connie told me to fight so we brothers would not lose our inheritance, especially my brother Arun in India, but we both refused. These days, I forget the strife and do not care anymore, but I want to mention how man's Greed is cursed on this land. How can greedy people live with their conscience and heart? My stepmother and a few others, who saw something in her, used to tell me, "Pradeep, you are fortunate to have Connie as your wife. She allows you to visit India every year." Wives in India will make a massive deal if their husbands go somewhere, even for two days.

Few of my relatives visited us in the US, while Connie went to India seven times. Each of our family members and friends was highly impressed with her manners, simple life- she never demanded any special food or any special privileges and accepted whatever was offered to her. It truly highly impressed them. Now, when I think of all these qualities and her exceptional intelligence, I go into the deepest pain of losing my Connie, and every day of our 40 years of marriage, love, and care moves in my brain, mind, and heart as if I am watching our lives as a movie. I am storing all these memories in my mind and heart. No matter how I try to explain it, no one will ever understand how I live with my memories. Even a doctor or a psychologist would never figure this out. This is due to the special bond between Connie and me: we had no boundaries, an unbiased love like the smile of a tiny baby, the soothing effects of the ocean, the early morning voices of the birds, or the beauty of stars, moon, and sun.

Many people told me they knew how lovely and great she was. I want to tell them that they would not be able to convince me of her greatness. Some feel they have already defined it to me- they could not have known her. Connie was one in ten million.

While traveling or staying in hotels, I often asked Connie replied" "No one would say no to a present or money- regardless." I found this to be true all my life, except for a very few situations. Connie also told me that we should leave a little early to go anywhere as unexpected traffic or other problems could arise. It is better to be there early rather than risk missing the flight, especially at the airport. Whether traveling or meeting friends at restaurants, punctuality was her theme.

I have to some degree, forgiven my stepmother since I met Connie, as her love, devotion, charm, external and internal beauty, and my true love and devotion to her made us extremely happy. My Darling Connie was my wife, friend, sister, and mother too. This may seem very strange to people—that a woman can be my wife, best friend, sister, and mother. She took all my pain on her shoulders and heart and started loving me so much and the same thing with me. My love for her was tremendous. We, too, were made for each other, and our love was true and pure. In the ancient Indian Vedanta, it is believed that a great wife could play all these womanly roles.

12

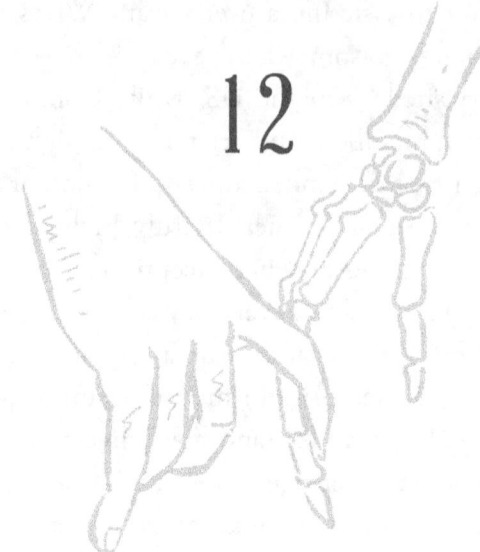

Remarkable Quotes for a Remarkable Woman

To prove this and as part of my tributes to Connie, I would like to share some remarkable quotes I studied and knew, but now I am taking them from the internet, to put the exact words.

This quote is by Chanakya in 520 BC. A **good wife serves her husband in the morning like a mother does, loves him in the day like a sister does, and pleases him like a prostitute in the night."** I would not use the word prostitute, but Chanakya went into depth by using this word, and maybe he was right. My world-renowned dermatologist uncle told me—"Son, marriage is an art, and you have to understand your wife as she is very sensitive and a husband's love is essential for her, more than anything besides the necessity of life and comfortable living." "A wife surrenders herself to her husband" I have written more on this under my uncle's advice. In our Vedanta, it is written in Sanskrit as:

A. Kaysha: Devotion, career, keeping the house in order. However, I also believe the husband must contribute more to the house and cooking and be the greatest help for his wife. I was very happy to do everything, including cooking, cleaning, and anything to make Connie's life easy. But she did a whole lot too, and we valued each other. She balanced her career, our travels, housework, and learning.

B. Kasrrmeshue: Giving good advice to her husband and others. At the same, I, too, was the same way, and we had the best understanding. Value everything equally.

C. Bhojeshue: Means good food for husband and the same I did for her. We both valued everything equally and had no egoistical sense that she was a woman and a man. She was everything for me.

D. Shaileshue: Means the love of wife and husband and in whatever forms it takes. In the old centuries, women and men married for physical relations emphasized having a good marriage and having kids. Love was there.

13

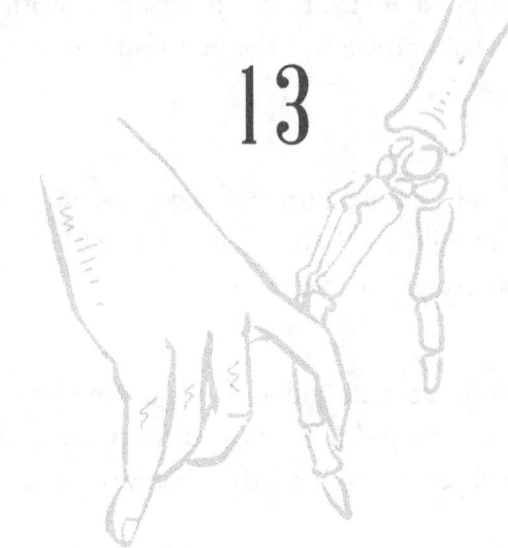

More Quotes by Chanakya

I read Chanakya's books *Arthashastra* and *Chankayaniti* during high school. Chanakya was an Indian politician and a great strategist and gained excellent knowledge. He was considered a great politician and one of the best strategic planners in 520 BC.

I. One of Chanakya's wisest aphorisms: **"A man is born alone, dies alone; and he experiences the good and bad consequences of his karmas- deeds alone, and he goes to hell or the supreme abode."**

This message Connie and Pradeep practiced throughout our lives. I am therefore 10,000,250,000% positive that Connie is with the supreme, which gives me some consolation. However, I still live with pain in my heart and soul. I would do my best to reconcile and survive by doing more good karmas and helping humanity, but I will never forget Connie as long as I am alive. She was everything for me. I genuinely do not want to go to those places we used to go to--- shopping, restaurants, and even roads. Everywhere I go, I miss her. It is tough for me to believe that I will never see her again, except maybe in my next life. But I want the exact Connie, with the same face and same external and internal beauty. My faith tells me God will fulfill my request, and this hope makes me strong to do better and better things.

2. **"As a single withered tree, if set aflame, causes a whole forest to burn, so does a rascal son destroy a whole family."**

Connie only had one brother. I believe that it was Connie's brother and his wife who destroyed her family with their greed. Her brother and sister-in-law destroyed the whole happiness of their mother and father, and most importantly, Connie's happiness. Now, when I think of Connie's brother- who is her only sibling- he and his four children and grandchildren were indeed proven with this quote. They were nice to us the first five to six years of our marriage, but later we had a love and hate relationship. Now, after the demise of Connie, none of them came for her last rites, and no one sent me condolences. Now, my 40 years of good or bad relations with them vanishes. I have no desire to talk or see any of them. Anyone who was not pleasant to Connie would never be my friend, nor would I like to talk to them or meet them. This is all due to my love for Connie. Was she alive, my bitterness would have been forgiveness, but not anymore. Connie is gone, and so are they gone from my life. Perhaps, they don't care as they only care for money.

3. **"Treat your kid like a darling for the first five years. For the next five years, scold them. By the time they turn sixteen, treat them like a friend. Your grown-up children are your best friends."**

I am convinced that this quote is true. When I was in college and studying my Chartered Accountancy, I was convinced that when your son or daughter is 15-16, especially when they reach 18, they are your best friend. I have seen this even at the age of six or seven. I was raised in a rigorous atmosphere, and my brother Arun and I were not allowed to disobey our grandfather or any member of our joint family; however, after finishing my undergraduate, Chartered Accountancy, NCC, Eagle Scout, and other things, I was treated as a friend by my family in India. Despite this, I still object to that friendship as my own Berry family- including my father and uncles and aunties- saw to it that my brother Arun, my sister Rita Revri, and I never got a penny from our millions of dollars of inheritance. It is bothersome, but after the loss of Connie, I don't want to think of nor need any inheritance. My loss of Connie is the deepest and most hurtful thing now. Other than my brother Arun and his family, no other family members of the Berry and Mehra family have a close relationship with me. If I call or meet them, they will go out of the way to meet me with love, hospitality and would respect me. Bluntly, I have no enemy. I am just outraged and devastated that Connie is gone. That loss takes over all of my happiness and joy, and I experience withdrawal. It would be nice if they came to see me; however, the old love will never come back. I was told an important saying by Mrs. Violet Hopkins, Dr. Behl's mother-in-law. She told me, "Pradeep, you can break a glass bowl either by accident or by falling. You can fix it with glue, and it will look the same; however, some marks of the broken bowl will also show. If differences come between friends and relatives, it can come back or not, but even if it comes back for the sake of formality, the true feelings are gone. Now I see the parents of young children treat them with love, and especially after 18 or even after they get married, they are best friends. I especially hurt, even more than Connie did, when she and I noticed her brother's behavior. His four kids were young, and we treated them like our own children. We were all very close as Connie's sister-in-law was (and perhaps still is) a wonderful host, but when the children grew up and had their children, her brother, I am sure on his wife's orders, began to create distance. All of this started some 15 years ago, and it got worse with time. They wanted us to come for a short visit of two days at their house in Wisconsin during the summer, at Christmas, and on Thanksgiving. Other than that, they never wanted to come to our home, even if they were in Chicago. Our sister-in-law was always the boss, and not even a leaf could move without her permission. Such was her control over her husband, children, and grandchildren. All of this was due to her power over money. Her money ruled her family. Connie told me many times, "Pradeep, when the kids were small, they wanted us to be there for the children. Now, since they have inherited money and their children are grown up, they have dumped us." Her brother, I would say, can only open his mouth and say what his dominating wife says. Even 25 years ago, I suggested that we should all go on vacation to India or Europe, or for a cruise, or even for dinner. He used to be very rude and hurtful, telling me, "Pradeep, we are busy for the next ten years>" in 1992, Connie went to the UK with her school teachers and friends, and I was happy that she should go. None of the other spouses wanted to go, so I told Connie, "Please do not deprive yourself. Go and enjoy yourself." I was delighted, but she was guilty that she went with her friends. I told her, "Don't I go to India for two weeks alone to see my brother and family?" at that time, my father, paternal grandfather, and Dr. and Mrs. Behl were alive, so I was happy to go. This argument convinced Connie to go to the UK for two weeks, and the five husbands of her friends went to the airport to drop them off and pick them up. I used to call Connie twice a day in the UK or a few times a day when she went with her teacher friends to Cancun, Mexico. Taking Connie to the airport, picking her up, talking to her on the phone, no matter how much it cost, was my true happiness.

While writing this, my memory is photographic, and I am in pain. My mind is 100% on the movie playing in my head. But that is not happening. Connie is gone. That is very upsetting and painful, but I have to finish her book. So coming back to 1992, Connie asked me to invite her brother and his family out for dinner. This would be a good opportunity for me to feel less alone. Because it was her wish, I called her brother, and he told me that he was in town with her brother, and I asked them to meet me at Hackney's restaurant. Her mother was not too happy that I was coming, as she thought I was coming for free food, and bluntly told me, "Pradeep, you would come for free food anytime." I told her, "Let me tell you, if you behave this way, I am leaving, and I can even pay for your dinner and buy you food for the next ten days. Please do not insult me. I only came because Connie told me to; otherwise, I was invited to the opening of a huge bank for dinner and social networking. I had to say no to the bank, and I was invited especially by the chairman and CEO for dinner, as they wanted me to help them shape up their commercial lending department and train the asset-based lending department." I left and met Connie's brother and his wife and mother. I remember asking Connie's brother, "Should we plan a trip together? We will go wherever you want to go." He immediately told me, "Pradeep, we are busy for the next 25 years," while laughing and insulting us as they are upper class due to their inheritance money. His ego and speaking style was hurtful, and I decided right away that we would never invite these arrogant people on a trip again.

We would never even give them the satisfaction of inviting them. I can assure you that if he had not been her brother, I would have said, "You can go to hell and do not ever even ask us to come exchange gifts and keep your inherited money and kids in the showroom. Goodbye, and never dare call us or ask for anything." Who needs these kinds of people whose god is money? I will never be friends with the whole family who never cared for their lovely sister, my Connie. I do not even have any good or bad wishes for them. They want to be connected with me over Facebook, but I would never want to be their friend. This relationship is over with Connie's death. I know their lovely Aunt Connie left them money, and they would grab it. Most people would die for that big amount she left to the four of them. I would say that they are shameful and unethical people. They would grab, and I am sure they will not even call to thank me or feel remorse, thanks to their mother, who has provided such a dirty foundation. God is watching. I am sure God will not forgive them, and they will have to pay for their bad Karmas in this life.

4. **"The life of an uneducated man is as useless as the tail of a dog which neither covers its rear end nor protects it from the bites of insects."**

5. **"A person should not be too honest. Straight trees are cut first, and honest people are screwed first."**

Connie and I have both gone through this message; however, we always followed the same message, regardless of the consequences. Although there have been so many painful things we suffered, Connie suffered more. This reminds me of an actual episode. In 1984, I visited a huge client of my employer (the largest finance company in the world) in California and took Connie with me. Connie would drop me off in the morning, pick me up in the evening, and go to the library and shopping while waiting for me. This client was one of the largest trailer homemakers in the USA and had taken a big loan from my company. I was introduced to the chairman of the board and all the senior management, with whom I spent the whole day talking about the business, plans, expansion, and all the related things about the loan. Later, they introduced me to their lady accountant. I was highly impressed with her knowledge and grace and thought that she knew the business very well. She was super.

During lunch, she asked me if I wanted to go for lunch, and I said yes. She told me that she couldn't go, so I ordered food for her, and I paid for that as part of my business expenses. We were swamped as a lot of work was to be done, and she closed her office, and we both were working while having lunch. She told me her story, which I will never forget. She told me that she and her husband owned this huge company. She trusted their employees and her attorney very much. She adopted that attorney as her son when he was a kid, put him through school, college, and law, and treated him as her son. She had a large customer in Mexico and owed the company many millions of dollars in accounts receivables. The customer was in tight cash flow, and she gave that account to her adopted attorney and asked all the employees to cooperate as a team. Suddenly, the company was forced into liquidation, and she and her husband were lost everything. She later found out that her attorney took all the money from that customer and later bought back the company and made the plant supervisor the president so that now she was reporting to him as an accountant. Her will made her husband strong to work as an ordinary worker at their company. She further told me that since they lost the company, she and her husband had never gotten a call from the Rotary and Lions Club and other charitable and arts and theaters clubs where they used to give charity and host dinners.

All their wealthy friends disappeared. She stated that the only people who came forward were the food vendors who brought their trucks to the company to sell breakfast, late snacks, lunch, and dinner to her 1000 employees. Those food vendors bought them a small place to live, gave them food daily, and met their expenses. All of their wealthy friends and cultured socials and music arts, etc., who used to invite donations were gone, but these vendors helped them survive. They went from riches to rags and lost their entire world. It was such a heartbreaking thing for me. While agreeing to approve the new loan for the company, I put in a clause stating that we would only lend the company this huge amount again if she were made the Chief Financial Officer, replacing the current one, who knew nothing and was making fifteen times more money than her. I openly stated that we would not grant them a loan unless she is in that position, as she knows all the customers and businesses better than anybody. I also stated that the attorney would have to face the penalty for his crime as he cheated on our previous loan. The deal was approved, the crooked attorney went to jail, and we recovered our loan, and the new CFO was there, making fifteen times more money and was extremely happy with her new life.

I finished my work early on Friday afternoon to be with Connie, who came after checking the hotel, and we enjoyed a long drive on Friday and stayed in California's Orange County for five days. Connie was in tears when she heard this story. I am writing this as a great tribute to darling Connie, who is no longer with me physically, but the whole scene of her picking me up and driving through Palm Springs is with me as a photographic memory. For forty years, the whole of our lives and love, our travels, and everything is a movie in my mind and heart 24 hours a day. Throughout my career, I dealt with many such episodes. Connie was very supportive and helpful in giving me 100% moral support and sometimes accompanied me on some very hostile borrowers, who played frauds and most unethical things for our worldwide largest fiancé companies where I was on the senior management team. I was given the most troubled, difficult large new and old borrowers with over 100 million and millions of loans to one borrower. Three of them were in Chicago, two in Michigan, two in Columbus, Ohio, three in California, two in Houston, different small and large cities all over the USA. Also, a few jobs were in France and Germany. One of my jobs took place in Columbus, Ohio, in 1987. The owner defrauded the lender for whom I was working. Many junior and middle-management field examiners went to his office. The owner had run away and was hiding for months, and he had given instructions to his two senior management staff not to allow \ anyone from the lender, and they were all denied access to his premises. Let me explain that since we were secured lenders, we had the right to enter, even to do a surprise walk-in; however, we had a practice that we should notify our borrowers that it was time for due diligence and ask if it was convenient for them to provide the documents we needed. We used to send borrowers a list of our due diligence requirements. Again, it was our courtesy to do so; previously, we had relied on surprise. Finally, since I was an expert in crisis management, I was asked to go. I showed up at the borrower's office and presented my business card. They were truly nice and asked me to sit and have coffee. I told them, "You three people did not allow my four juniors in, and now you are reluctant to let me enter and see your books." They said no way could I review the books, and I told them, "I have a right to do anything, and if you do not let me, I will report to my senior management, and we will take strong action against you that you will regret for the rest of your lives. Please know that I am not letting you play this game, and let me see whatever I want to see, period. They told me, "Mr. Berry, you are powerful and determined, but we are helpless as our boss had told us not to allow anyone." I told them let me talk to your owner and boss as I am not leaving like the others. You better be careful and let me talk to him, and if he has refused to give his number where he is hiding, tell him the senior management person is here, and he is determined to be here until the whole thing is discovered. They were panicky and went behind closed doors and talked to the owner, and slowly they told me yes, you could only see a few records, and we cannot provide anything else. I was determined and told them that I was even going to go through the locked room of your boss, and you better be ready to cooperate with me; otherwise, you would be supposed to be part of the fraud, and if we have to go to court and take orders, and you would all be involved for protecting your boss. Perhaps you should think of yourself, your wife, and your children as you do not want to be involved in the case is turned over to the FBI once fraud is detected. Now, please either listen to your boss or me. They both went to a room and came out after 20 minutes and told me, "Mr. Berry, we are going to do anything for you as we do not have the money, salary, and anything, and we would lose all so please, go ahead. Also, do us a favor. We have not been paid for three months and have been working free for him in anticipation that we would be paid all our dues soon. I assured them that we would make sure they got paid, but let me do my work, we can all go for lunch or dinner and have more discussion and talk and be friends, and I am here to save you and your boss if he cooperates with me. They were happy. I took them for nice lunch and the exclusive dinner. At dinner time, they told me, Mr. Berry, "It has been over six months since we had dinner and drinks and desserts, and you truly are a gem, and we feel that you are going to do good things for us. We are with you as we do not want to go to prison or pay heavy fines as we can't even find other senior positions and would be doomed forever." That was it. The next day, I worked and worked and went to the owner's room and drawers and whatever. I WAS THRILLED TO FIIND the stack of locked files, where it was mentioned and signed by the owner of his scheme of defrauding our lender, and there was a conspiracy between the owner and his largest customer that was the largest US company. I took all those documents and told them that I was going to the Federal Express office as some information is important for me to send to my office overnight. They said, Mr. Berry, whatever, and we leave at 6 PM and you to go the Federal Express, which is open until 8 PM and go to the hotel, and we will see you in the morning. That was one of the best things besides others in my life. Previously, I was also put into that situation and even different kinds.

Now, Connie Darling comes into the picture, and I told her about it, and she was worried about my life, and I was, as well. I kept flying from Chicago to Columbus for two months- Monday to Friday. Connie was instrumental in sacrificing all that heavy travel, and internally, we were both concerned. However, she too was strong and encouraged me that this is USA, Pradeep, don't think anything, you have been doing these kinds of hostile situations, and you have earned your name in your senior job, and that is why they had promoted to this senior position, and I take pride in you. I am with you, I can accompany you for a few weeks, and I even get my vacations and teach during school and college break. She did take a week off and went with me to be with me, staying in the hotel, dinner and all. I told my employer, and they were thrilled and told me, "Pradeep, please take Connie, and we would pay everything for Connie. It was advantageous to both of us, and they knew Pradeep would detect the extensive fraud. That perhaps was my last Friday, and I met the owner in the office at 9 AM. I did not tell Connie that I was slightly worried about what the owner would do, nor did I disclose this to my employer. God is great. Knowing that he is a six feet strong man, all my fear might try to harm me physically or throw me from the fourth floor.

Somehow or the other, he had found out that I knew everything. I went to him. Connie was sitting in the restaurant downstairs in case of some violent act or so. That was the greatest support I had that Connie was downstairs, ready to make a 911 call in case anything. Surprisingly, I went to the owner, and he stood up and shook my hand and asked me to sit down, ordered coffee, some bagels, and closed the doors. Only two people behind those big closed doors. I bluntly told him that I knew everything, and perhaps he knew too. He agreed to cooperate with me and requested me, "Mr. Berry, I do not want to go to prison. Please tell me how you can help me". I politely told him, "Mr. Z, please cooperate with us, and come admit to us and get the significant funds in millions. How are we going to get those funds as you have defrauded us and you know well that you can go to prison for life and please ask your customer to help you as they have deep pockets and would never like it to be seen in the paper or TV that they were part of the actual white-collar crime? He was asking me for mercy, and I felt that he was regretting now and was crying that he did all and was willing to do anything and cooperate. We also needed him as he was an expert in turning millions and millions of dollars worth of raw material inventory, working in process inventory into the finished goods and selling, getting paid on a COD basis, and starting paying our full loan.

We do not have to take any write-off in our P&L and Financial stamens—losses. The owner cooperated six months with us, and he and his company worked hard while we were funding the payroll and started paying IRS part of his liability of loans. In one year, we were paid back the large loan, and the owner had to sell his home, car, and everything for any shortage in our loan. He was practically on the road. We helped him to refinance his home, helped him find a decent job as he was an engineer and expert in his field. I took the initiative to help get his three senior management employees another job. It was one of the wonderful things in my career, and later on, I kept doing the same kinds of most difficult situations in my career until September 2005. Since then, I spent every day with Connie except 12 days each year going to India from September 1 till 16, 2005, 12 days in 2006, 12 days in 2007, and ten days till 2011.

In between all those days, I was with Connie every moment, even from India four to six times a day when I left my thing in my profession months. We collected all or loan any call to call the in the morning, The owner who was six feet tall and strong put all the expenses in expense account position employer if you feel that way, ask your employer to get anything. I would make sure you all are part of this and, perhaps, we had decided that we are coming on such a date. It was very hostile and extremely bad behavior of the company owner in Chicago. Another challenging but one of the best in 1981 in Chicago truly made my career and many others. How I handled I do not know how after MY CONNIE. The worst, of course, is losing "MY CONNIE."

The same episodes happened in Michigan, Austin, Columbus, California, Seattle, Indiana, Baltimore, New York, New Jersey, Chicago, Denver, Philadelphia, Phoenix, and many more cities. I will always remember and wonder how I was able to do all that. Perhaps, I would like to describe all of these as a case study for the coming young blood to gain knowledge in crisis management. These were extremely great challenges that I had gone through, and I am lucky that my employers and consulting work that these banks, finance companies, equity players gave me to do. It was a win-win situation for them and me. I know for sure that there are many other brilliant people with lots of things to teach, but I would also like to add some of my knowledge as a legacy in Connie's memory.

Michigan was special. For three months in 1981, I would travel to Michigan every Monday through Friday to liquidate our borrower or sell the company to avoid any write-off on our large loans. Connie was on a two-month vacation from teaching and was busy doing her research in the hotel we were staying in while I was working at the office, but we had breakfast, lunch, and dinner together and went sightseeing on the weekends. These things are important to me as my traveling job has become a joy. The best work travels I had were when I had to go to Germany and France and asked Connie to join me to be lonely. It was in September 1996 for over two weeks. I never felt lonely and was amazingly happy. Let me write, when I think of all these times, I practically start shaking and become devastated. Each and everything is fresh, every single day's activities- dining, driving in Germany and France, sightseeing on weekends, going to the winery. I can write an entire book about our traveling, which might have over 600 pages. I will see if God's and Connie's blessings are showered on me. Now, I do not think I can travel even for a night except to visit my brother and his family in India. How much has changed in my life due to one person,

CONNIE? Many people would never understand this, but I am happy writing for Connie and myself. If someone appreciates my book, I am extremely grateful to them and obliged to give tributes to Connie.

In 8th grade, we learned about the true story of Oh Master Ji (Oh My Teacher. During the early 1940s and concerns a Hindu teacher who worked at a small school in a village. This teacher took great pain to teach his Hindu, Muslim, Sikh, and other students with love and compassion. Suddenly, riots broke out between Hindus and Muslims. Villages started burning, and there were sectarian killings. At that time, many Hindu and Muslim bullies were fighting against each other. So it came to pass in this village that conflict began between Hindus and Muslims. One Muslim boy went to the teacher's home and brought his daughter to his own home. Later that day, when the teacher came home and found his small daughter missing, he was devastated. Then, his neighbors, who had seen the boy take the girl, told him where to look for his missing daughter. The teacher, thinking the worst, was extremely upset and took a big knife to kill his Muslim student who took his daughter. On his way to his house, he was sad and asked God, "Why would my student take my daughter? I gave love to all my students and took lots of pain in teaching them like my children. Why would he do that to me? What evil did I do to him that he should do such a thing?" All these thoughts were wandering through his mind, and the teacher was determined to kill his student. From half a mile away, the teacher saw the boy and started running to kill him. The moment he came across to him to kill the boy, suddenly the Muslim student said, "Oh Master Ji, I have been looking for you, thanks to God you are safe as your daughter is with me safe and sound. I brought her to my house like she was my sister before anybody could harm her. Please come and rest, and I would send you and your daughter with ten of my friends for protection." Master Ji was overjoyed that his devotion to teaching all the students paid off, and he apologized from the bottom of his heart for the negative things that had been in his mind.

Connie and I have tried to apply this true story throughout our lives. But, now it is bothersome that our selfless, unbiased love and respect for all our relatives and friends did not make them realize our pain in difficult times, especially when Connie was alive. God gave me the power to reciprocate my love for Connie when she became slowly more ill. That power, which came from love, was more than the strength of 150 people. This is all due to our true love for each other. I also chose not to inform anyone of her illness and decided to cope with my loss with all of Connie's power. However, each and everything of our 40 years is like an ongoing movie that plays in my mind and soul all the time- it is very painful. My relatives and some of my friends did not show me compassion even after her death. Only a handful of people came to give their condolences. I have been extremely angry with them and, perhaps, even with myself. I told my family that I would order food for them if they came to visit me. But they never came, and now that more than two months have passed, I don't know how I would react to their presence. I am angry and bitter over Connie's loss. If Connie could only return to me, I would forgive everyone and treat them nicely.

6. **"Whores don't live in the company of poor men, citizens never support a weak company, and birds don't build nests on a tree that doesn't bear fruit."**

    Connie and I have been very sensitive about this message throughout our lives, cared for the weaker section, and never cared for the rewards.

7. **"He who is overly attached to his family members experiences fear and sorrow, for the root of all grief is attachment. Thus one should discard attachment to be happy."**

    Yes, it is a good quote like many others, quoted by me many times. However, it is not practical for me, and I would perhaps never leave that attachment to my Connie.

8. **"O wise man! Give your wealth only to the worthy and never to others. The water of the sea received by the clouds is always sweet."**

    Connie and I applied this message all our lives. Connie left a generous donation for a charity to her alma maters, Carleton College in MN, and the University of Michigan to provide scholarships for needy students, the

Red Cross, the American Cancer Society, and Mayo Clinic. I have started giving on an annual basis to all of the organizations she favored. This gives me happiness. Connie always followed this message until her end, and hopefully, I will keep doing the same thing in the future.

Connie and I have never gone against the wisdom of this quote. I have seen people give great support to many noble causes after the death of a loved one. Hospitals, educational foundations, schools, colleges, churches, temples, and mosques are patronized in honor of the deceased, whether a spouse, child, or other loved one. I am sure that these noble gifts heal the loss of those people. I think there is great healing power in giving to charity in the memory of a loved one.

9. **"Do not put your trust in a bad companion nor even trust an ordinary friend, for if he should get angry with you, he may bring all your secrets to light."**

How true it is, and we both went through this in our lives. I have become more careful after Connie's demise. Among my friends and relatives, whom I considered our well-wishers, I see a big gap in their trustworthiness after Connie's loss.

10. **"The fragrance of flowers spreads only in the direction of the wind. But the goodness of a person spreads in all directions."**

Connie had that quality of goodness, and she did not have to practice- it was in her blood, in her brain, and she left marks on many people all over the world. I get so many letters and appreciation from all those people all the time, and they are a joy but painful as well. Connie went so suddenly I couldn't believe she was gone. I have to see the reality every day, then, every moment, wherever I am. In the health club, the grocery store, while reading books, checking the mail, organizing her desk, her chair, in our bed, our shower, our kitchen, our car, and everywhere I turn.

11. **"Education is the best friend. An educated person is respected everywhere. Education beats beauty and youth."**

Connie and I tried to live by this message all our lives, and I am extremely grateful for that. We both had great educations and kept actively learning to gain knowledge throughout life. Education stops after completing schooling and attaining degrees. Still, knowledge has no end. That is why Connie was reading so many newspapers, magazines and watching intellectual TV programs such as 60 minutes, the news, 20-20, Night Line, Mystery, WGN 11 public programs covering different world events and music. She also took intellectual, educational tours with scholars worldwide, listening to lectures, reading books, visiting the library, and watching intellectual movies, rather than wasting time gossiping, holding stupid conversations on shallow topics. She would research such diverse things as new recipes or new medical treatments from the books and internet for our greater knowledge. Although I have, from childhood, had a foundation of seeking knowledge, Connie instilled this even further in me. I will never be able to repay her in my many lives.

12. **"It is better to live under a tree in a jungle inhabited by tigers and elephants, to maintain oneself in such a place with ripe fruits and spring water, to lie down on the grass, and to wear the ragged barks of trees than to live amongst one's relations when reduced to poverty."**

    Connie and I always followed this great message, and to this date, we don't owe anything to anyone--- except our bodies, which we owe to our parents. People took lots of things from us, which we gave with happiness. Some borrowed loans and other things, yet today, January 17, 2016, no one has called to return those loans, and now I want to forget the debt. We managed, rather Connie, all the budgets and financial planning to never depend upon anyone except the supreme body that belongs to God.

13. **"Test a servant while in the discharge of his duty, a relative in difficulty, a friend in adversity, and a wife in misfortune."**

    I don't want to insult Connie's family, but her siblings really and truly were the most painful thing in this category, both when she was alive and after her death. Their behaviors were worse than the worst servant, friend, or relative to be tested. Connie and I went through this many times, and we tried to forgive them, as difficult as it was. Connie never expected that relatives, friends, and people we helped in any form would ever betray our friendship. Now, I don't know if I can forgive them for their betrayals. I would rather cut off my relationships with those who were using us and have disappeared from our lives when they got what they wanted- especially when Connie was sick from the middle of 2014 until the end. I am extremely bitter and angry because of their neglect, though perhaps time will heal this deep wound.

14. **"If one has a good disposition, what other virtue is needed? If a man has fame, what is the value of other ornamentation?"**

How true is it? Connie's internal and external beauty truly did not need any other ornaments or makeup to show the world her true self. Those people who knew her and anyone who came across her in life were amazed at her knowledge of inner beauty. No one I know ever had anything bad to say about Connie. Rather they esteemed her as the best of the best. She was gifted with so many inner beauties in education, knowledge, hospitality, housekeeping, traveling, and wherever she went, marked her name. It is the truth- I am not trying to brag or exaggerate her goodness.

15. **"The one excellent thing that can be learned from a lion is that whatever a man intends doing should be done by him with a whole-hearted and strenuous effort."**

Connie was a lion, and she did follow the above message throughout her. She took on any project- education, housekeeping, hospitality, shopping, bookkeeping, organization, duty toward her family, husband, friends, and neighbors. She did not lack anything.

16. **"Foolishness is indeed painful, and verily so is youth, but more painful by far than either is being obliged in another person's house."**

Connie reminded me of this message if I was having a hard time making a decision or faced with a user who sought to take advantage of our soft hearts.

17. **"Do not reveal what you have thought upon doing, but by wise council keep it secret being determined to carry it into execution."**

> Connie and I followed this message and practiced it throughout our lives. We were firm believers of this message, no matter how difficult or how impossible our course seemed. We never gave up once our minds were set on a course of action. We never gave up except when I lost my battle to save my Connie.

18. **"The world's biggest power is the youth and beauty of a woman."**

> I applied this message to Connie all my life and will continue to do so. She was beautiful both externally and internally. I agree with this message to some extent, but due to my lifelong love for Connie, I sometimes don't want to believe the truth of this. Connie was Connie. I cannot find any other person like Connie in my life. We will meet again. It is my faith. There have been movies and stories about rebirth and meetings of couples parted by death. God knows the answer.

19. **"Never make friends with people who are above or below you in status. Such friendships will never give you any happiness."**

> Connie and I never thought of this, as we sought friendships with people who were like us in education and intellect. We cared nothing for the income of our friends but only cared that they contributed something to the world. We had some very great and intellectual friends. I don't know if I will meet them again without Connie. Connie was so special and helped forge those friendships. Even if I meet them, my memories will haunt me, and our friendship will not be the same.

20. **"The serpent, the king, the tiger, the stinging wasp, the small child, the dog owned by other people, and the fool: these seven ought not to be awakened from sleep."**

21. "There is no austerity equal to a balanced mind, and there is no happiness equal to contentment; there is no disease like covetousness and no virtue like mercy."

22. "As soon as the fear approaches near, attack and destroy it."

> Connie was very successful in this message, except in November 2014 after Mayo, but she was still positive even then. The episode I described above was the most painful thing in our lives. She is gone, but my life has become unbearable pain, and I don't know if it will ever end. I do not think it will.

23. "He who lives in our mind is near though he may actually be far away, but he who is not in our heart is far though he may be nearby."

24. "There is poison in the fang of the serpent, in the mouth of the fly, and the sting of a scorpion, but the wicked man is saturated with it."

25. "God is not present in idols. Your feelings are your god. The soul is your temple."

14

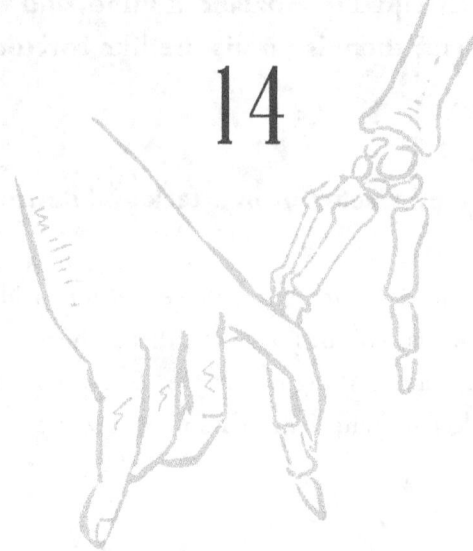

My Uncle's Advice

My uncle told me the qualities of a wife, "Son, a wife is precious if we truly analyze from an educated and intelligent point of view." How true it is. No wonder Connie is always in my heart and soul and would remain that way all my life. Now the world is different, so the divorce rate has gone up tremendously among the younger generations; lately, even couples married for decades. I wonder why and still cannot believe that divorce is healthy for anyone. There is an answer to solve this dilemma. I think marriage is an art, and we have to care for that every day or week as we give water to the plants and the gardens. Our cell phones and innovations such as the internet and cell phones are good for emergency talks and important things. What did we do when we had no cell phone 25 years to 30 years ago? What did we do when we had no TV or other gadgets 80 years ago?

    We had simple lives and high thoughts. It is terrible that a sacred marriage is so easily broken. How can we expect the world's people to be friends when there are fights between couples or families with kids? Are we progressing or going towards darkness? Gandhi truly stated, "Technology would ruin Mankind." Now the world is different. Perhaps newly married couples enjoy intimate relations and fun, entertainment, and kids but then end in divorce, though why? This is not the case with everyone. Beautiful marriages that last for lifetimes, which I truly love and give credit to those couples- they have my greatest respect.

In our marriage, it was love. To love and care for each other was the most important thing for us both. I want to mention openly, without offending anyone, that Connie had the same beautiful body until she got too sick for two years and was getting weaker and weaker until she found it hard even to walk or do anything. The two doctors spoiled her body with their mistreatment, and I hope God takes care of them. As she grew weak, her body became a god for me. I used to touch her feet and worship the same beautiful body as God. I was not praying to God so much as I was praying for her body. It was and still is my most painful memory. I knew I would have to live for her- her weak body was my God. Perhaps when Buddha left his palace as a child, he saw fragile bodies, death, and other sufferings. I was no different, but I did not become Buddha, nor could I. However, I would serve Connie's wishes for charity, education, and bettering humanity. Although we were from different cultures, I never thought that a wife is secondary to her husband. In my case, Connie was extremely important, and I cared for her as much as she cared for me. Perhaps that is why I am writing this book.

That is why Gandhi said, "I have the highest respect for woman as she is the incarnation of tolerance." I followed that message all my life. He further stated that "Woman can tolerate most of the things her husband does, including drinking, gambling, and cheating on her; although she would be extremely hurt, she finally may forgive him. However, if a husband suspects a woman's character, that is death for her."

As I mentioned before, I had forgotten our bad childhood memories once I met Connie, and my happiness was Connie. Now the tragedy of my childhood is nothing, but Connie's death is much more painful and unbearable. This is because of Connie's love, but Connie's death is unbearable. Now, my biggest loss and unhappiness is the demise of Connie. I don't care for all our wealth and would concentrate on helping humanity and teaching and following the path of Connie's honesty, loyalty, ethics, charity, and selfless work. I followed these same principles but, I would do more to get some ray of happiness from her memory. I will never be able to forget her goodness in my life.

Now I understand why the young in India consult their elders during crises and when facing problems, as they had a worldly experience that can't be learned in school. The knowledge of seniors comes from facing a life of problems. Perhaps, within my limits, I am getting ready to share what I have learned from my own experiences. I still have to learn more- I can learn from everyone I meet. Education reaches an endpoint, but knowledge keeps going if you seek it. Knowledge is like an ocean- there is no depth to it. That is what I have always believed.

15

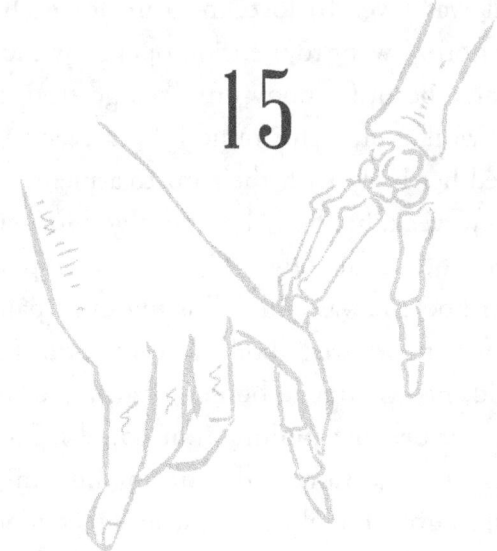

Beginning of Our Love

When I came to the US 42 years ago, it was an extremely difficult decision to make. Back home in India, I had an excellent education, all the comforts of a wealthy family, and the makings of a successful professional career. I did not feel in control of the unknown variables of my life is going to a foreign country, whether for a short or long time. A possible destiny had already failed to come to fruition- I had thought to go to the UK to study Chartered Accountancy from the Institute of Chartered Accountants of England and Wales. My grandfather, fearing that I would leave India, forbade me to study in England. He wanted our family to stay in India. Some of my colleagues and my Chartered Accountant left for the USA and UK, thinking that perhaps my future lay in the USA. With the encouragement of a friend who was teaching at an elite American university, I considered moving to the USA.

I eventually decided to come but postponed my move by six months to rethink my decision. Finally, I did it. I took a Lufthansa flight to Chicago with a stop in Frankfurt. I had a five-hour layover in Germany. Those five hours waiting for the flight to Chicago were the most troublesome hours of my life. Once the plane was on the runway, I became extremely homesick and depressed, thinking I was giving up my brother, maternal grandfather, aunts, friends, and education to restart everything. I would be like a newborn baby in a new place. I got up from my seat and started calling the hostesses, who tried to force me to sit down with my seatbelt on—their many attempts to force me to sit failed.

I was desperate to get down from the aircraft, and eventually, the captain came to me to ask me what the matter was. I told him honestly that I wanted to go back to India and please let me get off the plane in Frankfurt to take another flight for India. He tried to persuade me that it was impossible as the aircraft was on the runway, but my persistent request made him feel compassion for my predicament. (I would have been arrested for this behavior at the present day). He asked me to show him the return ticket and told me that I had a restricted ticket, so I must stay in Chicago for 14 days. He asked me how much money I had, and I said seven dollars. He responded that I would be stuck in the Frankfurt airport for a long time with no food, no hotel, and no flight. I told him that I could request any airline to take me to India, and upon landing, I would call my brother, and he would pay for the ticket. Captain told me it would not happen that way and advised me to go to Chicago, spend the 14 days, and take a return flight back to India.

After landing in Chicago, I asked my relative who came to pick me up whether he could arrange to go back to India the next day. He was dumbfounded and did not say anything. I stayed with my first cousin that night, and she was surprised by my behavior but calmed me down with Scotch and dinner. We talked, and I finally went to sleep at 12:30 PM and got up around 5 AM with a panic attack, feeling depression, homesickness, and terror at finding myself in some other part of the planet. I started thinking desperately of how I would go back to India.

Later, some friends and cousins came to welcome me, thinking I was happy to have arrived in the US, but I was in a depressed world of thinking of going back home. They told me to calm down, as homesickness happens to everyone. I wondered why they were no longer homesick and why they didn't offer to help me go back to India. After 15 days, I lived in my house in the Old Town, Chicago- right across from Second City, to supervise an Indian restaurant. The restaurant was in a four-story building, with the restaurant on the ground floor and five bedrooms and two baths on each of the upper three floors. It was one of the best-known Indian restaurants in Chicago. I lived in my bedroom, and the three Indian chefs who had the other bedrooms were my companions. I counted the days that remained to return to India, as my return ticket expired after four months.

At the same time, there was great pressure placed on me to go back to India for my professional career, help run the family business, and commit to an arranged marriage. This pressure caused me great stress. I was living in a very confused, puzzled state of mind and dealing with homesickness. I started meeting many

Americans and Indians who became my friends. Late at night, John Candy from Second City came to the restaurant with most of his cast. I did not know anything about him or Second City at the time. Later, they all became my close friends and were a great support to my troubled mind.   Each weekend a good-looking man would come to our beautiful bar for drinks and sit smoking by himself. I did not know who he was. One night, an American teacher I had hired as a part-time waiter asked me if I knew who he was. I told him, no, and he told me he is a famous film critic, Roger Ebert. I introduced myself to him, and he was extremely happy and was full of love and passion for his work. He started coming for long hours to talk to me. He became a good friend, showed me some of his work, and asked me to come for a movie premiere. The people I met- Roger Ebert, John Candy, and the Second City cast, Don Ross, Andy Shaw, journalists, and politicians like Honorable John Metcalf- helped cheer me up and show me that I had a place in the USA. Eventually, I fell out of touch with those friends, and I have not seen or met them since 1977.

Students of international languages at theUniversity of Chicago also came to the restaurant with their full class. Mr. Douglas Goodman, who was studying Indian languages, became my dearest friend. He started taking me out for my recordings on the audio to send them to my brother in India. Douglas got married to his college girlfriend, and both of them went to India and visited my brother for four days in our huge ancestral house in Old Delhi. The house is still there, but no one is living there anymore as my family is living in different houses today. I have not met Douglas since the late 1970s, but I would love to find him now. He and his wife would be great friends in my life now- although Connie can be replaced at any cost. I even get panic attacks and feel greatly depressed from the unhappiness I face by writing this book. I cannot even imagine that Connie is gone. It is heartbreaking, and I find myself extremely weak in writing this book. I am of two minds, unsure whether or not I should write. But I also feel that I must write this, no matter how difficult it is to put the words on the page.

I truly want to restart this life, taking me back to where I was 40 years ago. That would be the happiest thing—Connie and Pradeep in this life again.

Meanwhile, my Connie met me in the next two months, bringing me happiness, a new life, and passion. We had lots of conversations regarding my plans to go back to India, and she respected my desire to return but suggested I must see some parts of Chicago before I left. Connie told me about the Museum of Art and Science, the Art Institute, Northwestern University, the University of Chicago, the Shedd Aquarium, McCormick Place, Michigan Avenue, Lakeshore Drive, and many restaurants around the city. She also suggested that I enroll at an elite university for another graduate program, an MBA, before going back to India. I was reluctant to do so as I already had a great education from India. Still, it struck me that education has no end, and an American MBA would prepare me for more knowledge and advance my career worldwide. I have had the opportunity over the past 39 years to gain more exposure and advancement.

Further, Connie suggested that once I returned to India, I might regret it if I did not take advantage of my chance to know American culture and to experience European culture on my return trip to India, as I would have the chance to explore Germany and other countries on my flight back. She suggested that although I was well educated, there is a difference between knowing things and seeing them, meeting people, and exploring. She even told me that I should study foreign languages to advance my career in India or benefit me if I came back to the US after my marriage. She said that that would benefit me in the long run, and accordingly, I can choose my destiny with my future wife to see where we would like to settle for our careers. She told me that she had finished her education at Carleton College, the University of Michigan, and teaching plus doing another Masters in Spanish and French. Although she already knew the languages well, she was motivated to study further to advance her career. Meeting her changed my sorrow, sadness, and homesickness, and I was a different person with the most joyful life- I felt a new revival of happiness, and so did she. Now, I knew why so many obstacles, so much unhappiness, had kept me from India. It was my great and happy Destiny to meet Connie and begin a new chapter of my life with Connie. We were two bodies with one soul. That priceless happiness can't be bought at any price on this earth. All of the wealth on the planet could never buy happiness and love as we had.

My Connie also went through great happiness, but her happiness changed, and later she faced the most difficult time due to her sickness, which was made worse in no small part by her one sibling and his extended family. However, the disruption of our happy life by this family episode was minimal compared to her sickness, and in my strong opinion, her death came about through medical negligence. Although it is painful for Connie and me, the family problems with her brother and his family were nothing compared to the negligence. They could have been mitigated if the events of February 28th, 2015, had not happened. All these things are mentioned in different sections in this biography of my Connie, and they crushed me, leaving me to live in isolation with my unhappiness. Secondly, families have differences that get resolved, and the unresolved differences are not as painful to me as the family was once extremely good to us. I count that as a small issue now that Connie has passed. I am reminded of a true story of Lord Buddha, who came across a lady praying to get her dead son back. Buddha told the woman that if she could bring him a bag of rice from a house where there has been no tragedy for five years, he could bring back her son. After going from house to house day and night, she could not find a household free of tragedy. That is when Buddha made her realize the suffering of everyone on this planet. But even this story does not lessen my pain.

It is a miracle that our first meeting of one hour was the happiest 60 minutes of our married life. That miracle led to 40 years of life together, and yet it ended with one of my biggest regrets, a regret that I will have to relive the entire rest of my life. I left Connie's hospital room for one hour, 60 minutes, and that cost us both. In my strong opinion, her doctors came in my absence and falsified her medical records, ending Connie's life. I became a lonely person without my Connie. Sixty minutes brought us together for 40 years, and after 40 years, 60 minutes separated us.

I struggled to decide to stay or go, which became a boon, but that was the greatest thing of my life, as I met Connie and immediately knew we were one. We escaped and got married.

As a young man, I was an extremely qualified professional in Delhi, India, and was offered many senior positions in different parts of India along with other career opportunities; however, when a very senior school friend of mine, teaching at an elite university in the USA, came to Delhi and suggested I come to the USA., I began to see a possible future there. It took three months for me to decide if I wanted to go. I decided to come for exposure for two months with a senior job in the restaurant, food, import, and export business. I was responsible for accounting and cash flow, finance, and running operations with other employees. Although it was not in my profession, I decided to get some different work experience. I was ready to go back after two months, as I was very homesick, but my employer requested that I work a minimum of four to six months, and even that seemed too long. I was about to leave when I met Constance Fuller. It was true love in one meeting, and after dating for a short time, we married. It was our first love and last one... Constance Fuller became Mrs. Constance Berry, and Pradeep Berry became an exceptionally strong, devoted, true, pure, and loving couple. I would say our marriage was so much fun, love, and care for each other that many people we met were surprised to see that love, wishing that they had the same rhythm with their spouses.

I knew this special marriage would remain that way as long as we lived. "A great wife and a good friend are only for the lucky ones"-A great quote from Indian culture. My first employer did not pay my salary for two months, saying his cash flow was bad, which was not true. Connie spoke with him on my behalf, telling him that no one works free and better pays me. Otherwise, she would report to the IRS and Labor Department. I was not paid for a week. Connie told him a second time that he had better bring a cashier check with proper tax deductions that same day, or else she would report him to both the departments, and Pradeep would quit. I got the check right then and worked another two months with pay.

Connie wanted me to go back to my professional career and advancement for which I had the offer before coming to the USA. I returned to the field of finance, and I was promoted three months and after that. I never looked back. My employer paid for my MBA in an elite university while I was traveling close to 50% of the time all over the USA. During these two years, Connie sacrificed her life for my work and college, and we had very little time to interact, as she was also studying to advance her career. During that time, I noticed that many of my friends and coworkers were having problems with their spouses because they were asked to travel and be apart. Some of those coworkers got divorced, which was an eye-opening experience for me. Connie and I enjoyed our lives, took nice vacations, and had fun experiences that surpassed those of our friends, co-workers, and clients despite our time apart.

I want to mention a true episode that I experienced. I was extremely depressed when I was leaving for the USA, as it was something new, and I truly did not know if I wanted to go or not. My mind was set on no, but some people told me to go and try out a new thing. I was on a Lufthansa flight from Delhi to Frankfurt, with a five-hour layover before my flight to Chicago. I got depressed in Frankfurt airport as I had never traveled out of India. The moment they announced the Chicago flight was ready and I sat down, my depression culminated in a panic attack that was so bad that I got up from the seat when the plane was on the runway. A hostess told me to sit, but I did not, delaying the flight. I would have been arrested if it happened today. Finally, the plane captain asked me what was happening, and I told him the truth. He was nice and told me that I was causing trouble, but showing him my ticket so he could see what could be done. I showed him the ticket, and he explained that it was a restricted ticket for 14 days and that only after staying 14 days could I fly back to India. He asked me how much money I had, and I said seven dollars was the maximum amount the Indian government allowed due to India's lack of foreign currency. Now things are very different. The captain told me, "Mr. Berry, I can let you off at the Frankfurt airport, but with seven dollars, you would be stranded and would be in big trouble and would not even have a meal or hotel, and you would be suffering. He advised me to touch down in Chicago and live there for 14 days and then come back, as I had the round trip ticket. Those fourteen days became forty years in the USA, and now I am delighted that I came and met Connie and progressed in my profession. Without Connie, I would have come back to India after six months, or maybe even earlier. Sometimes destiny brings you to the most unlikely of fates in life. Again, I never expected that I, her husband, would have to oversee her cremation and last rites. I still remember my first meeting with Connie and how she brought a new life to me.

I want to recount a few more true incidents. One: It was in 1994, and I had to travel in the winter to Michigan to evaluate a new large borrower. I did not want to go alone, as other junior associates working under me were on their Christmas vacations, and some were in different parts of the world. I requested that Connie come with me, and she traveled with me, and I did a fantastic evaluation. The same kinds of things happened many times in 1981, 1984, 1993, and 1996. She knew how to entertain herself by seeing different sites, exploring shops, and reading on the hotel balcony. She would pick me up for lunch and after my work, and we would go out to dinner. I would work late in the hotel, and she would read her book and watch TV. Where would I find that diamond? I did the same for her mother since 1989 after her father died

In 2006, I left my career to devote myself to her and travel worldwide. Although we traveled from the early days of our marriage, she wanted to see the world, and with five weeks of vacation a year and my own consulting, we could not work and travel as much as she wanted. During the last three years of her treatments, although we traveled some at that time, I was 200% with her every moment of her life. It is so painful that she died before her time.

I must mention that our love was unconditional. We immediately knew that we were in love on our first meeting, and there was no need to have a second meeting. We knew that this was a nonstop flight to the world, and we couldn't even think of getting off the plane. Many people have many dates and meetings. Sometimes, their families inquire about one another or ask the family's permission before couples decide to marry at a huge wedding. We were successful without fighting the war of these hassles and compromising for family. I am always happy to see those couples who have been married for a lifetime. Our faith and values were that marriage is a lifetime commitment. We are lucky we passed our silver anniversary, but we failed to make it to our gold anniversary, in my strong opinion, because of medical negligence. That negligence was so quick that it did not give us time to save my partner. I failed in my battle and big warfighting alone against so many people. I wish I had had a strong army behind me, but I was alone, and the other side had too many fighters. One black belt, no matter how well trained he is in. After her demise, judo and karate cannot win if he is attacked by many enemies or betrayed by those he trusts. This is what happened to us—what a shame to humanity. Even animals have some principles. Kings many centuries ago, for example, Purus and Alexander, had some principles; however, at the same time, there is an old saying: never let your enemy go.

I loved it when the Purus won many battles against King Alexander and pardoned him. Later, Alexander won, and the Purus was brought as a prisoner of war to the palace of Alexander, who asked the Purus, "How would you like to be treated." The brave Purus tells him, "I want to be treated as one king treats another king." During that episode, Alexander'sbody guard wanted to attack the Purus. The Purus told the guard, "Don't you know how to behave and not to interfere when two kings are talking?" King Alexander was very happy and told the Purus that he would give him back all of the weapons and wealth he had taken. The Purus again tells him, "It means you are obliging me, and then you want me to be obligated to you and always consider that you showed your mercy, and I would still have to respect you as my king." Alexander immediately told him, "No, Purus, Alexander wants you to be his best friend, and now I want to come and shake hands with you as my dearest friend. I am desperate to have a friendship with an extremely brave man, and I would feel honored that the Purus is my dear friend."

This true episode reminds me of many things in our life, as we were always the best friends and never even thought for a minute that any differences, no matter what would come between us as long as we both are alive. We also thought that if something happened to one partner, that other would not only love but worship the one who is gone and wait until the next life to meet again. That is what I am doing with great pain but with hope for this love. In my 8th-grade studies of ancient civilizations and the Vedanta, I have seen these things, an open book for anyone to read and research and tells of various true episodes. With the technological advances of the 20th century, many Indian movies were made as much as 100 years ago and remain hits today for the older generation. It is said that now the new generation is not taught the principles expressed in such films. As Gandhi-ji stated, "Technology will destroy humanity," so he was not in favor of too much technology. One can see that we have lots of technology, but the destruction of humanity, greed, love of money, and materialism have taken over with technology. The answer is hidden in the above sentences.

It also reminds me of Julius Cesar and how his close friend, Brutus, betrayed him. In my opinion, in Connie's case, medical negligence and betrayal by the doctors during my one-hour absence was a much more serious stabbing to a crippled handicap like Connie after her cardiac arrest. She was fighting for her life, and medical staff and the hospital were supposed to be her parents for this disabled, sick person who could not speak or move as if someone had tied her completely in a small cage. Even a tiger or a lion cannot save himself in that cage. If you think you are brave, go alone or with ten people without any weapons and have a hand fight. I would call those brave people, and the medical staff was no braver than attacking a helpless, powerless animal with weapons or guns. I was also attacked behind my back when I was gone for an hour. I would have shown my power if they were brave and waited for me to attack me to my face. I would have jumped and attacked them like in wildlife. But cowards are cowards and attack from behind.

A brave person would always come in front, face-to-face, giving a full challenge—let us see who is powerful. But they were worse than Brutus. Her biological sibling and his family were equal to so many Brutus but would be her friends when they wanted something. There is a saying that some people are givers and some are takers. This was the case with Connie and her family. People never change. Greed is greed, and as time goes, it keeps increasing just as a wildfire always grows. A fire never says it is enough. Let me stop, as I have had enough fire. I am satisfied. I want this fire to become the cooling rain to help the suffering people in the heat who have no cooling system and are struggling to take shelter until some humanitarian gives them a cooling system for their hard work. They are not beggars, nor do they want to beg. But then the old theory of supply and demand comes into play for the whole population during bad economic times. Let's hope it gets corrected. As man has made the mess, only man can correct it.

I have to mention again that Connie was extremely adventurous, and ours was the first marriage, and she left behind the most precious memories of happiness in my life. Yes, happiness and happiness, but perhaps some punishment was also part of the package, and that was the last three years of her sickness. Now I do not know if I should be thankful to God or call myself grabbing punishment of my life that she is gone from my life, and my hands are asking for mercy to God to grant me one more chance and give me Connie back. I am lost.

Before coming to the USA, we all watched Hollywood and Indian movies with my brothers, college school friends, chartered accountancy, and my family. Girlfriends were banned, I would say, in that era. Forty years ago, it was the same way, then 30 years ago it was a new way, 20 years ago, the waves were beginning to move fast, 15 years ago it was moving towards a bronze medal, ten years back it touched silver, and currently it has exceeded gold medal. With hope, we planned to win the Kohinoor diamond. It would have been impossible for me to think of being without Connie as if I was falling from the top of the Himalayas. Connie would have saved me from falling; now, that is not possible, as we both see each other in our dreams and are desperate souls dying to meet each other. The movie "Who Kaun This" (Who She Was) was based on this theme, and I can only see her talking to her soul in my dreams.

We are like two desperate souls. I am reminded of the raga-based melody song "Naina Barse Rim ZIM," meaning "eyes and soul falling to meet each other as desperate souls." And that is what I am going through now, living the same melody and the scenes of that movie. Why does she not come to me? I try to catch her, but she is gone. Has she taken a new birth, or is her soul still waiting? My heart is breaking. I confess I realized this is Connie. I am going through that, I see Connie everywhere, but I can't touch her, can't talk to her, but I am seeing her soul coming to me. My heart and soul are making me go and catch her, but I can't get her in reality. Who was she? I am sure her soul is coming to me, and I am desperate to have her back, but I am upset that I can't even touch her. She was my wife, and she is still in my heart and brain, and I keep seeing her, but I can't believe that she is gone, and I see her soul, her face, and suffering. This movie can be easily seen on YouTube, and I am sure it is on Netflix. It would be listed under international movies or Indian hit movies.

Another touching Indian movie that I asked Connie to see with me in the house from Netflix was "Anupama," a love story of husband and wife. The husband has a similar situation to me after the demise of his wife. The movie shows the widowed husband blaming his newly born girl as the cause of his wife's death, and get isolated with all his wealth, servants, and business, and losing interest in life. My life has practically the same theme, making me bitter with my family and friends who did not call Connie or me for one year or some friends for six years to as, "How is Connie." They may wonder how many times did I call? Should I blame them or myself? My shock is so deep that I want to blame them without realizing that others may have many problems, too, and they are all justified. Yes- they are; however, I am not even conscious of my fault- never- as my loss has pierced my every minute of thinking about Connie. I would respect all of them, but nothing can heal my constant thoughts of my wife—my wife. I don't talk to them or maybe don't want to describe the trauma I faced. Even if my family and friends know or come to know, no one would ever be able to understand a fraction of that trauma. God, please forgive me if even God would be able to evaluate the trauma? I have to thank the Lord for not punishing me for my behavior. I surrender and ask for mercy and forgiveness that I am already going through that suffering of losing Connie, and I ask for forgiveness.

From our very first meeting, we were happy together without even going out on a date. We wanted to spend more and more time together, and we're happy to be alone together. We did not try to cultivate hundreds of thousands of friendships to be happy, but we were extremely happy in each other's company. Despite this, we were very social, going to parties, dancing, eating out, etc.; but we were honest and sincere and never let another man or woman come into our life together. We were pure all of our lives- we never cheated or hurt each other, and we were never jealous or attracted to another person. We took an oath, to be honest to each other no matter where I had to travel or if one of us had to work late or go to a work party alone. When I was out of town, Connie would drive alone to events and be sure to return by 10:30, so we could talk before going to bed. We both had to leave early for work the next morning, regardless of how late we stayed up talking the night before.

16

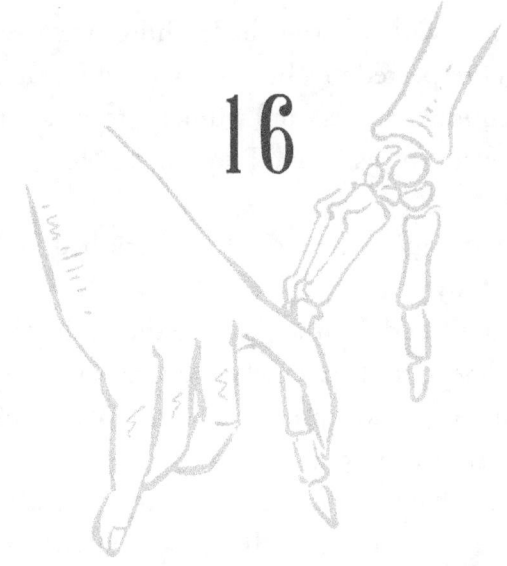

Connie was My Destiny

Again, I was happy after meeting Connie. Connie was my destiny and my reason for coming to the USA. She was the greatest thing in my life and helped me to forget all my childhood pain. Now the real pain of losing Connie is much harder than my childhood pain was. I would re-live the pain of my childhood for Connie's presence anytime now, and more realistically, in my next life. We had so much love for each other, and I am living with great pain now. Yet, I am living in the hope that we will both meet again. This faith I have and the revival of this faith gives me the strength to bear this pain. I know miracles happen, that reincarnations happen. Hope gives life- never deprive someone of their hope, and ask God to grant their wish. These are great tools and thoughts that wander through my mind at times. It helps to know that God knows all this and will grant this wish in our next lives to be the same couple- "Connie and Pradeep." I would be granted this desire of having Connie, even if I have to see hardship mitigating the joy of having Connie. It would be the best thing for both of us, and I am sure of that.

    I only had seven dollars when I landed in the USA. Neither my father nor the rest of the family has ever paid me a single penny from our inheritance. Connie and I got married. I was extremely happy and started working hard. I was smart and motivated to show her and my family back in India what I could. After three years, Connie and I went back to India once my family knew that I was doing great in the USA and comfortable with what we had. Things were very different with my family. They had always respected me, but now we were treated as if we were kings. That is why I must mention: "Success and winners are always respected." "We must play to win no matter what the game is." I do not care for that now, but the loss of Connie is deeper.

I would practice many great messages I have studied and known for years in Memory of Connie and my Peace.

I thought of what Jesus said: "Father, forgive them; they know not what they're doing." It is natural for me to undertake self-examination to remember and evaluate my past deeds and think of the holy preaching of the Bible, Gita, and Quran. Soon, the holy sermons came to my mind.

Surrender and accept when you are helpless, but keep the mind and body active.

Think of my past deeds to act correctly in the future.

I must prepare for mental and physical hardships to survive and do noble things for humanity, including teaching and sharing my knowledge and learning more for myself.

Pray for the self and humanity, and the world.

Keep busy, occupy my mind, and pray for forgiveness from Connie for anything bad I ever did that hurt her. I ask her blessings and keep doing good things for her sake.

Find a purpose in life to do things, which Connie would appreciate.

Lead a simple life of high thinking and deprive me of our great pleasures-traveling, dining.

I am doing that, and perhaps I will not go on cruises or any trips, except to India to see my brother and his family and other members of my family.

Lord Krishna had stressed an evenness of mind in all circumstances and situations, skill in action and overcoming the law of opposites, working without attachment, and considering returns, rewards, and prizes.

They told lies and got ahead in life, and here I am, telling the truth and stagnating.

Adam, in the Bible, said in a similar vein, "Allow your mind to think and say anything it will, only do not identify with it. Allow your body to do what it needs but do not react. Everything would happen on its time and accord."

Religion is not a business; it is a mission, a great way of life.

Manu said, "The whole world is kept in order by punishment, for a guiltless man is hard to find: through fear of punishment, the whole world yields the enjoyments which it owes."

17

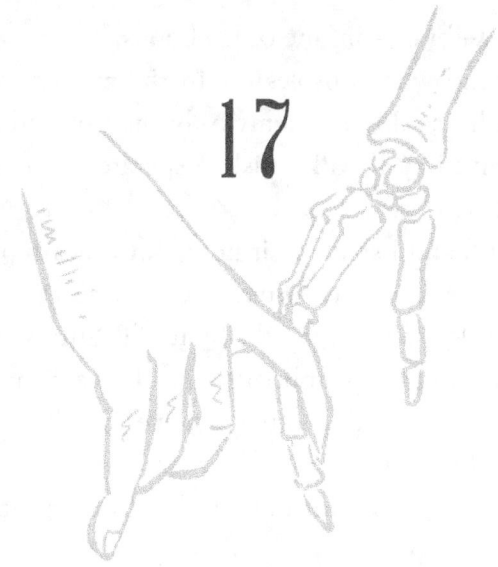

Some Nice Quotes for Our Daily Life

Further, it reminded me of wise quotations from my late uncle, Dr. P.N. Behl, "Darts, barbed wire and heated spears, however deep they penetrate the flesh may be extracted, but a cutting speech, which pierces like a javelin to the heart, none can remove- it lies and rankles. Bad language used in anger or otherwise hurts the person. The dagger wound heals, but the hurt caused by the speech leaves a permanent scar on the heart. Hence, control of the tongue and speech is very important. Never hurt others with your words. I strongly recommend austerity in speech, body, and mind. A man's job is to help one another and not to hurt each other. The latter is an animal instinct and not a human one. A good cheerful word can win the hearts of others; a bad word makes enemies.

Similarly, a dirty look can be killing: a cheerful smile is always appreciated. Women can seduce with a winsome look and a sweet word. Self-restraint is essential in all walks of life. Restraint in speech is important. If you hurt or abuse somebody with foul words, you hurt him. He becomes an enemy and vows to take revenge.

Further, if he returns your foul language, it shall hurt you as well. One can put knives and arrows in somebody's heart no matter how deep it is, but it can be taken away with medical treatment. But a bad deed and a bad word from the mouth rattles and rattles the whole life, and the person sometimes keeps a tendency for revenge." I would slowly try to follow the above great messages.

Further, Per Khalil Gibran—in one of his books.

"My soul is my friend who consoles me in the misery and distress of life. He who does not befriend his soul is an enemy of humanity, and he who does not find human guidance within himself will perish desperately. Life emerges from within and derives not from environs.

I came to say a word, and I shall say it now. But if death prevents in uttering, it will be said by tomorrow, for tomorrow never leaves a secret in the book of eternity.

I came to live in the glory of love and the light of Beauty, which are the reflections of God. I am here living, and the people cannot exile me from the domain of life for they know. I will live in death. If they pluck my eyes, I will hearken to the murmurs of Love and the songs of beauty.

I came here to be for all and with all, and I do today in my solitude will be echoed by tomorrow to the people.

What I say now with one heart will be said tomorrow by many hearts."

Prayers have a very soothing effect on a troubled mind. But sometimes, that fails, depending upon our love and devotion. I am going through that pain every moment of my life. My suffering is worse than ever, I thought after Connie's demise. I know that we all have to go one day, but I cannot accept that now because of my deep love for Connie.

18

Gandhi Ji – His Messages and His Teachings

Now I think of Mahatma Gandhi, Father of the Nation of India. His sacrifice and fight to get India's independence from British rule succeeded on the 15th of August, 1947. He was a barrister by profession and fought for equal rights in India and South Africa. A small built man can get freedom for all. Why, then, can't I get peace of mind and the power to bear the loss of Connie? However, this is a personal loss, and I cannot use this example. Gandhi said, "My life is My Message." "Truth always remains forever." "Non-violence." "My uniform experiences have convinced me that there is no other God than Truth." "God can never be realized by one who is not pure of heart. Self-purification, therefore, must mean purification in all the walks of life." "But the path of self-purification is hard and steep. To attain perfect purity, one has to become passion-free in thought, speech, and actions: to rise above the opposing currents of love and hatred, attachment and repulsion" I am bidding farewell to all the readers, for the time being at any rate. I ask them to join with me in prayers to the God of Truth that He may grant me the boon of Ahimsa in mind, word and deed". "I have nothing new to teach the world, Truth and non-violence are as old as the hills," By M K Gandhi. His messages were extracted from his Famous book "The Story of my Experiments with Truth," an excellent book for all readers.

19

Nelson Mandela

President Nelson Mandela was a big follower of M.K. Gandhi, practiced non-violence, and suffered for years in jail. But he forgave everyone, and his truth and sacrifices made him the President of South Africa. He was a world-renowned figure in the history of the world. When Gandhi returned to India, he mentioned that "India gave us Mohan Dass Karam Chand Gandhi, and we returned to India "Mahatma." The same Mahatma became Bapu and Father of the Nation ii.

In 1984, a great movie, "Gandhi," was released, where King Bentley played the role of Gandhi. This film and Mr. Bentley won Oscar awards. A wonderful true movie that helps elevate the mind and find inner peace. I might see it again to get more enlightenment to reduce some of the pain from losing Connie. How much peace I would get, I am not sure.

Great Dr. Luther Martin King, Jr. was a follower of Gandhi and fought for freedom and practiced non-violence. He, too, left behind a legacy for the world.

20

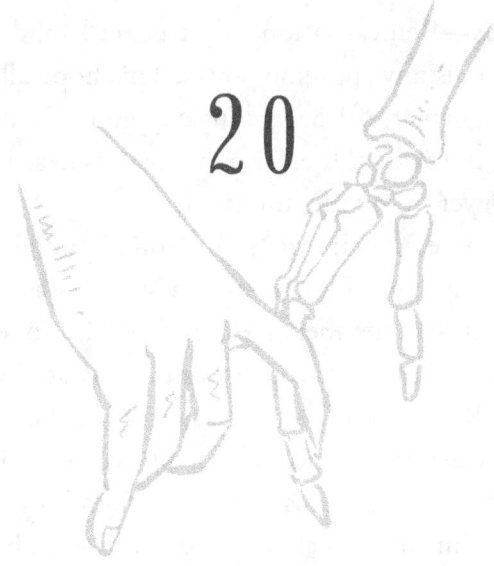

Swami Vivekananda

Swami Vivekananda attended the first world religious congress on Michigan Avenue, Chicago, Illinois, the USA in 1893, and said" "If you forget and forgive- that ends everything." He was the first person in history who said in his opening remarks "My Dear Brothers and Sisters of America" before his long speech. People were in tears. There is a street on Michigan Avenue, where the world religious congress took place in a hotel named "Swami Vivekananda Marg." He stressed, "Strength is life- weakness is death." "However long this life is, do something different so that that world can remember you- otherwise, where is the difference between you and trees and stones. They also live, die, and decay." From one of his books.

Marg is a Hindi word that means showing the right directions to youngsters, students, men, and ladies—showing them which direction to go in sorrows, to help people for humanity, to show new rays of hope when stressed, to show a way to go in the path where they can realize their bad deeds, to show new ways of living to the criminals who are ready to remorse their crimes, and to show a new way to all the purpose of life leading them to become good citizens.

I suggest that readers do further research on Swami Vivekananda.

These messages were great and meaningful to me when I was young and helped others, but it does not comfort me now that I have lost Connie. I hope I find some ray of hope, and that is—Reincarnation. My true and solid faith is that he could listen to our love if there is any supreme power. This hope allows me to have some peace once in a while. Further, if I have done any good Karma, the Supreme Lord would fulfill my desire in my next life. Also, my pain is heard by the Lord, for sure. That great hope is a power in my life now.

In memory of Connie, I want to share some thoughts on the great poet Tulsidas—we had to study his work in sixth grade. Tulsidas' poems can be read on the internet or in books. I remember the great Tulsidas, one of the most learned poets and scholars of the 16th century. He was too obsessed with his wife, and her absence was like his death. One night she had to go to see her sick parents. Tulsidasji was not able to stand missing her. He walked through the night in the rain to see her. Since it was late and raining, he used a rope to climb up to her room. His wife was very upset, telling him that it was 2 AM and you were here, and you foolishly climbed to my window. She told him that he was lucky to be alive; the rope he used was a huge python. Perhaps he was not hungry and enjoying the rain. Otherwise, he would have attacked and killed Tulsidas. She then told him to devote his obsession to God to learn and become something in the world. That was his enlightenment, and we surrendered to God and wrote many chapters on spirituality and education, which are known throughout the world in the Sanskrit language and have great meaning for soothing the mind.

21

Education and Career of Connie

Connie went to one of the best high schools and to Carleton College in Minnesota, one of the finest liberal arts colleges in the USA, for her undergraduate degree. She later transferred to the University of Michigan, another top college. After graduating, Connie taught junior and senior high school for a few years. Later, to advance her career, she went for her Master's in Spanish and French. Connie studied at top colleges in Mexico and Spain and then taught Spanish and French to the children at US military bases in Germany, England, and Spain for five years and then in California. Later, she moved back to her hometown, Chicago. That is how I met her, and she became the true love of my life. Connie exposed me to the American culture, dressing and polishing me to advance my career (though I equally had one of the best educations).

We both had professional careers—I traveled all over the USA but was home only for the weekend and sometimes more, but that didn't interfere with our love and understanding. We were in touch four or five times a day over the phone while traveling apart. Our Friday through Sunday night, we were always together, and depending upon the reports I was writing, I was in my Chicago office for weeks and home each night. It was a great life combined with our senior professional positions. Connie taught for 34 years and took early retirement but continued substitute teaching to keep her teaching license, and she was in great demand for Spanish and

French. She got offers of full-time teaching positions with different school districts, but she turned those down. I told her to forget work and to enjoy life and travel with me and have fun. She enjoyed teaching and had very close teacher friends whom I met and whom we had wonderful times. I give great respect to my wife as a teacher who did her duty.

Also, in honor of Connie's character and memories, I would like to mention some quotes I learned from my uncle Dr. P.N. Behl.' Book The Lord Of Darkness.

> Wisdom leads to freedom,
> Education to Character,
> Culture to perfection,
> Humanism to joyous living
> In a sense, human beings sometimes are crueler
> Than animals when greed comes.
> Our thoughts wander in all the directions
> And many are the ways of Man,
> The Cartwright hopes for accidents,
> And the physician for the cripple
> And the priest for the rich patron
> The blacksmith seeks day after day
> The customers endowed with gold
> Our thoughts all run towards profit
> For the sake of spirit, of mind
> Let go of all these wandering thoughts.

Character: Man is what his character is. A man of good character makes his life good, while a man with a bad character usually ruins his life and humankind. Character means the goodness of heart, tenacity, truth, living by your words, discipline, respect for others and elders and the weaker sections of the society, respect for the teachers and wise. A man without character is considered to be worse than a beast. People with weak character are usually feeble, meek, and easily changeable.

After retiring, Connie would go for weekly lunch with her teacher friends, and I was very happy- I also used to go with them as it was like a close family. Although she kept substitute teaching, she had more time to travel with me when I was traveling, which made my life great. I combined working and traveling to have great fun. I remember her going many places with me and her company gave me comfort. The most important time I needed her was when I had to go to Germany in 1996 for two weeks and then to France for another two weeks. We went to California, Dallas, Michigan, and many small towns. I think it was a great help to travel with me so that I would not be lonely. I would have never dreamt that loneliness was tolerable, but her demise has crushed me, as I will never see her except in my mind. All the 39 and half years of memories are painful. They are:

- Daily diary with beautiful handwritten notes of things we did
- Household notes of bills in folders
- Receipts of cash and credit cards
- Names of all the vendors and suppliers with phone and telephone numbers
- What day services such as painting, carpet cleaning, car service, and other utility stuff was done with notes of how much was paid
- Her different drawers of clothing with lists of the contents
- Her drawers of important documents
- Her makeup kits, with date, expiry, and all other details
- Our pictures of traveling and at the back, when and where and sometimes names of friends at the back
- Her letters from my family, her family, and our friends
- Important certificates and pictures for the future, just in case
- Years and years of our marriage anniversary, birthday, and Valentine's Day cards
- Separate books for household inventory, with the date of purchase and prices
- She would read different designs for ladies and men and accordingly would order new clothes for her and me
- Appraisal values of our paintings and the actual cost
- Medical reports and all the payments
- Medical reports and medical history for both of us
- Our business and pleasure trips
- Old canceled checks for future references
- Folders of her parents' pictures and their important documents for any future reference
- Folders of her grandparents and their pictures and letters
- Most important wedding cards from friends and relatives in special decorative plates

- Keep special napkins for different occasions
- Keep different greeting cards for different occasions
- Special thank you notes and special great quality dairies for different purposes and to write notes with her absolutely beautiful handwriting
- Variety of coasters, table mats, table cloths, special candles and silver, plates and glasses, etc. for different occasions
- Her beautiful writing for forty years, well organized, perfection in all aspects is one of the most painful things besides losing her
- All the brochures, the itinerary of all the cruises to Crotona, Italy, Ireland, Norwegian, Budapest to Amsterdam, Caribbean, Alaska, Spain, London, France, Germany, Seven times to India, Palace on Wheels in India, Jaipur and Agra twice by Air and Car. Khajuraho, Bombay, and our stay in Hotel Ambassador, Sun and Sand, Germany a second time, Berlin, France, Vienna, Switzerland, and fifty to sixty more

All are individuals and are in the files, intact in the separate folders in her big cabinets. I was just curious to clean some of the files on August 14th at 12.30 A.M. and was very upset to see how smart she was, and now all that fun we had is over with the demise of Connie. I see all those and get upset. Think and think and look and think and keep them back nicely in the cabinets. I do not want to throw them away, nor do I want to give them to any foundation or library. It has our diplomas where we studied the culture and food along with the history of these places. On the last day, all the people in the group had to prepare and present on the stage. You are honored with the diploma if you have done your homework and answered or wrote those in the one to two hours exam. I do not think those diplomas have much credit, but at least get into the door for some position if you have a post-graduate degree. It is a very tricky diploma. We never even tried to do anything with it. However, it's nice to show it to our friends. Now, Connie is gone. It's a monument for me for my happiness or sadness. I am going to keep them.

I found ten books of the world's best cuisines and recipes that Connie had been reading in the papers and magazines and nicely cut and paste in the books. I am sure restaurants, libraries, and educational institutions would be delighted to have them. I am sure they are like antiques. I would see what I would do with them? I would decide.

Connie also started doing volunteer work in Wilmette library work two to four hours every Wednesday, even when she was sick. She took that very seriously, as much I told her not to go when she was sick, but she said no and continued to volunteer. Later, I started dropping her off and spending time reading and buying books for donations too. Everything we did was wonderful as she was my obsession and was my love.

22

My Connie: The Blessed Lady

Connie was highly intelligent and intellectual, and I am only mentioning a very few of her philosophies. Otherwise, I would have to write another book with all the beliefs she applied in her life.

Connie always had Irish Blessings in her Book as a bookmarker.

"May the road rise to meet you. May the wind always be at your back. May the sun shine warm upon your face, the rainfall soft upon your fields. Until we meet again, may God hold you in the hollow of his hand."

These are other quotes from St. Francis De Sales in her bookmarks.

> "Make yourself familiar with the Angels, and behold them frequently in spirit: for without being seen, they are present with you." "God grant me the serenity to accept the things I cannot change—the courage to change the things I can and the wisdom to know the difference"
>
> —Salesian Missions.

"Remember your debts of gratitude" "Live in a way that leaves no regrets." "Everything people say or do is ultimately noted in the belief that those actions will lead them to happiness." "Your dream is possible." "Never seek happiness outside yourself." "Seek to understand your mistakes so that you may never repeat them."

These are a few quotations from
Open Your Mind, Open Your Life
—Taro Gold.

23

Connie's Passion for Reading

Connie was a great reader. She read the *Wall Street Journal*, *Chicago Tribune*, *Barons*, and New York *Times*. Additionally, she read a minimum of 16 magazines and health journals from elite universities and gave me important health care topics to read. I was a great reader, mostly of the newspapers' business sections and professional development topics, articles on different topics, and writing. Still, I also found time to read health care topics. I have always been fond of reading true storybooks, whereas she used to read both fiction and nonfiction and philosophy, besides all other genres. She would read *Consumer Reports*, *Chicago* magazine, and at least ten other magazines to get the most popular news and best-rated appliances, cars, TVs, and anything related to the home. Also, she would let others know the same. It was a great humanitarian cause. She loved exploring different cuisines and restaurants, attending Broadway plays, symphonies, and other things. She loved these cultural events and made me see all those with her. Now, I would have a very simple and plain life with all the withdrawal symptoms of my grief. The more I think, the more I want to write on every topic of her life. I am convinced that I will never find another diamond like that in my life. I hope and pray that God grants me, Connie, as a wife in my next life. I have a strong feeling that we will both meet in our next lives. This belief is the only thing that gives me happiness and the most upsetting life due to the loss of Connie. After her loss, I read those articles that she had suggested but was not originally interested in. Still, after reading them, I wanted to read the same articles many times over. Her awareness, intelligence, and common sense were beyond approach, and she was super smart and busy all day long. I am blessed to have such a gem in my life, and no one else can ever replace her, nor do I ever want to replace her. She was amazing and beautiful in my 40 years of life and always wrote and built her knowledge of different topics. Connie was a super reader. Her average daily time spent reading was ten to fifteen hours a day when she took early retirement, and before that, she read five to six hours each day.

Connie used to read many scholarly books; she must have read over 8,000 books during our marriage. She was very fond of the authors Susan Vreeland, Elizabeth Phillips, Jane Robinson, the Comedy of Woody Allen, Shakespeare, Ruth Rendell, Tom Wolfe, and Jon Krakauer, to name a few. Besides that, Connie also loved all cookbooks, health-related books about symptoms and their causes, and different recipes of world cuisines. She loved to read *Time* magazine, *Consumer Reports*, travel books for destinations around the world, and world history. Connie loved cutting recipes and trying them for her friends and me. She loves listening to old classical records, watching Oscar-winning movies, European movies, and listening to different music genres, including Elvis, the Beatles, the Beegees, Frank Sinatra, Mozart, and hundreds more. As I mentioned, we saw practically all the Broadway shows, including Joseph and the Technicolor Dreamcoat, Mama Mia, Miss Saigon, Elephant Man, Frank Sinatra, Irish songs and plays, and I would have to write 200 pages to write all of these down. This time, when I am writing, I have just pain in my heart and soul, feeling that Connie was truly one in a million. This diamond has left me alone as I will miss reading all that, depriving myself of all the world, including plays and Mozart, which was my passion with her. I was just reading about Turkey and its ancient heritage, where King Alexander and Cleopatra visited. I would be depressed and would get a panic attack if I ever decided to go alone or with any family member. I can't even think of going. I like now to go to the health club, do important household work, and stay home. I think I can think of seeing my real elder brother and his family and my grandnieces in Delhi, India. That is all. I now have realized that every author has written books in memory of someone, showing that authors write about their loved ones, which is wonderful. Otherwise, without two, such a book is not perfect.

24

Reading Passion and Her Polymath

I thought about Connie's reading habits and her interest in diversified magazines and knowledge the other day. Our whole family, including the entire Berry family, consists of about 200 people, three generations of my grandfather's sister's and brother's families included. Some of them, about 50-60, have settled in the USA, and some of them are smart- some are computer engineers, and some have graduate degrees. There are about 100 people on my mother's side. Overall, if we consider a population of 300-400 people, including some of her friends, I can prove it. Statistically, out of the whole population, Connie was the most intelligent person and the most well-read. I don't think anyone amongst the group can compete with her as far as intellect in every subject. The people I am talking about are very successful in their businesses and are intelligent. One of them is a medical doctor. I can even compare Connie with her and she is a medical doctor who studied in America, and her husband is also a doctor. I don't know why people think medical doctors are like gods, but this is the way they think, and this is the way they are. These doctors may be very good in their fields but do not know any subject other than medicine. In my opinion and experience of 41 years of my life with Connie, I spoke to my family members who are medical practitioners one day and found that they don't read anything other than their medical books. I don't think they know anything about the world, or about ancient civilizations, or about the histories of different countries. Their knowledge is just limited to the medical field.

I would say that Connie was a gold medalist in her knowledge. Business people, like doctors, are very good at what they do but know nothing else. So, it all boils down to the intellectual level of a person- what can they discuss, what do they know about diverse topics? I feel that an intelligent person should be able to discuss world languages and cultures. Connie knew every state in India- their languages, foodways, and cultures. At the same time, she was familiar with most world cultures. For example, she knew how different countries in Europe such as Ireland, France, Denmark, Germany, Norway, Italy, and Spain progressed, and what they did, Communists or Democrats. I don't think I have ever seen this kind of vast knowledge before or will ever see it again in my lifetime. When I think about it, I realize that Connie was brilliant. In this particular area, she exceeded me million times. She even knew the history of India; however, like me, she sometimes questioned whether the Mahabharata or the Ramayana happened. Some Indians believe that the histories recounted in these epics truly occurred, but some are skeptical. Some are confused, but most Indians, including me, believe that those events occurred. So when we had a question about these things, such as yesterday when I was watching Ramleela in Delhi, we asked ourselves what we believed. Most of my fellow movie-goers believe in the story of Ramleela, but some people don't believe in it- they said it was a show and considered it to be mythology. So, if I have my doubts, I don't think we should single out anyone else. Having said all that, Connie would put across her point in a brief moment and be done. Those who speak less and read more are often more intelligent than those who don't read. I mentioned this before, and I am repeating it now: listening is golden. Connie's intelligence was internal and external. I was very lucky to have Connie in my life. Her loss has rattled me, and I don't have any peace of mind even 8 months after her death. People want to see me become normal, but it will take me years to overcome my grief. The only happiness I get is from meeting new people. When I collected her medical reports, the people I met were much better to me than anyone else, even better than my friends. Our real estate agent, who I spoke to for a couple of hours recently, showed great compassion, and it was a mental stimulation for me. I am seeking out this kind of environment.

I just want to say this about Connie's reading- her knowledge was immense. I want to give you one more example. While reading about 20 magazines, I did not know that she was also giving a copy of that to our neighbor because she was a widow and could not afford to pay for the subscription as she looked after her family. Since Connie was already a member of those magazines, she subscribed to the magazines for our neighbor. The other day when I was talking to her, she told me that she knew I was going to India and would always get her a gift from there. She asked me not to get anything from India but instead to subscribe to the magazines that Connie would read. I was very happy to hear that. I had not known about this selfless charity of Connie's. I will continue her legacy of helping people. This gives me immense happiness, but at the same time, it makes me sad.

I was not sure that I would travel to India until I got on the plane on October 20th, 2015. On the night of the 19th, having only had two hours of sleep, I packed all of my papers into a briefcase and carry-on bag. I will now have to spend hours in Delhi sorting these papers and making copies. I will leave these documents in Delhi and take copies back to the US. Connie knew about all of the documents, and dealing with them made me very tense. Connie always helped me to organize my documents when I traveled. That was her greatness- she was the whole world to me.

I would mention this about her reading. I have said before that she must have read somewhere between fifty to seventy thousand books in her lifetime. She could read very fast, and she would always find time in the night to read. She would carry books with her on the plane; she would take them wherever she went. Sometimes I would get sick of her reading! I couldn't believe she read so much, and she wouldn't even talk to me. So she would tell me that there was nothing to talk about. She would then put the book down, only to start reading again after a while. I would get irritated, and then she would get irritated, and she would ask me why I couldn't pick up a novel and read. I would tell her that I liked to read the business section of the local papers and the *Wall Street Journal.* She would tell me that I needed to develop a habit of reading other things, like novels. She would say that instead of depending on her to explain why world events like wars took place, I should read it independently. Although I knew these things, I wanted to refresh my knowledge. Once Connie read something, she never forgot it. That was the difference between us. I want to reiterate that of all the people in my entire extended family. She was the most intelligent of them all.

25

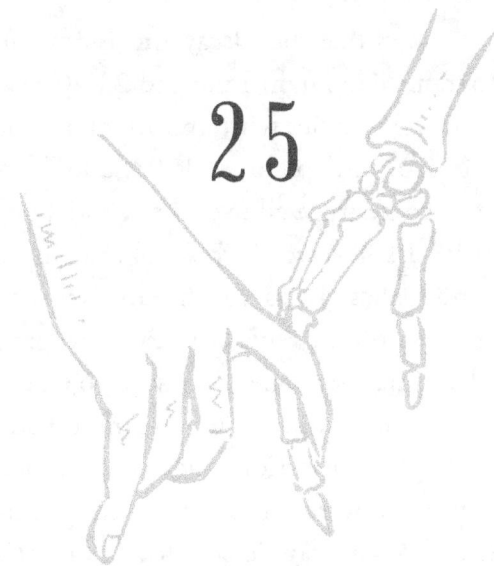

Connie's Love for Music and Arts

Connie loved old classical songs from many singers, such as Frank Sinatra, the Beatles, Elvis, Abba, Christmas music, Mozart, and many symphony and plays. She used to have two gramophones and 70-80-year-old records of singers like Cliff Richard, Tony Christie, and Ray Charles. I, too, was extremely fond of all that and our shared interest was a plus. I loved Broadway plays, and so did she. Of all the plays we attended, we never left early. We saw many plays, including Mama Mia, Miss Saigon, Elephant Man, Joseph, the Technicolor Dreamcoat, and Elton John's plays. Regarding the arts, Connie used to collect many artistic pieces for the house. She had special baskets for different places, like newspapers, magazines, small decorative art objects for the house, kitchen, study room, and bedroom. Connie collected several historical paintings. She took me to see many art and cultural shows. She was a member of the Museum of Art and Science and donated money to TV Channel 11, which the public supports and provides great programs. Channel 11 breaths of air music, history, Christmas programs, symphony shows.

Connie was curious about the subjects covered by different magazines and TV channels. She would read reviews and ratings of the channels and shows and knew which shows were popular and their ratings. Connie also knew which program would end, when a new show was coming along, and the ratings of films in theaters.

She would watch awards shows like the Oscar and Emmy and the country music awards. She enjoyed programs like Night Line and 20-20.

Connie also loved to travel to cities with important artistic events. Connie took me to Santa Fe, New Mexico, in September 1993, and I loved it. She knew that during September, artisans come from all over the world. She enjoyed shopping for herself and me in Santa Fe. I still have all those objects in my possession. Connie also took me to Austin and Dallas, Texas, for different cultural shows. She took me to a very exclusive furniture store in Florida in 2002 to get new furniture and to Wisconsin for different handmade watches. We went to Germany and to a German market in Milwaukee to purchase nutcrackers. Connie had season tickets to the North Lake club for stage plays, Marriot stage plays, and we often went to Las Vegas, where we must have seen over 70 beautiful plays. We saw Mama Mia! Twice- in Chicago and Las Vegas. We also saw Jersey Boys twice at different places. Each city has its cast while the show is the same.

26

Her Exposure to World Travel

Connie exposed me to world travel, which I truly enjoyed. She used to study and plan the best of cruises and other trips. I am extremely grateful and obligated to her for the beautiful cruises and other trips we shared both in the USA and in some of the most exclusive places in the world. Without her, I would not have traveled the world for pleasure. She often told me that I didn't take any initiative to plan anything other than trips to India. She came to India with me seven times and made me travel to the most beautiful places in India, including the "Palace on Wheels." It was a treat, and I would recommend this trip to everyone. It is a princely trip designed for kings during the British Empire. The Palace on Wheels runs from October through May and in the first week of January. We went in 1995, and the Palace on Wheels is one of India's best and finest trips. My readers can find more information on the Internet if they want to take this trip, from Delhi to Rajasthan. Connie was amazingly happy during our trip, and she mentioned it for the rest of her life.

Writing about my Connie, who is in my soul, and about her death and the medical negligence and seeing her dying is harrowing. At times, it feels I am just dreaming that she is gone. I am thinking of her cemetery. The most painful thing is her ashes under the green grass. I have to stand to touch her beautiful granite stone. That kills me even if I am not there. I am 7,000 miles away from Evanston and her grave in Memorial Park Cemetery in Skokie, Illinois. When I think of Connie, the green grass that has ashes kills me- that under that grass is my Connie, My Connie, HER body is under that grass. I am walking over that beautiful and intelligent Connie. Although her body in that casket was put in with the help of four professionals, I was truly to be part of that. Body and casket were together, hiding Connie Darling inside. How can I do such a thing to burn my Connie Darling in that? How do I know she is dead? It's very much possible that she was alive and weeping, crying. Pradeep, why do you put me inside, and please let me get out from this covered thing, as I am suffering from suffocation.

Like in the small tube of the MRI, I am sorry to do this sin. I recall a true episode of one of the most painful things I ever did with my first cousin, the son of my father's brother A.P. Berry, and from childhood, whom we used to call Kallo. Some called him Kallo Babu when he turned 25. We all lived in our big mansion in Katra Neel Chandni Chow in Old Delhi. When I came to the USA, Connie must have been waiting for me, and I know with 100% certainty that Connie was my destiny. Maybe God sent us on the Earth so that I had to meet her and marry her. Maybe both of us had some past relationships which were incomplete, and God gave us a chance to be together again for 42 years. The Palace on Wheels is an ancient place and love for the foreign tourists, mostly American citizens who are crazy to visit and wish they could see India.

In her seven trips, we traveled to the Taj Mahal, Jaipur, Kashmir, Khajuraho, and other places in India. I also traveled frequently throughout the USA for my professional career, and if Connie was on vacation, she used to accompany me. I was very happy and had a ball while I was working. Sometimes I would work long hours, and she was very capable of exploring and finding the best places by herself. Later, she would talk about her adventures and take me to see all that she discovered. If I had been alone, I would not have done anything. All these truly made me curious to explore more about travel and shopping. All these experiences made us compulsive shoppers for clothes and gifts, and we had a great collection of the best pens, picture frames, shoes, clothes, and many more items for the house and our family and friends. We were very social for a while, and later, we both were so happy that we didn't care if we were alone or not. We used to have a few evenings every week when we would go out for dinner and visit or invite friends and family, but we preferred to share our love and company by ourselves. We talked of different things, shared our knowledge and reading, and spent our time together writing, dining out, shopping, traveling, driving together, and going to the health club and small gatherings of friends. We were inseparable and used to feel lonely without each other. I think it was a great time and love, and even if we were sitting in the same room doing different things, as long as we could see each other, we were happy. I know that sometimes this kind of love is very painful because spouses who feel this way cannot go on if something happens to one of them, but we have no control.

As we traveled together, we saw practically half of the most important parts of the world. We saw Broadway and Las Vegas shows and symphonies in different parts of the world, including Vienna. Dining out in the best restaurants to experience new cuisines was a powerful part of our lives. Connie wanted the best but was financially conservative at the same time. She took me to Spain in 1987 for two weeks. We went on an Alaskan cruise in 1988 and visited Alaska a second time in 1989. We went on a Caribbean cruise in 1989. We also went to New Orleans in 1989 and spent time in the French Quarter. We went to New Mexico in 1990. We also took many mini-vacations over long weekends, traveling to Santa Fe and even to England. We took Michigan University Alumni trips to Tuscany, Ireland, Denmark, and Norway.

One of our greatest memories, especially for Connie, was my sense of humor and laughing when our friends of 30 years started calling me Doctor. Because of them, a cruise ship of 1400 people truly believed I was a medical doctor. The older ladies on the cruise, in particular, spread the word to all the ships that Dr. Berry was on board and not be afraid to climb a historic building. I told them not to worry, breathe deeply and climb slowly, and they complimented me as the best medical doctor. Other senior ladies told me they loved sweets and asked if they were harmful. I didn't want a lawsuit, and I had to improvise. I asked, "Are you diabetic?" and when they said no, I told them to keep eating and not to worry. They stuffed themselves with sweets, and I began to worry that I would be in trouble if anything happened to them. But God is grateful, and I started getting letters from many people cured by Ayurveda medicine and yoga. I decided that I would never do that again, and we started to no longer travel with our friends, except to Spain. Connie and I decided to focus on each other and began to drop the friends who were not close to us. They want me to join that group of friends, thinking that will help what I am going through without Connie.

Later, we took trips with Vantage Cruise- a two-week trip in Norway and another river cruise of 17 days from Budapest to Amsterdam. We took a Christmas Tree cruise for 12 days in England during the winter, and we went to the French Rivera, Germany, France, and seven times to India. I went home almost every year for two weeks to see my brother in India. But from 2011, until 2015, I did not even think of going back to India due to her health. I did not even think of leaving her for one day when she was sick. I left my high-powered senior position in 2006 to be with her, and I have no regrets at all. Rather, I am happy to serve her, which gives me the greatest satisfaction, but I cannot bear the pain of losing her. She wanted to go to Australia, New Zealand, and China, but some way or another, we could not go. I will regret this all my life.

We went to Door County three times and many other beautiful places in Wisconsin-- Lake Geneva, Crystal Lake, every city of California, including Palm Springs, where she found the standing table she had been looking for for two years. She was a perfectionist. We also want to all the Texas, North Carolina, and Nevada, especially Las Vegas. Living in Chicago, we saw all of the Broadway shows that came to the city. Later, in January from 2005 to 2014, we went to Sanibel Island for five weeks and to Marco Island, staying for three weeks at the Hilton Marco Island Resort to escape Evanston's cold and snow. It was nothing but fun, love, and billions of dollars worth of our happiness, which money cannot buy at any cost. Connie was very conservative and not concerned with high society. She never wanted to impress the world, as Connie was very modest and not a showy person. She enjoyed meeting interesting and intelligent people. We both shared the same rhythm. We respect every human being, whether educated or not. We both have been down to earth all our lives. Now I have lost that momentum and will not enjoy the same life without her. Many family members and friends tell me that life keeps going, but there is a big stop to see how our life together was.

27

Connie—Her Charm and Beauty

Connie was charming, ethical, honest, giving, faithful, and extremely intelligent, and a great reader, in addition to being an incarnation of tolerance and strong will. She was exceptionally beautiful, both externally and internally and from every angle, and a wonderful wife and best friend. In addition, to being well-rounded and bright in every aspect, she was the darling of my family and friends. Whosoever met her became her fan and friend and, accordingly, became our friends too. Connie was born in Glenview, a very affluent suburb of Chicago. She loved her parents and was very faithful, and always offered help at any time. She used to invite them to our house every week. I also enjoyed having them, and we were all very fond of Indian food, which we both used to cook for them. In their old age, Connie took care of them. I, too, was involved in helping Connie care for them. Her father got sick first, and we were there every moment for his help and support, including doctors' appointments and trips to the hospital. We were there when he died in December 1989. We asked her mother to stay with us after his death, but she refused.

Let me clarify, her mother was crazy, and after becoming a widow, her life revolved around her four grandkids from her only son. She wanted to stay with them, but they refused to have her, and she kept on trying but in vain. I think it was a pathetic and dirty thing for Connie's brother to deprive his mother of her old age.

We brought her mother to live in our house for months and months when she was sick. Otherwise, she was living in her own house. Later, Connie's brother and his family took their mother to another Wisconsin, a three-hour drive from our home, and put her in a nursing home against her will. They feared that otherwise, Connie's mom might not leave all her money to him. Connie had told her brother that they were welcome to see their mother's will, that their mother had left an equal share for them both. Despite this, her brother and sister-in-law did not trust us. "Greed of Man is A Curse of The Land." The rules of greed sometimes rule the world; I feel Animals are better than human beings. Animals will kill their prey only when they are hungry, whereas man keeps on exploiting and killing out of greed, even when he has had enough and has satisfied his hunger.

We visited her mother every month, sometimes twice a month, stayed in a hotel for two nights, and took her out for lunch. We have satisfaction and happiness, knowing that we made her last fifteen years of life extremely happy, even after her husband's death. We both were instrumental in arranging her cremation and service in the peace chapel and then putting her ashes next to her husband. Connie was extremely upset after the loss of her parents and did much charitable work, which gave her happiness. "It is extremely important for me to mention that Connie and I would have brought her mother back from the nursing home if Connie was not suffering from a rare skin disease, pityriasis rubra pilaris (PRP), in 1999 and 2000. That disease was more painful than her fight with cancer, except in 2014 and 2015 when she suffered from spreading cancer. Connie was extremely hurt that her siblings and their kids were not nice to Connie's mother, who sacrificed her life and money for them. I am not trying to write bad things about her siblings and family, but we were both upset, and it was a tragic thing for me to see my wife's agony during this time. I would mention more about more painful episodes in "Another Painful Chapter for Connie and Pradeep."

28

Connie's Character and Thinking

There is no end to the greatness of her thinking and her character. She was loyal and honest, never lied and always forgave, gave without taking, had a great work ethic, and maintained our household without asking me for help. She never depended on anyone but always found a way to cope with her. She was very brave and bold. If someone were in error, she would tell him to his face and make him realize his mistake. Connie did not care if someone was wealthy and would be friendly with all intelligent people. She did not run after wealth or social power-that was not in her blood or mine. We cared for what people were and not what they had.

I give my tributes to Connie by quoting the following messages from Swami Vivekananda. Swami Vivekananda quoted the following messages. These sometimes give me strength, but still, they do not heal my pain.

1. "Have faith that you are all brave lads, born to do great things. Let not the barks of puppies frighten you; no, not even the thunderbolts of heaven, but stand up and work."

2. "Your country requires heroes; be heroes—stand firm like a rock. Truth always triumphs. A country wants a new electric fire to stir up a fresh vigor in the national veins. Be brave."

3. "Trust not the so-called rich; they are more dead than alive. The hope lies in you- in the meek, the lowly, but the faithful. Have faith in the Lord. Give me a genuine man; I do not care for anybody to help you. Is not the Lord infinitely greater than all human help? Be holy- trust in the Lord, depend on Him always, and you are on the right track; nothing can prevail against you."

4. "Faith, faith, faith in ourselves, faith in God- this is the secret of greatness. If you have faith in three hundred and thirty million of your mythological gods, and in all the gods which foreigners have introduced into your midst, and still have no faith in yourselves, there is no salvation for you. Have faith in yourselves and stand upon that faith and be strong."

5. "All truth is eternal. Truth is nobody's property; no race, no individual can lay exclusive claim to it. Truth is the nature of all souls. Who can lay special claim to it."

6. "Look upon every man, woman, and everyone as God. You cannot help anyone. You can only serve. Serve the children of the Lord Himself if you have the privilege. If the Lord grants that you can help any one of His children, blessed you are."

We both applied these messages throughout our lives, and I will continue doing so for the sake of Connie. My message to all my readers- Please have a bond of love, care, respect each other, have full trust and honesty, plant your relations as we give water to the plants. Connie and I did all that; however, without Connie, I am suffering as a fish without water, the pain an animal feels when slaughtered, or the pain of human beings and animals killed by others. Gandhi-ji was right when he started his movement of nonviolence- fighting never brings peace. Living by the code of an eye for an eye would destroy the world. Would you mind trying to understand how sensitive the relation between a woman and her husband is when they are married? Most wives only want love, care, respect, security, a faithful, caring husband, comfortable living, and a nice family who cares for her. Wives can sacrifice many luxuries and material things in return for their husbands' love, but they must have that love. Yes, there are exceptions, but in my opinion, the first one holds. Husband and wife must admit and say to each other- three words. "I love you."

29

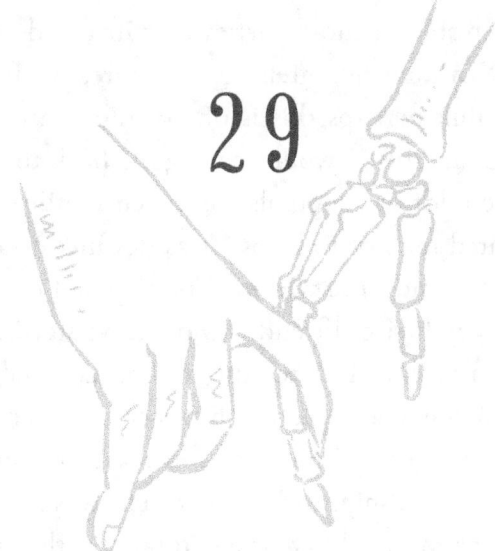

The Wanting to Feel Connie's Presence

Connie's Character—Part Two

I want to write more regarding Connie's character. I think I can tell you we were made for each other. I was raised in an environment with very strong values and with an emphasis on character building. Our grandparents were very strict about focusing on studies, sports, and other activities like the Scouts and the National Cadet Corps (NCC). I was extremely good in Boy Scouts; I was the NCC battalion sergeant and had a lot of other extracurricular qualifications. We were given the strongest foundation possible to build our character. That also meant not having any relationships or attachments to the opposite gender. The priority was to get educated first, and all other things could happen after one was well settled in life. In reality, because we were brought up this way, we never really thought of having any female friends. It wasn't unlike today, where it is very common for people to have boyfriends or girlfriends where they might or might not marry each other. In any case, that was a different era.

Connie was also brought up in the same way. Her focus was only on her education and her research. She was keen only on her studies, and she was not interested in parties or meeting men. She was very happy with her close-knit family and girlfriends. Her mother was very strict, and Connie herself had a moral code that meant she was not interested in those parties that involved drinking and dancing. In addition to her education and intellectual nature, we found this a common aspect amongst us. I think perhaps this is one of the contributing factors behind our getting together. Ordinarily, I would have gone back to India for an arranged marriage, as there were a lot of proposals from rich families which had come my way. Perhaps God wanted me not to go as I was destined to meet this girl Connie who was beautiful both outside and within. Connie liked to say that I was her first boyfriend, and she was my first girlfriend, although we started as only friends.

To this day, I don't know how I gained the confidence to talk to a woman because if you are from India, talking to a woman is the most fearful and dangerous thing. Of course, after I came to America and met ladies in my corporate life, I developed the courage and faith to form friendships with women. The reason is that in America, men and women have been raised in a different environment- they have been brought up full of confidence right from their childhood. I remember that when I first came to this country, one of my colleagues, who was working under me, told me, "Pradeep, let me tell you one thing, in this country, children are given the maximum freedom." I was astonished to hear that because even though we were given freedom in our era, we were watched like hawks. We were always kept track of—our activities, where we went, etc.

I noticed a big difference in our cultures. If you talk to people over here, you notice how confident they are, irrespective of their age, because they have been brought up in such an environment. I'm not trying to criticize or hurt anybody's feelings- I'm just sharing my own experience and knowledge without offending anybody. When I go to the health club or shops or even in my professional life, women talk to me as if we have known each other for years. There is a lot of joking around, and our conversations are full of fun. I have not seen that kind of atmosphere with Indian ladies, whether they are married or otherwise. They tend to be very reserved, so I think it is a big cultural difference which I find very interesting. Once again, it is not a reflection of these cultural ways of communicating. I have traveled worldwide, whether in America or Europe, and I find that outside of India, people are friendlier and more open with strangers. It is not as if people in India are not like that. They are very wonderful and hospitable, but there is some kind of a rhythm missing. I find that sometimes even young Indians are reluctant to talk. Even in America, I meet many Indian school and college students—often, they don't even say hello. At times, I ask them if they are from India—to which they mumble yes and claim that they need to get back to their work. This has happened several times, and to some degree, it has upset me, but then I decided that this is a cultural difference, but that is no answer. A simple smile and a little hello are always good.

30

Making Good Use of Time

Connie told me, "Make good use of your time."

During the late '70s and early '80s, both of us were working very hard to build our careers. Although I didn't need to do any work on Saturdays, I would get up in the morning and work on my reports because I wanted to increase my knowledge and advance my career. I used to put in that extra effort, I gave 200% instead of 100%, and Connie would do the same. The only difference between the two of us was that while working, I would turn on an Indian program called Chitrahaar. I used to watch that programme from 8 o'clock to 9 o'clock while I worked. Connie would let me watch it and not say anything. She was very selfless; she probably thought that since I enjoyed it, she should not interfere. Those were very interesting days for both of us.

One day in 1979, my uncle, Dr. Behl, came to our home when I was watching Chitrahaar. He turned it off and said to me, "Why on earth are you wasting your time watching this useless program? I know that you are working from 8 am to 9 pm, but instead of this junk Chitrahaar, why don't you watch some financial programs, so that you can do both, just like I do. I listened to some lectures while writing my book, and this is the way you teach yourself." His British wife told him, "Pran, leave him alone, let him enjoy his program." He replied to her, "Listen, Marge, you don't know, this is about his career. He is my favorite nephew, and I love him very much like my son. I want him to shine, and I want that Connie should be proud of him. So he should stop watching Chitrahaar." Turning to me, he said, "Pradeep, you forget about this lousy program and concentrate on your work." I enjoyed watching it for one hour, and I thought at that time that my uncle was being very tough on me. Later, at the age of 55, I realized what he was trying to say then. Now I don't enjoy those kinds of programs.

In 1984-85 I got into the habit of watching Indian movies. Connie was initially happy that I was enjoying watching the movies. Later on, when she saw that the habit was increasing, after about one year, she told me, "You waste your time watching movies which have no theme- girls are dancing, and boys are running. These are not intellectual movies. If you want to watch interesting movies, watch those movies based on true stories which make sense. Those movies have some sort of intellectual ending. You are not learning anything from Indian movies. It is the same plot: a hero fights with 100 people, the hero can do anything, then a villain comes, then they have a flight, the villain hits and hurts the hero, and finally, the hero meets the heroine. The actresses are gorgeous- I love their dresses and sarees, but they lip singing the songs, dancing unlike the actresses in a ballet or Broadway show or stage play, where they are properly trained to sing. These Indian actresses are undoubtedly beautiful, but the background dancers are not so beautiful because they want to contrast the background dancers and heroines. Our American movies are not like that." I used to watch many American movies when I was in India. We never missed American movies.

After coming to the USA, maybe because I was homesick and away from my family, I started watching all the Indian movies we used to see in the theaters in India. That habit persisted for a year or two. Connie told me, "If you use the time you spend watching movies to reading your reports, business documents, the New York Times, the Wall Street Journal, or even novels, you will get knowledge." I said, "I don't like to read any novels. They are useless fiction. I like reading the autobiographies of people like Nelson Mandela, John F. Kennedy, Mahatma Gandhi, Dr. Rajendra Prasadin, Mark Twain, US Presidents, and people who researched different fields, medicine, and other books. Still, mostly I preferred reading business books relating to my profession. She said, "Read whatever you want, but keep the habit, because it will give you a hobby, it will keep you occupied, and it will stimulate you, and you will become an intelligent person." Her average reading time was 4-6 hours a day when she was working.

When she took early retirement, her average reading was 14-15 hours a day. She used to read magazines, books, newspapers, and very selective and intellectual books and articles. I used to read during the days I was working, but after taking time off, I started writing articles for MBA students and many institutions. I would write on my passion and subject area: commercial lending, merger, and acquisition. People used to ask me questions on the internet and ask my advice on how to solve them. There were questions from people about banking, internet banking, and the commercial loans sector. There would be questions about hostile mergers, how to buy companies, how to run a company, how to start a company, leverage it, and many other things, including improving sales.

I used to write because I had lots of knowledge; this knowledge did not come because I am a special man of God but because I worked hard. I went to an elite university in the USA for my MBA. I passed over 80 professional development courses while working for different large finance companies and large banks, which were mandatory to promote and build knowledge. Without bragging, I can talk about any subject or topic, whether my career, spirituality, ancient Indian civilization, Buddha, Shakespeare, the Bible, the Koran, Indian classical music, Mozart, or Broadway shows. Thus I developed my personality a lot, and all the credit goes to Connie. If Connie were not there and not helped me, I would not have changed myself. I started feeling embarrassed that Connie may see me as the same person who was not well cultured, well developed. Thus I ended up outshining both of us.

I don't mean to offend anyone in my lifetime. Still, I see certain people in my own family. About fifty of them don't do anything on weekends and don't read or research papers- the only thing they do is gossip and waste their time all day. I am surprised that some of them were born in the US, but they have not adopted any elements of American culture. Their knowledge is limited to their job. Even though they were born in the USA, some were fired 10-15 times, despite their qualifications. I wonder why that happened; they were doing their job half-heartedly from 9 to 5 and not doing much to enhance their career. For the last 10-15 years, they have been begging me to find them a job. I often helped them find one, only to learn they were fired because they did not know the subject.

Nothing is easy in life. The only thing that pays is hard and smart work and innovation. Education is a constant daily habit. Degrees have finite completion points, but education, systems, and technology keep changing, whether in banking, finance, or computers. For example, in banking, different structures have been developed for different kinds of lending. I know all these new systems because I am interested in learning. This is all because I want to be proud of myself, and I was also doing it for my wife to say I am also an intellectual person. That was why, when we were going on different trips all over the world, I used to interact with people more than she would. She was sort of quiet. When the final exam at the end of the trip would come, Connie would answer the questions. She would answer because I was not well prepared. She did a fantastic job, so she used to tell me, "You should also take some initiative." Then I would stand in front of 100-200 people and talk about the subject area. I worked very hard for that. These incidents I am narrating would not have happened unless Connie was there.

That is why I feel that Connie was special, and I will never find Connie again, except in my next birth. I am praying every day that I get Connie again in my life. This is very important to me; I am willing to sacrifice anything for that. As I have repeatedly mentioned, her loss has been the most painful thing in my life, and no one else will ever understand what I am going through. Our love was one out of million people. When I say this, I want to ask for forgiveness because people will think I am talking nonsense. They will say that their love was also the same. I agree that their love was maybe the same, but I don't know their stories. Our love was great because we were known as "Connie and Pradeep" everywhere. At least 50,000 people must have told us over the last 40 years, including friends, family, and colleagues, that we were too attached and that God would bless us. Many people used to tell us that both of us were special.

31

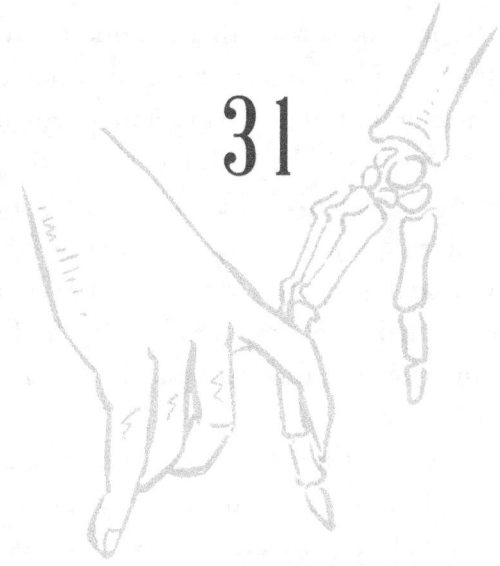

Yearning for Connie's in One Form or Another

My love for Connie was very deep and pure. We had the greatest love for each other. I sometimes feel guilty or selfish about my grief, but I have seen many tragedies. Those tragedies also affected me very badly, regardless of whom the tragedy had occurred. I always thought about these tragedies- why did they occur, and why do such things happen? After the death of Connie, I don't want to think of all those tragedies. Connie's death mitigates all those tragedies. I don't want to remember them. How has Connie's death changed my way of thinking? I don't want to say it is selfish, but you only understand the grief when it happens to you, when someone very close, like a special wife who meant the world to you, passes away. Connie and I were inseparable. I don't think I should feel guilty about it. Even if I feel guilty about it, I don't want someone pointing it out because it is solely my point of view.

God forgive me for what I want to say, but if something happens to someone, I would not feel sad or sorry unless I truly care about it. Connie's death has made me bitter and angry, so perhaps I will not care deeply for the grief of others. I will probably only feel sorry for their pain. The new realization in my life is that there is a difference between feeling sorry for someone and truly feeling their pain. I know that we all have to die. If someone is older than me and my relative, I do not know how to react if something happens. Even if I go to their funeral or their last rites, I am not going to say a whole lot of things. I will stand quietly in the corner thinking about it, and maybe my tragedy will be with me at that time. I will be there as a bystander without any emotions. This is because so many people I thought were close to me did not care during my three years of pain, so I will not feel for them. Even if someone is very close to me, yes, I will feel sorrow, but nothing more.

Nobody will be able to match my love and the depth of the feelings I had for Connie. What I'm writing is very difficult to put down on paper, but this is how I feel. Some people will hate me. Some people will think it's good, yet others will think I'm correct and say I was very much in love. Some people will think I'm selfish and have a one-track mind, but I'm not going to worry about them. If someone says something to me after reading this, my only response will be to say sorry. No one can compare my loss with any other person's. Connie was very special to me and will remain so.

Today, September 29th, 2015, I went to visit her at the cemetery. I used to go there two or three times a week, and I decided to go again. I think I was there for 30-45 minutes. Whenever I go there, I have noted that I get some peace of mind. Maybe what I feel is not peace of mind exactly, but it is just a shadow of letting go of the grief for some time. I feel that I am with her when I go there. The pain inside is deeper since I had never expected that I would have to live to see this situation. She was alive 6 months ago with no inkling that she would die so soon, and today she is no more. It was just yesterday that I used to take her to the hospital and doctors. I remember how we used to sit together and chat, and suddenly in one second, everything was gone. Going to the cemetery makes me feel that.

I think that mentally I'm ready to live near her headstone. People will think that I've gone mad, but I'm not crazy. I have seen how people have lived through after the death of a loved one, such as in Egypt. I think if I had a choice, and they allowed me (which I think is next to impossible), I would live in a small house near her. Even if that life would be very hard for me, I would still take it. I have never had that experience, nor will I ever have it. It might look like the most stupid thing to do, but every individual has a different way of expressing grief. Many people don't think as I do about this subject.

I want to write everything coming from the core of my heart that I have already conveyed. I have thought many times. I had shared this with my brother and everybody when I went to India for two months. When I think of going back to India for a month to change the scene and get some work done, I will see how I feel. When I leave the house for a long time, the things I used to do with her, such as preparing her meals and praying in her room, haunt me. I will feel that her soul is still around. I know that her soul is in peace, but my mind is not at peace. So, I think it is going to be very difficult for me. In India, the girls weep and cry when they leave their parents' home after marriage because they will be missing their family.

The girls cry for maybe one day, but I am grief-stricken whenever I go out of the house for more than a few hours, except when I go to the store or health club when I know I'm coming back home shortly. Similarly, I weep whenever I have to go anywhere. If I have to go anywhere for an extended period, or if my relatives come to visit me and I go out with them, at least I will be in the USA, so the gravity of the pain will be a little less, but I will still be thinking about her. However, if I go overseas, then the gravity of the pain will be a million times stronger as my mind will be at home.

After I reach my destination, maybe I will handle it for a few days, but I will get restless and return home. So many times, I think that I should go for one week or a couple of weeks, but then I realize that it is not a short journey; it takes a lot of time to reach India. It is not always easy to go for a week or ten days. It was a different era when we were working, and Connie and I would both go, or I would go alone to India, but I would never be gone more than two weeks, including travel. Later on, I cut it down to twelve days, including travel, because then I knew I was responsible for my work and Connie. Now there are no responsibilities. I have left my senior position, I am not working anymore, and Connie is no more. The attachment to home has caught me differently, and it isn't easy to get out.

I don't think my grief will lessen; rather, it will become worse as time passes. Many people told me that it would take me six months to one year to overcome this, but I feel it will take much longer than that. It is a sign of my love for Connie. I don't know what Connie must have gone through when she was sick with that cardiac arrest and how she held my hand, and she wanted to say something but could not speak. I don't know what she wanted to say and that bothers me. This would not have happened if she had passed away in the house without any mistakes made by the doctors. I would have been very affected, no doubt about it. But the trauma I saw, the medical negligence by the doctors, the way they delayed their response to her cardiac arrest, and the three weeks I spent fighting with them, that trauma is worse than anybody can go through. I pray to God that no one should go through it. I am very upset about it, and I cannot believe it happened in the USA. Things like these happen; some people say it was destiny, some say her time on earth was finished, but I don't buy that. I used to believe that when the time comes, you pass away. I refuse to accept this kind of death after doctors' suffering and negligence, so I now say that the end time is in our hands.

I think I am being naïve, but my love for Connie is still there. I'm being very honest. Some people will appreciate this, some people will say I am stupid, yet others will realize true love. Hopefully, they will learn something from this. This is how I feel, and I think I will put in the heading 'realizations of my pain and the pain of others. The only way I keep myself very happy is by talking to people I meet. They listen to me, especially young ladies over here, and they get touched by my story. Then I casually ask them if they want to tell me about themselves if they are comfortable enough to do so. I think that they are very honest, and once they trust me, they share their stories. They say that they wish they had a marriage like ours. They wish their husbands were like me and say they are still searching for the kind of love Connie and I shared. I think that in that respect, I am extremely lucky. Many people in stores and restaurants, who don't know me, have told me that I am lucky. When I make phone calls to various companies and talk to various people, I have observed that my story touches 99% of people. Maybe 2% of people say that I should get on with my life, but I don't think I want to hear that. I need sympathy all the time for this incident. I know you show your weak points whenever you ask for sympathy, but I don't care now.

I am going to write what I feel. When you read something written from the heart's core without worrying about what people will think, it becomes a gem of a book. That is how true stories are written, and so many movies are made about real-life incidents. I ask that people listen to me, and I hope that they will understand my emotions at this time. It is 5 a.m., and I am now going to sleep. In the past, I would wake up at this time and go to the health club. Yesterday, I was awake until 7:30 AM writing, but I didn't have to worry because it was a weekend. But tomorrow is a working day, and I know I have to do a lot of work. Even then, I could not help writing her biography because I wanted to get it published as soon as possible. One day, when this book is published, I will go back to my original routine of sleeping by midnight and waking up by 9 am.

My main priority is to keep talking to the attorneys; I am ready to go to the highest court of law. I will not leave any stone unturned in my efforts. The rest, I leave it up to God. I beg Connie to give me the power to succeed for her. I pray that I can find some attorney who will take my case and that we win the case- then I will be somewhat happy, and Connie will be happy. That is why I am determined to go through with it. People ask me the point in pursuing the case, and I tell them it is my satisfaction. This is the way I feel about the tradeoff of my love with other tragedies.

32

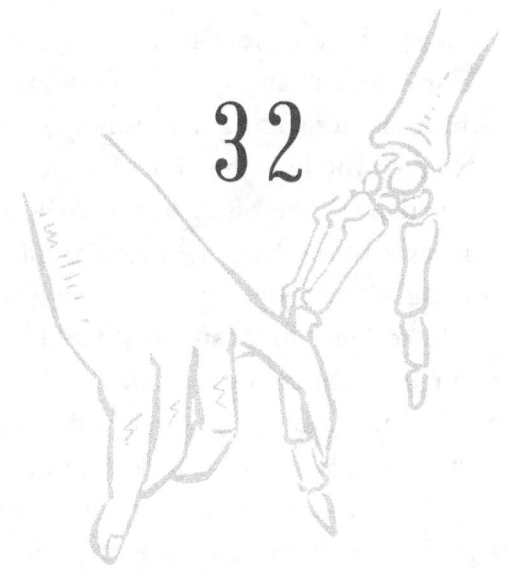

Connie is Still With Me

For the last eight months, I have noticed that Connie has gone away; however, while I am at my house seeing her pictures, I feel as if Connie is still with me and talking to me. Yes, it's a good feeling, but more than that, it's a very sad and upsetting feeling, too, and that is stronger than the good feelings. The other thing I have noticed is that for the last four months, from July 2015 onwards, when I turn on the lights if I wake up in the middle of the night, I feel if Connie will get disturbed by the lights, as my first thought is that she is asleep. I then feel a shock and realize the truth, and that is a double-edged sword and like an arrow in my heart. It takes me more than an hour to go back to sleep and again in the morning the same arrow- one can see better in the morning as all the house is empty. I leave the lights on in her office until 8:30 in the evening, and at 8:30 in the morning, automatic lights come on until 10:30 a.m. and then turn off at 10:30 in the morning when there is enough natural light. These days, of course, my sleeping hours are extended well beyond the usual 1 a.m. I go to sleep at 4:30-5:00 a.m., and even on occasion as late as 8 a.m. That was when I had written an email to some legal advisors as they were already at work at 8:30 a.m. When I was working, I was in the office by 7 o'clock, and at other times, I was at airports at 5 a.m. or the pool by that time of the day. This shows how life has changed.

There are people I know, who are older than me, and who maintain certain daily habits. They get up at 4 o'clock and go for a walk and then work at 8 a.m. Although this is not a universal fact and daily routines and waking hours change from person to person. Not everybody is the same. People are different. However, I am only relating my experience. The other day at 6:30 a.m., I was preparing to sleep, and when I went over to my balcony, I saw people walking dogs on the sidewalk. It was bright and early, and people were going to work, and that reminded me of my earlier life back in college and mostly with Connie. We both used to get up at 6:30 a.m., and Connie would leave by 7:40, and I would leave at 7:45 or sometimes earlier. Since I had to travel in my great profession, I started my car or took a train depending on where I was going, or perhaps at 5-6:30 a.m., my Limo was waiting for me at the airport. Later, when Connie took early retirement after teaching for 36 years and doing volunteer work at the library, she kept the same schedule until 2006. I also left my career to be with Connie for traveling, enjoying life, going to her medical appointments, dining out, shopping, and other things. We were together all day and night. Yes, I used to visit India for two weeks every year, and my last trip was on November 6th through November 20th, 2011, for 12 days. My next trip was on May 17, 2015, after her demise and when my world was over. It was the same for Connie, too.

Time changes, the economy changes, and nobody can predict nature and its changes. Morning is followed by night, and that in turn leads to morning the next day. Nobody can control rain and snow or sunshine. So these days, I feel as if Connie is around. I can feel the vibrations, and these days the vibrations are increasing in intensity. I sometimes feel that I should wake Connie up as she is getting late for work. When I realize she isn't there anymore, I still tell myself that perhaps she's in the bathroom or her room watching TV and reading her books. But when I am lying down, I suddenly realize, "What am I thinking? Connie is gone. She's no more!" It takes me 20 minutes to one hour to digest this, and it is the most painful experience one can go through. So these are the experiences I am going through right now. I am in Delhi today, and last night I woke up unsure where I was—at my house or elsewhere. I thought later that I was sleeping at home. I eventually realized that I was In India, and it was so surprising that I dreamt of Connie thinking I was at home. I think it will take me a certain number of days to understand that I am in Delhi. But my mind is somewhat happy to be in Delhi.

I am happy to be with my nephews, grandnieces, and brother, but other than them. I have no desire to meet anybody else or to do anything else. I'm slightly tired right now, but I go out with my brother and nephew to the market to get some snacks or go somewhere for a couple of hours. I might go to the health club, but other than that, I am in no mood to meet or be friends with anybody or to attend parties and gatherings. These are all sad occasions for me. People tell me, its ok, Pradeep, it is your grieving period. I'm not sure how long the grieving period is going to last. Perhaps it will last forever and will become part of my life as long as I am alive. This may be why I am so keen to arrange things that my house, art, furniture, rugs, and other expensive collections are taken care of after I am gone. It often worries me as to what will happen to all of those things. People tell me to look after my health instead of worrying about all these material things. But they don't understand that I am not talking about material things, but Connie's soul or blood is in every single one of those items, which have been collected over the years. So it's not just about the material possessions, and I am not crazy not to want to sell them and get money in return. These have Connie's life and soul in them- how could I possibly ever get rid of them. So this is the tremendous hardship that I am facing, and it is worse than anything else I've ever experienced before. I have faced many other tragedies, but I have forgotten about them or at least tried to. I will never be able to forget Connie's loss.

There are two kinds of losses, in my view. One is related to money and property, and there are disputes over them—leading to lawsuits and overall ill-feeling over money. But I am not talking about money. Money is nothing to me now- it is just a way to live. It is just a way to maintain myself and my lifestyle of simple living and high thinking. I am content that way. Even if I suddenly get millions and millions of dollars, they will not bring back my happiness or Connie. If there were some means, and I know it is impossible, I would get Connie back if you donate all your money somewhere and get your loved ones back. There are countries where you can donate money and get into schools and colleges. This is mainly for the private institutions, not necessarily for the good institutions. There are good places in India, and of course, America has got one of the best educational systems in the world. So there are a lot of vocational courses where you can get a degree, but you have to donate a lot of money. But it is not possible that I can donate money and get Connie back because I would have given away all of my money if it were possible. I watched Ram Lila, an episode from Indian history, and my brother and his daughter-in-law were discussing it with me. They mentioned that the characters in it could curse others and take their lives back. I wish I could find some of those people so that Connie might come back. They said it was not possible as they had made a lot of sacrifices for a very long time to achieve that ability. I agreed that their sacrifices were more than mine. Although, as I have said in other chapters about the story of Savitri and Satyavan—if they could do it, why can't I?

The answer was given to me by my brother's daughter-in-law. She said those people were different at that time. They had special powers because they had never done anything wrong in their lives. She said I must have good karma, but it is possible that without necessarily intending to, I may have done something wrong. I agreed with her- perhaps sometimes I lied, and other times I did not listen to Connie. There were occasions when I did not follow her advice, if not giving her a tough time. She used to ask me to develop new things, as she was very interested in my progress in life. Maybe I have sinned thus, but she indeed tolerated many things from me. I don't know the answer. Only God knows the answer, but there is also true nobody who can bring Connie back. And that is very painful. I just marked that I should keep talking about this chapter for as long as I can, but at the same time, more is not always good. "More is not always better," Connie said to me. I know there is a lot of repetition in my story, but it's all right to repeat things, especially as people get reminded of things once they read again. Also, I don't use words like "my wife" or "her," which sounds impersonal. That is why I use her name, Connie, again and again. Perhaps it is not the best way to write, but it is the best way for me.

Those other words don't carry the same weight as the name Connie, at least for me. I don't expect everybody to like my writing or that I will be a bestseller, or that this will be the best book in the world. I am writing and expressing myself and hoping that even if only one person can understand my pain, I will be very happy. I won't say there is only one because many people have already requested a book copy. Most of the people who are asking for a copy are unknown to me. There are people from technical support, computer technicians, or customer service representatives for different airlines. Some call centers where I used to call for my banking needs or companies like Visa/Citibank/Bank of America. They listen to me as I have to tell them honestly that Mrs. Berry is no longer here.

The other day I spoke to this person from *Consumer Report* magazine for almost an hour and a half! He was almost in tears, and he gave me a prize for the subscription. I promised him that I would begin reading all the magazines that Connie used to subscribe to, which are very instrumental in building knowledge. There is another book called *Health and Nutrition and* another to do with wellness and health. There is another magazine called *Men's Health*. There are magazines to do with women's health and nutrition, and I don't want anything to do with the magazine for women, as I don't want any other woman in my life, but maybe I will subscribe to the others as it'll give me happy when I read them. This is a new experience for me.

I will also give away some of the other magazines that others have requested, as I will never turn down any request that has anything to do with Connie, except, of course, a request for some of her possessions like her jackets. The other day she wore a jacket and asked me how she looked. That picture makes me cry, and I have had it framed. It shows Connie laughing. That was true love. I remember she'd gotten a brand new jacket, and she was very weak. She always worried whether she looked nice or looked bad. She looked very pretty and kept looking at me. That picture goes through my heart like a sword or arrow and makes me break down.

So before I came to India, I carried that picture with me, a small one in my pocket and my briefcase. I will keep looking at that picture; it has become the most important part of my life. People will think I am talking about emotions, mental issues. I don't care, but I know I can still do many constructive things, especially Connie. These are not just emotions but are facts of my life. The other day, I had gone to the store to return some things I had thought we would enjoy. As per their policy, they took them back, but the man asked why I returned them. When I explained, the man was touched and went out of his way to help me. The other thing was that I went to the cemetery on the 19th of October, 2015, before departing from the US. I had decided on the flowers that I intended to buy. I went into the store and told the young man what I needed. I showed him Connie's picture, and he was bothered by the story. He complimented Connie saying she was beautiful, and refused to charge me for the flowers. He said that one flower would be from the store in Connie's memory out of two different colors. The young man said that because I was a regular customer, the store wanted to give me something as a token of appreciation for the memory of my wife. It was only $6.50, and I took the two different flowers. I went to the cemetery, and it was very dark.

I took pictures and sought Connie's blessings so that I could go to India in the morning. I slept for barely two hours, and now I am here in Delhi. I hope the day will come that I will be in my own house back in the USA. I'm confused because if I stay there, I am very unhappy, and if I'm here in Delhi, there is some happiness but some sadness. So I am living in those four parts of the world, with happiness mixed with sadness. I have no idea when it'll get better, but I have to take it one day at a time.

33

Her Home was Her Life

To Connie, her house needed to be decorated with the best of things. Her taste, I believe, was much better than that of any professional. She was very selective in choosing the right items and matching things- furniture, decorative items, paintings, carpets, kitchen and bathroom appliances, floor, tiles, and millions of other things. We got much praise for her decor, the cleanliness of our house, and the quality of our home. Friends used to wait for the invitation to come to our house to see the soothing atmosphere and great food. We were extremely happy about our hospitality. She was extremely organized and would keep lists of everything. She kept the carpets and windows clean and kept a detailed schedule of what to clean when. I have to say. Our house has always been absolutely neat and clean. Perfection, quality, cleanness, changing styles on certain things were in her blood. I have not seen anyone like that, nor will I ever. I remember that when she renovated her kitchen with granite stone and tiles in 2006, it took both of us over two months before she chose her matching materials and fixtures. Later, she hired the best company to put tiles on the floor, granite stone on the kitchen counter, tiles on walls, appliances in the sink, and the kitchen. Friends gave her many compliments on the renovation. She invited all of our neighbors and friends for drinks and snacks. They all said that our house was the best house they had ever seen. These were all our American friends. We received the same complimentary remarks from

30 Indian families when they came to visit. In addition, they asked us to invite them back again and again. The same thing is applicable for her furniture, tables, lamps, chairs, and other things. A few years ago, she wanted a walk-in shower and hired the best company and materials. It took one month to finish, and we had to live with just one bathroom. After that, she replaced the air conditioners and other appliances, which, perhaps, I would never have replaced. I was extremely helpful and happy for her to get the best. Since she was my life, I was getting the greatest happiness to see that she was happy.

Serving her, making her happy, healthy, and not depriving her of anything was the only happiness I enjoyed. It gave me the most powerful motivation to deal with the world and all human beings. My happiness was to teach the new generation and share knowledge. Guiding new professionals was a great time, and I was extremely happy as Connie was with me, either at home or out together. I am not going to enjoy all that now. I will explain why that is in her "demise chapter;" however, I would like to teach and share my knowledge, education, and our life experiences, which might take away my loss and pain for my happy days.

Later, I am lost again. Temporary happiness and sadness are going to be my life from now on. I have seen the suffering of spouses married for a long time after the death of one or after divorce. How effective that pain is, I now know more. I am suffering from that pain and withdrawal symptoms, which are incorporated into my mind and heart. This book is a little happiness, but the sadness is much more with me. I don't know what I can do, and I am waiting for what life I will face. I would live to fulfill Connie's wishes, which is still painful as I can't see her. In ancient Egypt, mummies were a great example of how people dealt with losing their loved ones. I think it was right for those people- at least they could still see the body, which might have given them a feeling that their loved ones are still with them. I don't know if I could have done that or not, as she wanted to be cremated. I never thought that her husband and her love would have to go through the pain of handling her cremation and other things. I don't know how much pain and suffering I went through, and I would like to know why I had to experience that. Her pictures and our pictures around the house are my life. My life combines happiness and sadness, and I cannot choose which emotion I feel. I will have to go through my whole life to find the answer if I am meant to find that answer. Now, my pain and withdrawal symptoms are incorporated in my mind and heart.

34

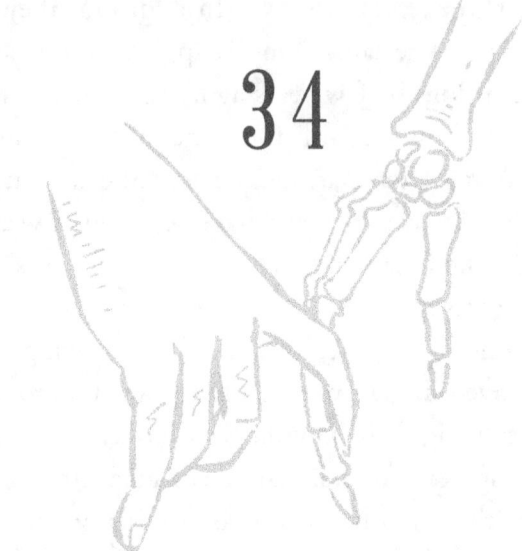

Cleanliness and Housekeeping were in Her Blood

While talking about Connie, I must say how neat and clean she was in the house. She kept our house as a museum. She used to take a keen interest in the house. Her collection was just unique. Sometimes it used to take her years before she could decide on the fabric she wanted, the kind of covers to use, the kind of kitchen design Connie wanted, the kind of granite she wanted to use, etc. She was very selective in the house. I would say that Connie's taste, thinking, and the way she used to perceive things were many times better than any interior decorator. She was very particular about cleanliness in the house. She could not tolerate dust in the house.

She was very particular about the laundry, so that she would change bed sheets every couple of days. She was so efficient and organized that cleanliness was ingrained in her. No matter what time it was, night or day, she would take a shower and change her clothes. She would wash laundry every two days, including my clothes. She was very particular that I wear a shirt for only one day, and she would say, "No! It is more than enough!" Sometimes I used to argue, "No, I just wore it for one day. I can use it for one more day!" She would say, "No! Look at the collar at the back! You have a professional job; people notice the small things like your collar." I would say, "I don't think so because I wear a three-piece suit." She would say, "You are not going to compromise. It is better that you buy, or I will buy for you, ten or one dozen white t-shirts and shirts. You will not wear them for more than one day." Then I would ask her, "Is it not too much work for you to do the laundry?" She would say, "I can handle it. It's not that difficult. Doing laundry in the house is very simple. You have to put it in the laundry room, and then you have enough time. I just do two loads every other day. It makes no difference."

She was very organized; she would iron my shirts, t-shirts, socks, and handkerchiefs. I think these things show how dedicated she was to me, and she would make such an effort to see that her husband looked great all the time in his professional job. She used to feel very proud of me. I used to get a lot of compliments from my office, especially when I was working for Heller. They would say, "Mr. Berry, we see you as the most fashionable person in our whole organization. How do you do that?" I would say, "Well, my wife Connie is very particular about my suit and what kind of tie, scarf, and pen matches it." He would say, "Well, she has made you a model. I think you should be in the model industry." So I would say, "Well, it's not like that, but I like being well dressed." I got many awards for being the best-dressed person of the year. I dressed like that from childhood, wearing three-piece suits, so I carried on that legacy.

When I think about it now, I realize how much energy she spent caring for me and how much pain she had to bear. God bless her! I don't think I could have done all that with so much affection. Sometimes I would be upset that she would even polish my shoes. I used to feel like a criminal that my wife was polishing my shoes. I did not polish my shoes as I thought that it was just dusting. Here, shoes don't get dirty. But she would say, "No, I think the first thing people notice is shoes, and a well-dressed person is always liked. You have so much intelligence and personality. Being well dressed will be like the icing on the cake." I think that attitude put a sparkle in me. I used to take pride in it.

Regarding her clothing, she would rather buy two clothing pieces that were expensive and pretty, rather than buying several cheap ones. She always emphasized, "Pradeep, I think it is better to buy good quality and buy less. Whenever you buy, buy the best quality because they will last longer and look good." We had friends who held good positions, and they would wear polyester shirts and cheap suits and ties. She used to be surprised that they could thrive in the corporate sector. Eventually, she could not tolerate it any longer. She told them, "I hope you won't mind my saying this, but I think in your profession, when you are holding a good position, you should not wear those polyester shirts and polyester jackets. I think you should try to learn how to dress up professionally. This is not a blue-collar job."

Also, I remember once in a year; when we did inventory accounts, we would be delighted that we wouldn't have to wear a suit. We could wear casual clothes. Most people used to come in jeans. She told me, "Jeans are unprofessional." She never allowed me to wear a pair of jeans. So she was very particular, even for casual clothing. She bought me so many different kinds of pants and shirts. I think I must have over 100 shirts, and they are sitting with me. Some I never wore, and some I wore maybe a couple of times. I will never give away those shirts because they are great memories and gifts from my dear wife. I think I can go on writing about clothing. I have lovely pairs of socks by Nautica and Pierre Cardin.

She was very classy, and I think all the Italian ties she bought were lovely. She used to buy at least 1 or 2 ties for me every month. Whenever she would go out, she would buy something for me. She would never ask me to pay for anything. I used to tell her, "Well, you are spending so much money." She used to say, "No, it is my love for you." I used to reciprocate that. I used to travel wherever I would go, sometimes I used to go to India, and I would bring many things. She was so considerate. She would say, "No, I think I want to pay." I would say, "That is not right. You spend so much money on me, and when I want to give it to you, you want to pay." She would say, "No, this is the way I am. I generally feel bad." I would say, "No, please, in the future, don't ever say to me that you have to pay me because this is my love for you. The way you love me, I love you." So she would say, "I will accept it but don't buy too much. If I ask you to buy 1 sweater or 2 bracelets, you get so many!" She was very fond of silver. So she would say, "Ok, you can buy me one necklace, one bracelet." I would buy maybe 10 bracelets and 10 different kinds of necklaces for her. So she would say, "You know what, you don't know the difference between 1 or 2 or 10! When I tell you to bring 1 or 2, you always like to bring so much. What a collection I have!" So I would say, "Just keep it. Or give it to your friends, or give it to your nieces." She would say, "I think next time when we go, we will try to return them."

Just as she was very considerate about my money, she was also conservative. She would use coupons and save money. About our house, she used to say, "I would rather travel all over the world and be house poor." That's how we started enjoying life, and we went all over the world on different cruises. I can name hundreds of them. We went with the University of Michigan, with Carleton, with different alumni, and with professors. It was all intellectual, and there were lectures, studies, and sightseeing. The cruises gave a lot of intellectual input in every area of our life.

This is one of the great qualities which she would combine in her house. She used to combine housekeeping with my dressing.

These were some of the qualities she had. I am going to write in more detail about many episodes and stories where she used to excel. We went to Ireland, and she said, "You have to dance this Irish dance because it is a cultural activity. Irish culture will ask you to wear these green clothes, and the girl will ask you to dance with her." She was not jealous that some young girl would dance with me because it was a part of the Irish culture. She was very happy to see me dancing. She took pride that her husband was dancing and he could dance in the Irish style.

I want to mention these things. I want to continue writing to leave a legacy about how much we love her and how much love she could give you. I always consider my wife Connie as my wife and my best friend, sister, and mother. In Indian culture, in 500 BC, Chanakya wrote about the same four qualities of women and how they can play these different roles. It is also written in Sanskrit, in our Vedanta, that a woman has four qualities I already mentioned. There were times when her love was like a mother, and her advice was like a sister and friend. As a wife, she was a great companion. These kinds of qualities, I would say, are very rare. I am lucky that I had this opportunity. It was my destiny. There were a lot of girls that my family had chosen as prospects for me, and if I had gone back, perhaps I would have been married to one of them, and I would never have seen Connie again.

I lived all these years because Connie was with me, and now after her demise, everything is over. This is most painful, and I pray to God that He can take anything from me, but He should give my wife back and Connie back. I hope that in our next life, we will be together again as husband and wife. If there is any power, if there is a miracle, we keep on taking new life every time, and we are always husband and wife and enjoy the same kind of life. If that happens, I am going to get over my anger. After a few years, we will meet again. This is great hope. It would be best never to deprive someone of their hope because hope may be the only thing they have.

35

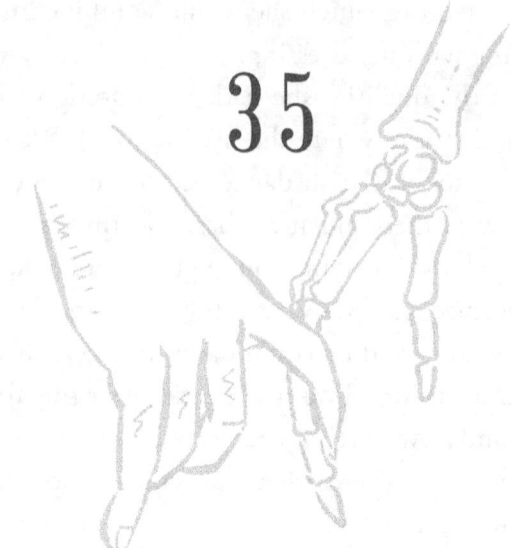

Her Love for the Best Cuisines

Connie was extremely selective about the food we ate. She liked to cook and eat the highest-quality food, including vegetables, fruits, meat, fish and desserts, wine, and hospitality, both at home and in the restaurants. She was an amazing cook and made different food and homemade desserts, which I would never be able to get in my life without her. They were fresh, not fat, and healthy and organic. She was the engine for taking me out to the best of the restaurants for excellent food. Her selection was extremely great, and she didn't care about the prices, although she was very conservative in many ways and knew to save for old age and rainy days. Cutting coupons to save money was her great hobby. Her passion for reading about new restaurants and recipes and trying different foods from all over the world was unique. I enjoyed all of that a whole lot. At the same time, she looked after the house- shopping, cleaning, doing laundry, and taking care of my professional clothing and accessories, including ironing clothes. This was a gift of God to me. At the same time, her choice of casual and traveling clothing was another unforgettable gift of my life. She truly loved me to do all that for me. I had never been blessed with that kind of love, except my elder brother, who cared for me in India. I would have to write a whole new book covering each of her qualities. I also helped her with everything, as she was busy and we both were partners in cooking and shopping. It was only due to my love for her that I learned excellent cooking and shopping, with her or alone. When I came to the USA in January 1976, I didn't know anything about cooking except making tea. It took lots of self-teaching, and I can say that now I am an excellent cook. Now, I doubt I would cook as I have lost interest in food due to her absence.

Morels are one of the finest foods in the world. They are very expensive, even dried mushrooms. India is one of the world's most important producers of morels. Even in India, they are considered a delicacy, and during my grandfather's time, they would be served at every marriage and major function. Guests expected to be served morels, and a host who couldn't afford them would have to apologize. I may ask my niece, Mona, to bring some for me when she visits, and I am sure she knows how to use morels to prepare vegetable dishes and rice pulao. I used to bring some for Connie, and she also used to buy them from Whole Foods or Spice House in Evanston. Another healthy delicacy that we loved was saffron rice. Saffron rice was a favorite dish, and saffron, like morels, is a rare delicacy.

36

Great Deeds and Ethical Values of Connie

Connie Darling did so many great deeds of karma. That includes, but is not limited to, a charity for different organizations, schools, colleges, low-income families, hospitals, the Red Cross, the Salvation Army, the USA Olympics, and foundations for children and education. She was instrumental in looking after her parents, besides taking them for doctors' appointments, buying groceries, cooking for them, and bringing them to our home for dinner. After Connie's father's death on December 20, 1989, we both insisted her mother come and stay with us permanently. We would have been very happy to look after her. But her mother refused, hoping to be near her grandchildren, whom she adored and got the biggest joy from while sacrificing many things. In reality, she cared and loved them much more than Connie Darling and Pradeep. It bothered us. It was painful, and we felt betrayed. However, we both decided that if that gives her happiness, let it be. We used to do whatever she wanted us to do whenever she asked. She often behaved badly with us, taking the side of Connie's brother's family and being nasty to us. We tolerated that for her happiness. Later, Connie Darling told her mother, "Mom, you better be nice to Pradeep because when you are old, Pradeep and Connie will come to rescue you as he has been brought up always to respect elderly people." Connie's mother still had one hobby, and that was her grandchildren.

When Connie came into my life, it was a mind-blowing experience for me right from the beginning. Connie told me that her mother is extreme, and I didn't understand this because our grandparents brought up my elder brother, and I and I came from a joint family system. Connie was so right that after Connie's father died, her son and grandkids didn't want to do anything with her. Her son told me many times Connie was in tears after I told her. She told me, "He has so much money that he and his family does not have to worry for generations, but our mother and father, who did everything for him, haven't a penny." I, too, was extremely hurt and perhaps told him something jokingly, as they were in our home for Thanksgiving. Later, again, he told me the same thing. It holds. He did not spend a penny for his father or his mother, not even for their funerals. He has all the wealth for his family, their spouses, and grandchildren, and even for his three sons-in-law, whom he and his wife shower with money so that they can have full control over them as they are or so possessive of their kids and grandkids. Money buys everything for them. It would never have worked for Connie and Pradeep. Connie and I decided that we would do anything to make her mother's old age happy. It truly happened. Connie and I were instrumental in looking after her mother. It was great to serve the elderly. True love should be selfless, and we should sacrifice to see others happy. I have seen many examples of these kinds of sacrifices.

During our lives, when Connie and I met, it was true love on the first meeting. We both wanted to be together and hopefully marry. Connie asked me if I had another person in the USA or India, as arranged marriages were common in India. I said that my parents and family had selected many girls and their families to marry; however, I didn't know if I had that desire. She told me, "I don't want you to regret anything later, and I am willing to sacrifice my love if you have someone waiting for you in India." She also stated that she would then never marry anyone except me. I immediately told her the same thing. I would only marry Connie. It breaks my heart and upsets me that I am writing this after 40 years. Where is my Connie? Where did she go? Why am I left alone, and when will I meet her?

I will forgive everyone in my life and start all over everything if Connie comes, which I know is naïve thinking, but I want to think for my happiness. In her absence, I am reminded of the cruelty of Connie's brother and his family towards their mother. Connie's father always told Connie and me to care for his wife if something happened to him. He also told me, "Pradeep, my son and his wife have so much money that they can buy or do anything." Her son, too, admitted to me that "Pradeep, my kids are well set, and they don't have to worry for anything in their lives, including my grandchildren." He was pretty sincere and honest. I truly admired him and told him I was very happy for you all. Connie's brother told me to tell his mom to make her friends, as neither he nor his kids have time to spend with her, as he has built a mansion on the lake to enjoy and wants to travel the world and have their own life of fun. Connie was extremely hurt for years about this, and so was I. Let me clarify that it's a unique family, and I have not seen any other American people behaving this way. American people, I know, in general, are helpful and full of compassion.

I tried to forget all that and gave Connie the maximum support and love to help her overcome her troubled mind. Further, I would have never written this if Connie was alive. Her demise has brought to light many hidden painful episodes. Now, all these things are new wounds in my life. Connie used to bring her mother to our home to stay for months. I was very happy to see that Connie was happy, and Connie's happiness was my happiness, and it gave me the joy to see them both happy. Most of the crimes in the world have many reasons. However, in my opinion, the majority of them are due to money. Greed, property, love, and jealousy are pretty common.

Connie and I were extremely upset when her brother, who hadn't cared for his parents, suddenly decided to take his mother, against her will, to a nursing home rather than his own big home. Their own home and the nursing home were three hours away from our home and their mother's home. There are plenty of nursing homes near our home. The motive was kidnapping her for money. Mother was not keen, but her son and his wife played on her weakness, her grandchildren. Connie and I knew their motives. Connie got a rare skin disease in September 1998, and it was difficult to diagnose. It was PRP, and that restricted Connie's ability to bring back her mother. She wanted to come back to her own house. However, her son and his wife were determined that their mother lives in the nursing home to have a hold on her money and ensure that she did not give anything more to Connie. They wanted to grab everything she had so that Connie would get little of her share. Money is a disease, and it proved true. Connie had told him that Mom is leaving an equal share for her and him after she dies and that he was welcome to verify that from the will and the bank. Greed is a curse on this land. Her brother and his wife didn't want to believe what Connie told them, so they planned to keep the mother under their control so that the mother may not give more money to Connie. How wrong and dirty they were.

Connie was the most ethical, honest, selfless, charitable, giving person I have ever met. I truly mean this. I might have lacked somewhere, but Connie was perfect. She was looking after her mother without expecting anything in return. Rather, she used to buy her what she needed and spend money on her. Connie told me that her parents put her through school and college, and that is enough- I am extremely grateful to them for spending money on my education.

Further, due to them, I can make my living. It is amazing and true that Connie never took a penny from her parents. Instead, she worked part-time jobs to pay for her Master's and other education. I was new in the USA and was surprised to see that. In India, we were used to asking for everything from our parents or grandparents. It was a new wave for me, and it took me a few years to learn about it. I am now the same kind of a person—a giver who expects nothing in return and wouldn't take anything from anyone. Many people wanted to give me a token in the past, but I couldn't accept it. I am sure God will take an act of extremely powerful revenge on Connie's family, as they are not human beings but have animal instincts.

37

Our Love Destiny Would Continue— But With Unhappiness

Our life was a true story of pure love. It was wonderful to feel and vibrant to enjoy each moment, even while we both worked on highly professional senior positions. Everything looks different now she is gone, and I am lost. I will not go to the places we went; it will haunt me like Dracula, making me go through more pain and suffering. I wonder if I would find an answer to my loss. In memory of Connie, I might start humanitarian acts and teach undergraduate and MBA students and professionals in commercial financing, mergers, and acquisitions, buyouts, crisis management, and, if needed, spirituality or world economy.

    Sharing knowledge is the best way to survive Connie, and she always loved to share her knowledge with others. I will always seek her blessings and forgiveness for any mistakes I make. Her life was to live for me, and mine was to live for her. I am thankful that, with a broken heart, I was able to do her cremation in two days and inter her ashes in her plot, next to her parents. My happiness and unhappiness were a necessary combination. I wanted the best cremation done in two days to cut my pain as she was special, and God kept me alive to do that. It tears me up to think of what would have happened otherwise. She was very special and not a charity case. Peace comes, and pain starts after seeing and praying to her. For thirty-nine and a half years, our life was ingrained in the house. It is full of her memory: our pictures going to different places, her cemetery, and the maintenance of her best-designed house, with very selective furniture, the kitchen, the bathroom and carpets, and other selections of these 39 years. Living here is a double-edged sword; however, these are my lifelong possessions. I am sure we will meet again in our next lives. And currently, though physically she is not with me, spiritually she is here and still guiding me.

While she was going through medical care, I left my high-powered income and professional career. I truly enjoyed every moment with her, including taking her to the doctors, shopping with her, and other things. Serving her was a great joy. Although I was very upset about her health and for the last two years, it was painful for both of us, but still sitting and looking at her and the satisfaction of being with her was happy enough, and I was devoted to her. I was extremely hopeful that Connie Darling would be alive for another 10 to 15 years, and I always used to worry about her and pray to God to keep me alive to take care of her. I never thought she would go so fast, and I was shattered and practically broken down, and I didn't think I could survive my loss. But I prayed to God to keep me alive to do her cremation and chapel of peace ceremony and to bury her ashes on her plot next to her parents. I told the funeral home and crematorium that I wanted the best of everything for her last rights and would not compromise on cost and quality. It has given me happiness and lots of pain, which I will experience as long as I am alive. Each moment, Connie is in my mind, and my heart is broken when I think of the last few months. I start shaking and lose all my happiness. I don't think I will be at peace anytime. I have no desire to remarry or have a great social life. I get both peace and sadness at our house. Even when I am visiting my family in India, my peace of mind is not there. My brother and his family give me all their love, but Connie remains in my mind, body, and soul, and I don't enjoy anything. Yes, my brother and his family, and my two grandnieces, 9 and 4, are keeping me happy, but inside, I think of Connie, too. Now I realize why people enjoy their grandchildren. Still, I have seen many relatives and friends missing their spouses and not gaining much happiness from their grandkids. To each his own?

Some people immediately go for second or third marriage after the death of their spouse. It is an individual choice, depending upon the love they shared and other factors, and there is no universal law governing the choice to remarry or not. In my case, I took the demise of Connie extremely hard, and I have known for years that true love happens only one time in life. This is the way I feel, and I don't expect everyone to agree with me. I am not perfect, and I think of many things I should have done but could not do for her due to circumstances. At the same time, we did so much that others can't even imagine or think of it.

38

Connie and Her Devotion to My Professional Help in Many Places

Connie bought so many things for me to make sure that I always looked great. The experience of traveling was her great gift to me. Her exposure to American culture and my personality development was a precious gift for my career and advancement. She never lied, cheated, or hurt anyone. She did so many selfless things to help me and to help others. If I start writing all the other things she did, I would have to write another book. In reality, there is no end to her good karma and deeds.

My mind is blank, and I can't wait to write that Connie Darling was extremely exciting and fun. I have never seen such a great person. She was a wonderful human being and super bright and beautiful. I, too, did good karma. That would justify why I am upset that God didn't save her when there was a hope that she would live and do more in the world. Why didn't God save her from death?

I truly believe that my success and advancement were only because of Connie. I am certain of that. Last night around 3 A.M. on July 29th, I was just sharing the childhood lie of my elder brother and me. Immediately, I realized that had I not gone to the USA, even with my advanced education and joining my family's booming business as my father's elder brother had offered and desperately needed me to join with a 25% share. After the death of our 85-year-old employee in 1975, the 25% share that my grandfather had given to him because of his devotion and intelligence became available. I was told that he was a 6-year-old kid when my grandfather hired him to work with him in the business, as he had no one to feed him. Later, he was trained and was the engine and the right hand of our business.

My uncles were neither educated nor bright, and that's why my grandfather gave him a 25% share. That is how I was offered the opportunity to take his spot. My father didn't encourage me, saying, "Son, you are exceptionally bright and should go for your career." The truth was he wanted that share to be given to my half-brother. I refused as many variables were uncertain. How would my father and his young brother treat me? Then I decided to go to the USA. Had Connie Darling not met me, I would have been back to India, and everyone would have been badmouthing me and whatnot. I am sure I would have been a failure and had so many hassles in my life, though getting a great job was not difficult. Connie was my Destiny. I am sure I would have been extremely unhappy in India without her. Thanks to Connie for my success and destiny, and I know we were meant to be husband and wife. A special reward and gift of God.

I want to write about an incident when Connie and I were traveling towards Palm Springs, and we came across the most powerful sight you can imagine. We were driving in the mountains, and the roads were very curvy, and I asked Connie, "Do you think there is any problem in driving? Do you think people take that many chances in driving?" She was familiar with the surroundings, so she told me, "Oh no! I don't think you have to worry about it, because it is pretty safe and it is not like in underdeveloped countries where people worry about driving. It is just this time of the year. Unfortunately, you are not finding too many cars, so don't worry! Just relax! And also, if you are uncomfortable, then I can drive, and you can watch." But I told her, "No, let me gain some confidence." So it took us about two hours, and then we finally reached Orange County. That was one of my most difficult driving experiences in the United States on the mountains. When I came back, I said, "Oh my God! That was a piece of cake!" And Connie told me, "I told you that!" I am mentioning this incident to point out how Connie helped me gain confidence about driving, about every aspect of it, and how to control the car. When we returned from where we stayed, I was ready to drive anywhere, especially in California and San Diego. So this is worth mentioning how much Connie helped me in every aspect of life.

My friend Palli, who lived in New York, invited me to visit him at his house (now owned by the Clintons). I was 40 miles away and was scared to drive there at

8 P.M. for dinner. Connie, who was in Chicago, asked me to please not go, as I was driving a rental Lincoln, and New York can be dangerous if you get lost. I thought I had good directions, but I didn't arrive until 9:15 P.M., and they were waiting for me with 10 dishes on the table. I could hardly eat as I was worried about the return trip. I was such an idiot on this occasion- I did not have the telephone number or address for the hotel I was staying in. I was lost for hours and drove until 2 A.M., and I was convinced that I would never reach the hotel. The only choice was to call my friend at 2 in the morning to come to rescue me, but then I worried that he would think me an ignorant fool if I called him for help. Palli was extremely rich because of his inheritance from India and his large, wealthy family, but he respected me because I had no inheritance and the best education. I have not talked to Palli since Connie died. He used to call once or twice a week to check on Connie and me. Perhaps I should fly to New Jersey and surprise him with a call asking him to meet me at the airport. He would never let me stay in a hotel but would have me stay in his house. He was a childhood friend of Arun Berry and thus also my friend. I have thousands of friends worldwide who loved Connie and respected me, but I do not want to tell the whole story about her illness and the negligence that led to her death. I would get so very upset to have to tell all of my friends. That is why I am happier living in isolation for now.

We were trying to find different places to go, and Connie told me, "You know, the best way is to call the hotel people or let me get the magazine." She was very good at reading and finding out directions. So we stayed for two weeks in Palm Springs, Orange County, and San Diego, and we enjoyed every single part of it and a couple of other places. So I must say Connie had a super-intelligent brain. Later on, we went to Carlsbad, which Connie knew and had read about. We made many trips like that. I am just sharing her experience, and after that, she also told me, "Next time, next year, we should go to Santa Fe." Let me tell everybody that Santa Fe is one of the most charming places. It is the third-largest place on the earth as far as art and crafts are concerned. Number 1 is considered either France or New York. Even if New York is number 1, then France is second and then Santa Fe. In Santa Fe, people and artists come from all over the world. I was amazed at the art I saw in Santa Fe, New Mexico!

The other great experience she gave me was taking me to French Quarter, which was magnificent. We stayed in the French Quarter, and the food and the culture there are different. We had a ball, and she showed me everything because she was very adventurous. I must say that I was not adventurous, whereas Connie was very adventurous. As a result, I was able to enjoy many new experiences because of her adventurous spirit. A similar incident happened later when I was working in San Antonio, Texas, and my employers told me, "Pradeep, do you want to come back or do you want to stay there?" So I said, "Well, I don't know." To which they offered, "If you want, you can have Connie fly over and just put it on the expense report." So I called Connie, and she flew over. I picked her up, and we stayed there for one week, and it was a ball! I was working, and she would drop me at the office, pick me up for lunch, and then go and do her shopping. In the evening, we would go back to the hotel. I would work for half an hour or an hour on my report. Then we would go and have fun. Again in the night, when we would come back, she would watch TV, and I would do my reports. So this way, I think Connie was a great contributor in traveling with me so that I was not lonely.

Connie told me, "Pradeep, having the best quality clothes, shoes, suits, ties, jackets, matching clothes that show you to be a well-dressed person is extremely important, especially in the USA for people working in a professional career." I knew all of that; however, she taught me much more. Connie and I were involved in gaining knowledge and sharing it with the world. According to Chinese and Indian philosophy, it is a sin not to share knowledge. Our primary duty is to share knowledge with those who want to learn; otherwise, you waste your time and theirs. People who think they know everything are the most ignorant. Connie and I have come across many of them, and they only want to gossip and tell useless lies that they are overqualified for jobs and try to fool other people. They do not realize that others are smart, and they have made a fool of themselves with their bragging and lies. Such people are left without respect and only a handful of family and friends, often depending on their parents. These circumstances can ruin marriages. A wife wants her husband to no longer be a mama's boy, and mothers should make their sons realize that their wives come first and mothers second. Some mothers provoke discord, telling their sons that they are henpecked, and these small things may break a marriage. No wife can tolerate a husband who ignores her and is always with his family. Why did he marry her? It would have been better to stay a bachelor, living with his parents, and lead a miserable, lonely life looking for a wife. Even then, only a desperate woman would marry such a man, and that too would be according to her conditions and might be a marriage without love.

I could write an entire book on this chapter, based on the research of Connie and me. We never thought of publishing with our work and travels, especially when Connie began to fall ill, and we decided that youth and time would ebb like time and tides. I am glad we did, and the results are this: My Connie died unexpectedly on February 28th, 2015. No more travel and dining out for me, and I will have to live in pain, although I may make jokes and pretend to be happy when I am with someone. Sometimes I am extremely happy, especially when I am having an intelligent conversation with intelligent people. I like to talk to everyone, regardless of their education or wealth. I love people and animals, and I respect every human being as part of the planet. I am not so great myself that I have to decide about people. I must have many faults, and I want to teach everyone my faults and weaknesses.

39

Sympathy and Empathy —But Pain

I would like to add in my memories that I am trying to understand the pain of some of the people I have met in my professional life, who have gone through more tragedy than one can imagine. Though even at that time, I understood how much pain there was, after the demise of my darling wife Connie, I can understand the gravity of the pain that they went through.

It was sometime in 1983, and I had flown to Charleston, Virginia, for some work. I flew on Sunday night because of Connie. She had gone with her students to show them the political system in this country. In those days, she was teaching Spanish, French, and political science. She had to leave on Friday and was supposed to come back on Monday. They were to visit the White House, among other places. Since I was not doing anything, I left on Sunday afternoon. My clients, the borrowers, were the second-largest trucking company in the United States. They were desperate to get a loan at that time, as the trucking industry was deregulated. This company was struggling in their business, although they were very wealthy. To expand their business, it was important for them to show certain credits in their financial statements. When I reached there, the borrowers picked me up and took me out for dinner, and then I stayed in the hotel. One of the senior partners took me to his house and treated me to dinner the next day. Now here is the real story that I wish to share: on Wednesday, as I remember, one of the main owners, who was extremely wealthy, took me to his house. He said, "Mr. Berry, I want you to have dinner with me, and then maybe you can sleep in my house." It is very rare that a borrower, who is unknown to me, will take me to his house. I think he must have liked me very much- my professional approach, conduct, and behavior. He was highly impressed. He said, "Mr. Berry, let's go out tonight, and I will show you something." It was pitch dark when he took me to a place, and he stopped his Audi car. Then he got out of the car, and he said, "Mr. Berry, please walk with me to this place." As I walked, he said, "You know, this place where I have brought you is where my young son, who was 24 years old, was killed in an accident. As a result of that, I have lost everything. I cannot function because of this tragedy. My son was going to take over my business. All my hopes have gone. My daughter, though she's working, is not capable. She is not highly educated. My younger son has no desire to do anything except to become a truck driver. I have bought him a truck costing $250,000." We were chatting in the night, and he said to me, "I don't know, Mr. Berry, somehow or the other I feel that you should join me. I will pay you to double the salary or three times the salary you earn now plus I will pay for your wife's salary and buy you a house, and I will give you 30% to 40% stock in my company. Finally, I will give over this company to you as I cannot work anymore because of the tragedy of my son." He was practically begging me, really requesting me to accept, and said, "Please listen to my pain and please move to Charleston, and I can assure you that you will be very happy, and because of you, I will get a new life." I felt very sorry for him, and I was confused. It was a good offer, but at the same time, I thought of Connie's career, of the repercussions of leaving Evanston, her parents, and everything else, so I declined the offer.

It continued to bother me that this person had gone through such tragedy. I've been trying to contact him, and I found out later that he closed his company due to his shock and grief, and then he sold it and just disappeared. For the past 25 years, I have been looking for him, but I cannot find him, and I have no idea where he is. If he is alive or out there, I would love to go and share his tragedy and my tragedy.

Now I can understand what he was going through at that time. It is something you understand only when it happens to you. This is what I want to add. I have many other stories that I will mention related to pain. When another person is in pain, that pain does not seem that deep to you as an outsider, but when the same thing happens to you, you realize how painful it is. I will never forget this realization which relates to me and is affecting me deeply.

40

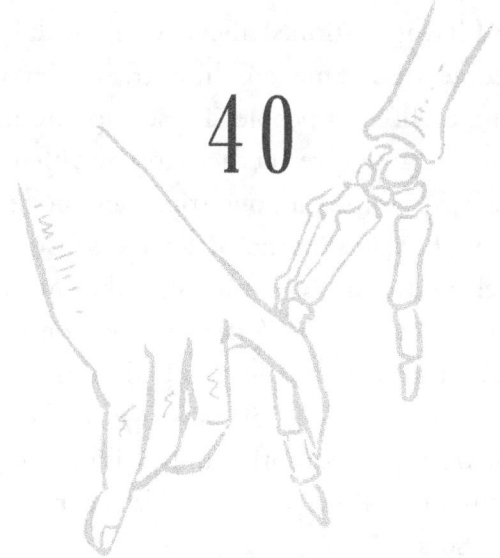

Cruises—Part of Her World Travel

Cruise Trips with Connie

Once again, I want to say that Connie was instrumental in putting this love for travel in my blood. I went on many cruise trips with Connie, as she was very adventurous. Connie took me along and gave me the opportunity of going to different parts of the world. She used to be interested in reading about which cruises are available from the University of Michigan, which is supposed to have some of the best cruises. Recently, I heard Carleton has also started offering cruises. We also made some trips which were not cruises, for example, we went to the Black Mountains in Germany and France. We also made trips related to my business. During one of our trips to the Rhine, Connie desired to take another trip from France, which would go through many countries up to Amsterdam. From Amsterdam, it would go further to Switzerland, from there to one more country where you would rest overnight in a hotel and return to the United States of America the next morning by flight. They also provided the option of adding extra stops if you wish, as we did in Norway. We flew with them, and since we were part of the Advantage group, we stayed four days in Bergen. It was such a wonderful thing and a beautiful country. Connie and I stayed in the hotel with about 30 people. On the final day, when we had to depart from Bergen back to Norway on a ship, 98 more people joined us.

All these trips that I have mentioned above were not the kind of trips ordinary people make. The people that came on these trips with us were interested in learning, and they were intellectual people. These trips are not just ordinary trips, and there would be many lectures given at each stop by different professors speaking about different topics. For example, on one trip, they spoke about different lakes. They would explain how the dams on the lakes were constructed, how the water is controlled in the Daniel and Rayan Rivers, and how they must match and control it. It is a magnificent thing to see how the York men have controlled the water system. In addition to these lectures, there would also be beautiful sightseeing excursions in small boats that carry only 120 or 130 passengers. The tourists on these trips were intellectual people from the sponsoring universities who graduated in different years and were mostly seniors- there were no kids on these cruises and only very bright people and professors.

There were doctors, professors, banking and finance professionals, and teachers. We would share common tables during breakfast. We would sit with different people for every meal to have stimulating conversations with different people. Sightseeing would also be done with different groups. In the buses, the drivers, coaches, and guides would guide us, telling us the history of the places we visited. We would also visit different schools and colleges, meet the professors there, and listen to them speak. Finally, there would be a small exam which we had to pass. As a result of that, we learned so much about the country and its history.

I don't mean to say that they would give you grades so you could get a degree, but it meant a whole lot because nobody wanted to fail those exams. So we had to study for the exam! Cultural activities would also be included in the program. For example, we would have to dance according to the particular culture. When we were in Ireland, it was part of their custom that girls aged 17-19 would ask the guests to dance with them. I was sort of embarrassed when one girl just grabbed me and said, "Come, man, we have to dance!" So I had to dance with her for half an hour in the Irish way. Connie was watching me, but she didn't feel jealous. She didn't think, "Oh my God! My husband is dancing with a young girl!" It was acceptable to her because Connie had a lot of faith in my character, and I also had a lot of faith in her character. However, it is not very popular in Irish, German, or French culture for men to ask ladies who are not their wives to dance with them. So when we had to dance in France, I needed to dance with Connie, and we were very well dressed for the occasion.

I knew the different kinds of dance steps to some degree, but Connie taught me a lot of different steps. She also told me, "Pradeep, you should take some dancing classes," which I did. So look at how many cultural things she exposed me to and cultivated a love for dancing and experiencing different cultures. This, I would say, added to the experience for me. With so much experience now, I can talk about it in schools and colleges for hours! I can explain different points of the cultures, how Irish, German, English, Norwegian and American cultures are different. This world is a magnificent place if you know where to go; however, some people will go in the buses, and they don't get that same experience because they are not educated, and they don't have professors and coaches to guide them in the trip.

I recently got a mail from Carleton College announcing that they are taking a trip to the Rhine and Switzerland. We have already been on this trip, although they are covering slightly different cities this time. I would love to go with Connie if she was alive. We would never have thought twice about it, and we would just have made the reservations. The trip will start in November, but I don't think I want to go because I know I will be depressed. I also received a brochure from the Carleton Alumni Association about a cruise going to Sri Lanka for 19 days. I thought that if I was already in India, I could take a flight to Sri Lanka and join them there. I'm not going to go on my own accord without approval from Carleton. Carleton would love to take me because it is not a business but also based on feelings for their former students.

Connie's connection with Carleton will give me the power to say that Connie is with me, and she would be happy that I'm attending a cruise. I know that I will not meet Connie or meet Connie's match; however, I'm sure there will be a younger batch of people. I will feel like there is some sort of a bond in our conversations during lunch, dinner, or other times. I will have some background, a great tool, and power to talk about Carleton and why I came to the cruise. Then I can talk about my wife Constance Berry, how she was part of Carleton, and my memories of her. Since people are so compassionate, they will respect me for this. They will give me moral support, and they will say, "Oh Pradeep! I think you should do this more, and it's a good tribute to your wife Connie, and it will be the greatest thing you can do!" So they might encourage me to travel more. Otherwise, I will be sitting in the same big hole.

Connie went to Harvard, and she went to top universities in Mexico and Spain. She finished her MBA in Spanish in both Spain and Germany. Both of us were there when she was teaching. I had gotten myself transferred there since we had offices all over the world. So we were together, and I would say in my married life of 40 years that she accompanied me for travel on an average 30% of the time. My company used to pay, so they made my life very easy.

41

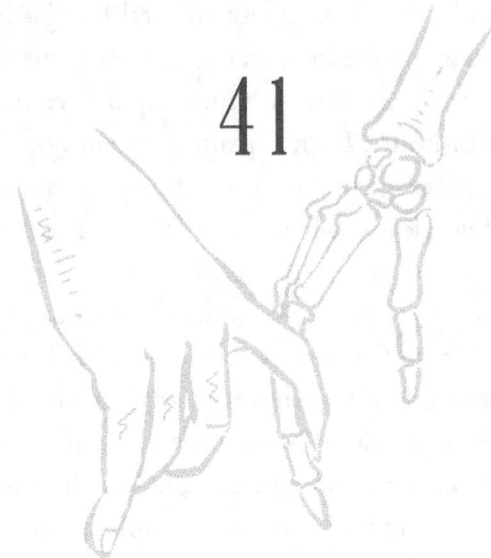

Connie's Character

Regarding Connie's character, I think I can tell you we were made for each other. I was raised in an environment with very strong values and with an emphasis on character building. Our grandparents were very strict about focusing on studies, sports, and other activities like Scouts and NCC. I was extremely good in Boy Scouts, was the NCC battalion sergeant, and had a lot of extracurricular qualifications. We were given the strongest foundation possible to build our character. That also meant not having any relationships or attachments with the opposite gender. The priority was to get educated first, and all other things could happen after one was well settled in life. In reality, because we were brought up this way, we never really thought of having any female friends. It wasn't unlike today, where it is very common for people to have boyfriends or girlfriends where they might or might not marry each other. In any case, that was a different era.

Connie was also brought up in the same way. Her focus was only on her education and her research. She was keen only on her studies, and she was not interested in parties or meeting men. She was very happy with her close-knit family and girlfriends only. Her mother was very strict, and Connie herself had ethics where she was not interested in these parties, which involved drinking and dancing. In addition to her education and intellectual nature, we found this to be the common aspect. I think perhaps this is one of the contributing factors behind our getting together. Ordinarily, I would have gone back to India for a pre-arranged marriage as many proposals from rich families had come my way. Perhaps God wanted me not to go as I was destined to meet this girl Connie who was beautiful both outside and within. Connie liked to say—I was her first boyfriend, and she was my first girlfriend, although we started as only friends.

To this day, I don't know how I gained the confidence to talk to a woman because if you are growing up in India, talking to a woman is the most fearful and dangerous thing! Of course, after I came to America and met ladies in my corporate life, I developed the courage and faith to do so. The reason is that in America, men and women have been raised in different environments. They have been brought up full of confidence right from their childhood. I remember when I first came to this country, one of my subordinates, who was working under me, told me, "Pradeep, let me tell you one thing, in this country, children are given the maximum freedom." I was astonished to hear that because even though we were given freedom in our era, we were also watched like hawks. We were always being kept track of—our activities, where we went etc. So I noticed a big difference in culture. If you talk to people over here, you notice how confident they are, irrespective of their age, because they have been brought up in such an environment. I'm not trying to criticize or hurt anybody's feelings, but I'm just sharing my own experience and knowledge without offending anybody. When I go to the health club or shops or even in my professional life—women talk to me as if we have known each other for years. There is a lot of just joking around, and conversations are full of fun. I have not seen that kind of atmosphere with Indian ladies, whether they are married or otherwise. They tend to be very reserved, so I think it is a big cultural difference which I find very interesting. Once again, it is not a reflection on anybody, whether Indian or otherwise. I have traveled all over the world, and whether it is America or Europe, I find that people are more friendly and passionate except in India. It is not as if people in India are not like that. They are very wonderful and hospitable, but there is some kind of a rhythm missing.

I find that sometimes even young Indians are reluctant to talk. Even in America, I meet many Indian school and college students—often, they don't even say hello. At times, I ask them if they are from India—to which they mumble yes and claim that they need to get back to their work. This has happened several times, and to some degree, it has upset me, but then I realize this is how they were raised, so it is unfair to blame them. Connie also told me the same thing.

She told me that when I met some Indian friends, it felt like we were glued to each other like brother and sister. I'd say that it may seem like that, but in reality,

I felt as if I was imposing on them, as it was I who made an effort to talk to them, whereas they were reluctant.

Our interactions were full of such exchanges because we were of such innocent character. Possibly because of this, I told her that we should get married. Connie thought about this for a while, but she was not sure. She wanted to know how long I intended to stay in the US or if I'd leave her high and dry. She said to me, "Pradeep, you know I like you, care for you, and love you. But I don't want the possibility that you may leave me alone, and if you do, so I will not be able to bear the loss. I think I will go crazy if you leave me, and you never know what I can do because I am not one of those who can remarry again. To me, marriage is sacred."

She said I should take a few months to think about it. Even when we were about to get married, she asked me 10 times if I was serious. She did not want to be betrayed. She asked me repeatedly if I had any doubt whatsoever or if I was marrying her under some kind of pressure or force, then we were better off remaining friends. I remember reassuring her that I would never leave her under any circumstances. I will treasure the memory of Connie in her bridal gown as she said all these things till the day I am alive. When I think of those days, I feel hurt, and it reminds me what a wonderful gem my Connie was.

42

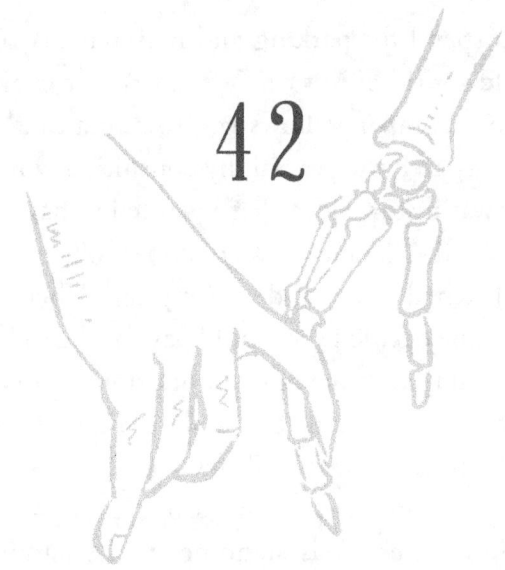

The Truth Always Wins

I held the last position in an organization as the head of the Midwest region, General Manager, or Head of the Division, for leverage funding. Before that, I had my consulting firm. When their offer came, Connie told me, "Pradeep, I think you are making a big mistake by joining this large company. They offer a very good package; however, you are doing much better in your consulting and already have projects lined up for the next 6 months to one year. I think that you shouldn't get tempted because it will be very hard for you. Just think about it- right now, you have your consulting firm, you travel when needed, and then you can come back home. You have a choice whether to go to the office or work from home. You are only looking for benefits. These benefits are mitigated by the fact that your freedom will be compromised. Your consulting allows you to spend more time at home if you don't want to work for a few months. This sort of thing will not be possible once you join." She was totally against me joining, but this company persuaded me, and I was confused as it was difficult to make. It was in December 2002, and I remember not being able to sleep for the whole night. Connie was so upset with me in the morning, she said, "I don't think you ever want to listen to me, and you will regret it." I think Connie was right. It was a 45 min drive to the office. We always had two cars, one car Connie would use, and the other car I hardly drove because I was flying most of the time. After that, Connie told me, "I think considering the amount of money you spend for parking and maintenance and the fact that you hardly drive, you should get rid of this car. We have one car, and if you are working in the Chicago area, your company allows you to rent a car. You can always rent a car." It was not mandatory to have a car in my consulting work because they would pay for mileage. But it was just my idea that I wanted to have a car if Connie drove the other one. But she said, "Where do I go alone? Wherever we go, we both go together!" So finally I listened to her and sold my car. When I got this job, we had to buy a second car. Connie decided she would pay for the car. Look at her sacrifice! She told me. "It is your duty to buy your car, but don't worry, you have been very kind to me, so I'll buy you a new car." She bought a new car in two days, and she would drive her car, which was also brand new. So again, we were stuck with two cars. So on the first day, I wore my suit and drove the new car to reach the office about 20 minutes before time. I was standing in the parking lot and thinking, "Should I go inside or not?" I was just about to leave when suddenly the Vice-chairman, who had hired me, saw me and said, "Pradeep, what is happening? We are all waiting for you, and we have hired 10 new young blood MBAs and some graduates. They are all waiting because you are going to be responsible for starting a new division, so please come inside, and we are going to welcome you." So I thought for a minute I felt happiness. In the office I met everybody; they were all excited and happy. They told me, "Now that you are here, we are going to learn from you, and we are going to grow." So the first day was totally enjoyable. But on the way back home, I thought, "Oh my God! Now I will have to start going back and forth again every day." It meant getting up early! I was used to my independence earlier, and now I had lost my independence, so I went into a serious depression in January 2002 that lasted about 6 months. Connie told me, "I told you! You might as well quit the job." I talked to my other consulting clients, and they told me, "Pradeep, people make this mistake. Don't worry about it. If you want to quit, quit right away and start our projects." I think I should have listened to Connie and started on my projects right away.

I was independent. I was getting paid more. If you compare the benefits between working for an organization and self-employment, they are equal. Overall, even if they were giving the benefit of Medicare, I think with my practice, I was still ahead. So now, since I was committed, I did not quit. As much as I wanted to, Connie wanted me to quit. She sacrificed her wants for my decision. I was miserable. Later on, I started liking the job because training all those 23-24-year-old young people was the only thing that gave me happiness. Looking back, I think God wanted me to train them in 3 years compared to the 10 years it would have taken them otherwise. Another person was working there as a senior, but surprisingly he did not know anything. He used to think that he was my boss, and I told him, "Listen, I am not working for you. Rather you are going to be working for me." There was a lot of politics involved, so when I told this incident to my senior boss, who was the chairman, he told me, "Since I hired you, you are reporting directly to me, and all the staff of 20 people will be reporting to you. You are their boss." This man still thought that he was my boss, so I was unhappy and about to quit. Then they told me that they warned this guy and told him, "If you don't behave with Mr. Berry, we will get rid of you immediately." So finally, he apologized to me. I am mentioning this because I don't know how political connections work. I left that position in 2005 when Connie became sick. After that, I took an oath that I would not work and dedicate myself to Connie.

Now I will recount an incident that shows the dedication of Connie. I had left the job I described above, and I had to find new medical insurance. My old company offered me coverage for 18 months. I said, "I will take it." I was in a senior position, so they gave me COBRA insurance, and I had to pay more than what they were paying. I was paying the full cost because the program was very good, so when it ended after 18 months, I was fiddling around getting quotes from different insurance companies. I found out that there are a lot of loopholes with these policies. Sometimes they can say, "We don't cover you for this, and we don't cover you for that." Medically, I was fit, I didn't have a problem, but still, you should take precautions. When these companies have to pay a buck, they are very careful, and they can also say, "Oh, it was a precondition." That way, they don't have to payout. I had heard that from many people.

My insurance company, though, was very clear, and they had sent their policy in writing. But Connie told me, "Listen to me. My insurance from the Education Board System and Illinois Teachers Association is very large. You better take my insurance because my insurance is the best in the country." Of course, they used to subsidize her insurance coverage. She said, "I will pay." It was very expensive, almost double the amount I was paying. I was paying $300, and it was about $750. So I said, "Why to pay $750 when I am not sick." She said, "Listen, you never know. If God wills you to be sick and you have to claim, they will say you have a precondition. So don't get involved with all this nonsense. I will pay." So I said, "No, I will pay." So she said, "Listen, I am telling you. If you wanted to pay $350, you pay only that much. The rest I will pay from my pocket." I declined, but it was greatness on her part, how much she loved me and how much she cared for me.

Otherwise, in this day and time, I have not seen anyone offering that. Since she truly loved me, she paid for part of my insurance for several years.

Later on, I think she was not getting the government Medicare. Medicare is a system where everyone has to pay when they are working as Social Security, where you pay 50% and the same way with FICA, which is also the same thing- the revenue from the taxes all goes to the government. So we all have to pay. It is the law here. Only if you pay do you get a check, whereas in my case, I had to pay for every single thing on my own. I used to get a 1099 form, which is only issued in the United States of America- other countries don't issue 1099. They send you a statement showing how much you have earned if you have a foreign account or something like that. So I was getting my 1099, and I filed my taxes very promptly. Connie would tell me, "I don't want you ever to miss any income because by chance, if the other company has not sent you the 1099 form, then it is your responsibility to pay." I said, "I know that." She said, "Otherwise, if we get caught by the IRS, there will be a lot of trouble, and I don't want to get into trouble." And I know that both of us were ethical, so I said, "You don't have to worry about it." One time, one of my clients told me, "Mr. Berry, we are not going to file the 1099 form. As far as we know in Human Resources, we don't report that." I said, "It's not possible. Someone must be reporting it because you have to report this as part of your P&L. You are wrong. I will not take any chances. Either you send it because someone might find out electronically, or there will be problems. I want to be honest, and I want to sleep well." So we were both ethical, and everything was going fine. So the time came when I decided to take my earlier benefits, which is called Social Security. Connie was paying into the Education Board System, where she was not qualified to get Medicare. She was missing maybe 10 credits and maybe one year of teaching.

Connie had worked very hard at a private institution taking care of her social security and Medicare. I made a big mistake which I regret- in my consulting, she used to lot of work for me. When I was so overwhelmed with the reports, Connie used to edit my reports. She used to print them out; she used to make the folders for me. She used to email my borrowers, she used to do a lot of other work, and I should have been paying her some money as a secretary, and I would have put it as an expense, and I would have saved on my income tax. During this time, she would have got those credits for her Medicare. She would have been independent to get in a year or year and a half what she did free of cost for me. I wish God I would have paid her enough money because it helped my taxes and helped her get Medicare. She was so nice, she never even asked me to pay her. Where would you find a rare person like Connie?

It was bothering me today while swimming; I thought what a big mistake I made with that great precious diamond. I was very upset, and I said, "I pray to God that Connie will forgive me because she did so much work for free, selfless work, but I did not realize her worth." Later on, when I got the rest of my Social Security, she was eligible to go into Medicare. But there was also a problem because there was also a time factor, which we did not expect. The Medicare people told us, "Once you get your benefit, Mrs. Berry will also be entitled to Social Security and Medicare right away." I have a full record of all those people. But they refused to pay, and I decided to fight, so we fought with Social Security. They said no. They were charging her more premiums, and they would not give her the benefits for another 2 years. So finally, I appealed, I had to fight for the right thing, and Connie told me, "Just forget it." But I said, "No, you have done so much for me. Now I'm going to do the same thing for you." So I filed for an appeal, although they say that in the appeal, you generally lose. But I thought if we have done some good karma, we will win. So there were two choices: we could go for trial in front of the judge or have it over the phone. We just thought that if God is there to help, we will win regardless, whether we go to court or over the phone. So we got a letter that on such and such date, at exactly 11:30, the judge would call us.

Luckily on that date, exactly at 11:30, the telephone rang, and the secretary said, "Are you, Mr. Berry? Is Mrs. Berry with you on the line?" I said yes. So then the Honorable Judge came on the line, and he said, "Mr. Berry, Mrs. Berry, how are you?" We replied, "Hon. Judge, we are fine. How are you doing, Sir?" He said, "I am fine. I understand you have been appealing. It has been the most difficult thing, and I think the final verdict was already given to you. I do not know why there is so much confusion, and I don't think I can do anything for you or reverse it for you because the final judgment has already come." I told Hon Judge, "If you listen to us for 15-20 minutes, both of us will be very grateful to you."

Then I started telling him that we were both very ethical people, we had been paying our taxes for the last 40 years, we were good citizens of this country. We always paid our taxes in time; we were not involved in crime. My wife had been a teacher and professor for 34 years. She had gone to the top schools. I had so many degrees. I told the Hon. Judge, "My petition is this. Hon Judge, we will never tell lies. I have the names and dates of these people." He said, "I got all that in written letters. How do you prove it?" So I said, "Well, I told you under oath, you earlier asked us to take the oath. I said all this under oath. This in itself is a big thing in the United States of America that we are saying this to you on the phone under oath." I said, "I don't think you need a better explanation than that. I have my handwritten note, which I can mail to you or fax it or send a copy, whichever way you want. But it's a small amount. We are not going to lie to you, Sir. This is the mistake of this person. She was very rude to us, and she was jealous, maybe that Mrs. Berry is making more money in her retirement than she will. She was spiteful and asked me why she needed Medicare since her income was so much, she could pay any money premium. She had no business to be so rude because she was just doing her job, and we are entitled to our rights. We have paid our taxes. It is not as if the United States of America is paying us for free. It is the money we have contributed to this system. My wife contributed to a different system, and she is only getting the pension. But she is not getting any benefits, and she is maybe short of 1 credit of maybe one full year, and I think you should reconsider." The judge listened to all that and said, "Both of you are very ethical people. You people deserve it, and I will have to look into further investigation. I will make calls and talk to those people. I will give you my answer in the next 3 or 4 weeks. Good luck to both of you; it was nice talking to both of you. Let's see what happens." We were still confused, but from the message, I could understand that we would hopefully receive a positive answer because he mentioned it when ending the phone. We were both convinced that we were going to get a positive reply.

With great help from God, in two weeks, we got a letter that we had won the case, and it was written that whatever extra Mrs. Berry had paid in premium, whatever was not covered, they had to send us a check back. So the amount we lost, Mrs. Berry got everything back from the hospital and the Medicare system. So this is called the United States of America. This is called karma. So this is why we should be honest because honesty always stays through the person's life; dishonesty is caught very soon, and people lose their trust. Especially in America, there are two things people don't like: lying and not asking for an apology or showing remorse. If you apologize right away, they will forgive you, but this is why this country has an advantage.

I'm sure this is the way in every country, but it is true, especially in this country. Whenever there is a trial, and a murderer says, "I am very sorry, I think I made a big mistake, and I apologize to the family members of the people whom I killed, and I hope that they will forgive me." If he shows remorse like that, the judge will give him a lesser sentence. If the murderer says, "I am not going to apologize, I am not going to do this, I have done the right thing." then the judge will increase the sentence. People reading my book and in the United States will not take much interest because they already know, but if someone is in India or another place, I think this will be a great example. I'm sure, even in India, people are very intelligent, and they will know. But still, I think it is important for me to write this incident, a tribute to my wife, because of the beautiful things she did that we got rewards. Unfortunately, despite all these things I'm saying, the truth is that Connie is no longer with me. That is the biggest thing.

No matter how much I praise her, it is not going to bring her back. I hope that I become her husband in my next life so that my purpose will be successful. I pray to God all the time. "God, give me Connie. My the only Connie, same beautiful, externally and internally beautiful Connie that she should be with me, and, in our next life, we should meet when we are very young, as young as in kindergarten." That would be a wonderful thing to happen to us that our childhood would start as little children, later we would grow up together, fall in love, and get married. And if that happens, I think I will be the happiest person. I don't have any other wish like being born into a multimillionaire family or being born rich; I only want Connie, who would be my sweetheart from a very young age. If that happens, my sorrow, my pain will go away. Today if I hear God telling me, "Pradeep, I grant you, after your death, immediately, when you are reborn, and Connie is already there, she may be elder to you by a couple of years, and you can meet her." I will accept it, however much older she is to me. I will accept that if I hear a voice coming that she may be elder to you in the next life, but she will still be your wife, would you accept it? I would say yes. I don't care if I'm 15-16 years old and she is 30 years old, even then I will accept it, I love her that much. Miracles do happen, and I'm ready for anything. Even if she meets me like a sister or becomes my mother, I would still take it, regardless of whether she is my wife, sister, or mother. That is why Chanakya quoted that, "A wife can be your wife if she can be your best friend, sister, and mother." The same thing is written in the Vedanta about the duty of the wife. So this is my pain. It doesn't lessen if I go to a support group or read; Connie is on my mind all the time.

43

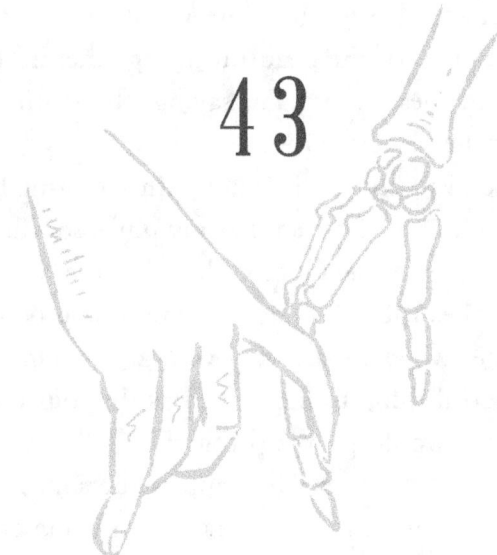

Realization and Enlightenment of Pain After Connie's Demise

I wanted to share one more thing, and that is about my paternal grandfather, my father's father. He was a very learned man, very spiritual, very knowledgeable. He had four sons and several grandchildren, and we were, of course, his first grandchildren. We lived together, all 17-19 of us, in a very big house in Delhi. My grandfather was pretty wealthy; he supported everybody, and his sons worked in the business. We were students then, and we're just about to finish our education. When my grandmother died, I remember he did not go to the cremation, but he asked his elder son and everybody in the family just to take her away. He managed to say some goodbye. It was clear then that he was very upset, but I still failed to understand why he did not perform the last rites or even attend the cremation. After the cremation, he asked if everything was done properly, which we confirmed. He used to stay alone on the ground floor, while the rest of us stayed on the other four floors of the house. I think we were all ignorant at that time, but he was alone in a dark lonely house with many rooms. I remember asking him if I should stay in the same room that my Grandmother used to be in, but he declined. He said that he was fine, and he was very knowledgeable, adding, "You people have to study, and as a result of that, I don't want to do such things that ruin your studies." I think I asked him a couple of times, but perhaps I did not mean it very seriously. I doubt if I had thought of the pain he was enduring then because I felt he was very knowledgeable and capable of handling it. He was the one who told us about the inevitability of death, and I felt that such a learned man would cope. However, to my surprise, within no time, he started deteriorating rapidly. He had the support of his family, but he was just not himself, and despite being surrounded by so many people, he was very lonely inside. I think he especially struggled at night, a time when we were all alone with our thoughts. We never thought it would happen, but quite unbelievably, he also passed away after 2 months. When I think about it now, I realize he went through much pain before he died. I feel today that he must have suffered terribly, but he never said a word to anybody and bore the pain silently. He did not write a biography or share his feelings with anybody. I am sharing this to tell everybody that one should not be silent and share their pain to let others know that they should be prepared to face this kind of unexpected tragedy.

That is why I think I am feeling more pain because although I have seen these kinds of painful moments, I had not imagined how difficult it would be. I thought that I would suffer perhaps 50-60% but not 100%. Now that it is happening to me, I am enduring it with more than 100% pain.

I saw the same thing happen with another family member living in the USA with his children and grandchildren. He was also very close to his wife, and I think close to his grandchildren as well because he was happiest when talking about them. When his wife died, however, he turned around and felt very lonely. I don't think he had any great love for his sons, and I doubt he was crazy about even his grandchildren. Additionally, I think there was a dispute about money amongst his children, and it gradually became worse as his children wanted to grab his money. As a result of this, there was deep enmity amongst his daughters-in-law. It was around this time that he moved out of the home. Sometimes, he was living back in India with his daughters or with some friends in the USA, and at other times in a hotel. He used to tell me Pradeep (he used to call me Pappi), and he used to call me every day, and I remember I used to call him at least 6-7-8-9-10 times a day. I used to call him uncle and made sure I called him irrespective of whether I was working or traveling. He got a new lease on life from me. I don't know the connection, but he trusted me, perhaps because we had an old relationship. I did a lot of work for him when he was going through this crisis. I settled his accounts; in fact, I even spoke to his children about why they were misbehaving with him. I spoke to his daughter-in-law and other family members, reprimanding them for stealing money from his account. I doubt if that made much of a difference, though. I remember a time when I called him at the hotel he was staying in. I spoke with an Indian Gujarati gentleman attending to him. He said to me, "Mr. Berry, I want to worship you and touch your feet. Why don't you come over here?" When I wondered why I should do that, he told me that Uncle thought of me every minute. He told me Uncle used to wait for my call from the moment he got up in the morning. When I called the next day again, the gentleman said, "Why don't you come here—I want to meet you because you are something; you have the power to heal his wounds."

He told me my uncle looked forward to my call in the morning at 8:30. I used to call him from my office, and we would speak for half an hour. I used to call him in the afternoon and night as well. I was doing it out of my love and compassion, as at that time, I felt very sorry that he was missing his wife. I had no idea in reality as to how much he was suffering, and because it was 20 years ago, I can only guess. The difference between these two examples and mine is that they were still occupied with their families. Such was not the case in our lives because we had decided not to have that kind of extended family. Thus, in our case, our love was 100% split between Connie and me. We had time for each other only.

Their love could be 50%-40% towards the wife or 70% or 30% towards the children. There was surely a distribution of love between them and their children and grandchildren. His wife was so fond of their son that she used to fight with her husband over them. So I think they suffered so much despite there being a division of love.

Sometimes I compare that with my situation and wonder how much suffering there can be if one is 100% devoted to someone as Connie and I were to each other. Even in the other cases, if there was a 100% devotion to the other person, it's just not possible; for example, if you travel with your grandchildren, your wife is alone at home. Similarly, if the grandmother leaves her husband alone for months while she is with her grandchildren, there cannot be 100% devotion to each other. So it is not an apple to apple comparison, but I can see that he still suffered after his wife passed away despite there not being a 100% commitment.

I have seen another case that is somewhat like mine. I have seen a few cases where a husband was married to his wife for about 40 years, and when she died, the husband had no regrets whatsoever. He missed his wife as you would expect, but not as much as I thought he would go after 40 years of marriage. He used to say, "Oh, Mr. Berry, it is fine, you know." He was thinking of making more money, which sickened me, but I suppose different people behave differently. There was another person who was married, who supposedly could not live without his wife. This woman was sincere to him, and I was shocked to death when I found out what happened after she died. Some 5-6 years later, he went and brought in another bride. He thought he would be happy and look what happened- his bride took all his money and left him on the road!

So these are different variations of life, and everybody goes on with their own thing. I can give you a thousand examples, but that is not the purpose of my biography. Although I saw many people's pain, it is irrelevant as my biography is meant only for my wife. To some degree, pain is always there for your dear loved ones, whether your wife or your children. It is a different kind of pain, but it isn't easy nevertheless. Some people have overcome the pain of their loss, or perhaps they are just acting. Some others manage to keep ongoing. I spoke to one friend of mine who lost his son because he committed suicide, and he did not want to talk to me, saying it was a topic he wanted to avoid. I respected his wishes, but he called me the next day, apologizing for his rude behavior. He said his son was his darling and shared a few of his feelings. After that, I was careful not to bring up the topic unless he wanted to talk about it himself. I suppose everybody is different, and people handle their grief differently. Some start giving to charity; some others marry again, certain people start doing humanitarian work- that's the way it is.

In my case, I don't think I will haphazardly do anything. For example, I have kept busy writing articles, meeting people about important matters, talking to attorneys, etc. So there are some diversions, but the moment I leave the office, the pain starts right away -Confusion, and according to psychologists and psychiatrists, sometimes when you start thinking about one thing, that stops you from thinking about other things. In my case, I do not even want to go to those places where I used to go with Connie. I have written that I have stopped reading the newspaper and stopped watching TV. IT TRULY BOTHERS ME whenever I read the name 'Constance Berry' in the magazines we receive. I begin to think perhaps I should start reading them, but I don't think I'm ready right now.

I am determined about one thing, though—whenever I receive a letter from MCR and other organizations in her name, I will donate some money to the extent possible. Connie passed away at HH hospital close to our home. Connie had given good donations to the HH hospital, and that is the same hospital where in my opinion, medical negligence took place, and she died. I am sure she would not have given a penny. I still get letters from Connie asking for charity. I do not want to give a penny to HH. Reading her name, going through her drawer, going to her room, not finding her in her bedroom washing her clothes is the most painful thing in my life. The other day, I was sitting at my desk looking for certain papers, and I found her degrees. I could see how much love she got from her students, how much appreciation she got from the Dean, and how many prizes she had won! I knew about these things, but at that time, I was not appreciative of their value. Now, all those things are like a monument to her. Last night, I saved all those things in her room and got busy organizing all of them. I sorted out all the degrees and gifts and letters from her students and school authorities. I look through Connie's tributes from her College and the Dean, noting how she was highly regarded. When I read these things, I lose control and wonder—isn't all the knowledge and education that one has futile? All of us have to go one day. None of us is special. I think the doctors made a mistake with Connie. If the doctors had acted differently, Connie would have still been with me today. The main problem with me is that Connie did not die of natural causes, but her life was snatched away by these doctors.

44

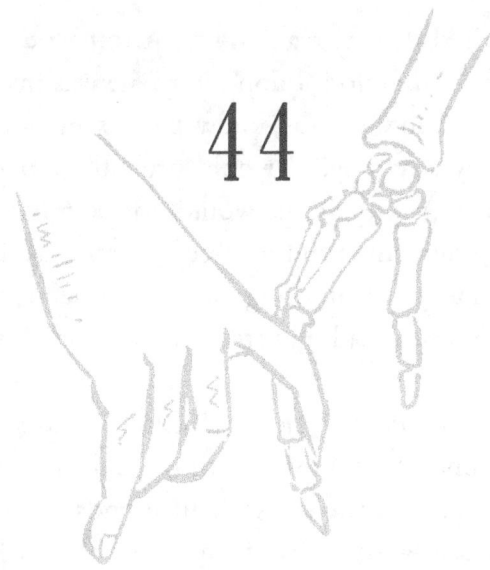

Grief-stricken Reactions

I have seen many painful circumstances, and that is why I want to understand how people who have lost their spouses, who are very important to them, react to their painful situations. I am trying to find out my knowledge, but their experiences will not help me. People tell me to read books about Buddha, where he asks disciples to get rice from any house that has not seen death. I have read it, and I know all those things. People tell me there is no house where tragedy has not taken place. I know that, but all my knowledge has vanished because of my unconditional pure love for Connie. I don't want to compare events that happen to different people to my circumstances, but at the same time, I am curious about people who lost their spouses and how they dealt with it.

I know some people dealt with it very positively. Some friends and relatives just accepted that they have to carry on now their spouse is gone. I was really surprised because they were very close to each other. I don't know if these people were close to their spouses or they pretended to be. Sometimes people pretend they are close, but they are not very close. When the wife of one man I know died, I don't think it made much difference in his life. He was very upset, but at the same time, he just carried on without mentioning her to me. We met many times after that as he was my distant relative, but I don't think he ever mentioned her. I used to ask him how he felt without his wife, and he used to say, "I'm OK, she had to go, and she had to go." I was surprised that he regularly went to parties, drank, and would be there wherever there was a function. I don't think he was in any pain. Now people challenge me. They say, "How do you know he was not in pain? Maybe he was suffering but did not say anything!" I would probably reply that if the person is suffering, or if that person is in pain, he would not be mixing up with people and acting normal. In my judgment, I did not see any remorse in his life that he had lost his wife. So sometimes reaction brings action, and action brings reaction. The whole family told me that he had adjusted and was not missing his wife much, which was surprising.

I also want to share one more incident. I think it was some time in 2012; we were in Captiva Island, one of the most beautiful islands in the United States, south of Fort Myers, Florida. There are two excellent islands, one is called Sanibel, and the other is Captiva. The islands are very small, less than 10 miles in length, and there are beautiful resorts that preserve some of the natural settings, with beachfront views of the Gulf of Mexico. It's just beautiful, and they don't allow any fast food, they don't allow any large buildings, they don't allow any commercial shopping centers. It's a very isolated place for people to relax, and it is mostly a second home for the rich. It's a very rich place, and people who have gone there really love it. It is one of the world's most important places for collecting seashells. So people come there from all over the USA, and I think it is just beautiful. So we used to go there from 2005 on, spending 5 weeks on Sanibel and then 3 weeks on Marco Island. On one of our trips, we were both having lunch at a very famous place, and it was very special to Connie. A special kind of fish called grouper is available only in Florida, especially around Sanibel and Captiva. It is a special delicacy available only in Florida. This grouper fish you will not get fresh anywhere else in the USA, just like salmon comes only from Alaska, and we had the best quality grouper when we were there in 1987 and then again in 1989. They catch the fish in the ocean and immediately prepare it, just out of this world.

Similarly, in New Orleans, they have white fish, which is delicious. So going back to our incident in Captiva, there is a restaurant called "The Bubble Boy." They make their fish in a brown paper bag and grill it. It is just magnificent, and perhaps one cannot get that taste anywhere. It is fresh, like fresh coffee in Hawaii.

When we went to the big island, Kona, Hawaii, in 2006 and 2007, we visited many Kona coffee and chocolate farms to taste different types of coffee and chocolate. We bought both coffee and dark chocolate of different types, only grown on Kona Island, Hawaii. Similarly, Kona has other delicacies which are just super. In India, mangoes are the best in the world during the summer. India also has many different fruits and vegetables which are seasonal. Nature and God have been very kind to India. I think India is the second-largest producer of fruits and vegetables in the world. The largest producer of potatoes, milk, fiber, jute, cotton, silk, jumbo shrimps, leather hides, iron ore, and basmati rice. The South Indian coffee in India has a completely different gorgeous taste. I know every country has regional differences in climate, food habits, and food. The economist Thomas Malthus mentioned that every 15-20 miles, people's language, food, and culture are different. Since we live globally, the distance probably might have gone up to 20-30 miles. If I go 30 miles or 40 miles from where we live, people over there have different ways of living. The houses are different, and the standard of living is different. If I go 100 miles away, then local lifeways are completely different. I think Malthus was right when he said that India is a rich country inhabited by the poor.

So coming back to this point, we met a person sitting by himself in a restaurant in Captiva Island in Florida in 2010. I'm sure he was close to 80 years old, handsome, good-looking, he had maintained himself very well and looked very educated. He was sitting next to us, and we kept looking at each other. Finally, I decided to talk to him. He asked us, "Why don't we sit together for lunch?" So Connie and I started talking. When asked where he lived, he stated Spain, but that he came to Captiva every year for 3 months in a small house for vacation by himself. After I asked him if he has family, he said that he has two daughters and six grandchildren, and they all live in Spain, and when he meets them, he enjoys them; however, more or less, he lives alone. I asked him about his wife. He said, "I lost my wife 20 years ago and did not marry again. She was my darling, she was my love, and I would never remarry. I am alone, and I am fine." I was very much taken aback. So I said, "Pardon me for asking, but what was your profession?" He looked at me and said, "Do you remember seeing my face in the 50s and 60s?" Then I suddenly remembered that he was one of the most popular journalists covering India, China, and Asia. He was one of the most intellectual journalists and TV personalities who would announce the world news. He told me he had met Prime Minister Nehru and Dr. Rajendra Prasad. Later, he also met Prime Minister Shastri and many other politicians. He knew everyone. Then I recollected and said, "Yes! My God! What an accomplishment for you!" Then he said, "No, I don't do anything now. I used to travel extensively and was very happy. But after the loss of my wife, my darling, who was my baby, I don't travel so much anymore." I did not have the experience of losing a spouse at that time; hence I couldn't sympathize. Now, I am recollecting that incident—what he must have gone through, or maybe even now he must be going through. I think it is one of the examples I want to give.

After Connie and I said goodbye to him, we were still talking about him. The young waitresses were looked after well, who treated him like their father and helped him if he needed something. I don't know whether these kinds of experiences make me strong or weak. I will not compare his life with my life, and that is my message: we should not compare our situation to others. It is good to compare to get some knowledge, but if you think you can follow the same principle as another, it does not work if you follow a particular person and he is your idol. If someone says, "Look at him, take that example," you cannot be that person. The doctors gave me examples of people who worked their way out of grief. I am not ready for that because their pain may be different. My pain is different. I think people should not compare losses, and when people are grieving, other people should not say a whole lot except to tell them, "Please look after your health, do whatever you want to do, whatever makes you happy."

One should not dictate how one should lead their life because one cannot understand others' pain. I want to let people know this important message- Do not play with somebody's sentiments by giving them false hope. Some people recommend that I read some autobiography or biography of some person. I have read these, and I am still reading them, but it has made no difference. That is an indication that our love was unique. I can only say that. Perhaps many people have never had this kind of love, this kind of feeling we had for each other. I don't want to make this a very negative book; I don't want people to feel that I am talking about my pain. I think in this kind of hidden pain, there is a hidden message as well.

The hidden message is that one should try to understand the grieving person's mind, who was so happy with his wife, his first girlfriend, and the last one. People should appreciate what I have been through rather than just telling me, "Oh! This is God and life. Forget about the past. Life goes on." I don't want to hear all that. I don't have any other choice than to go on, but I want my own very simple life, and I don't want to go anywhere except India because it gives me some happiness to be with my brother, his family, and my family grand-nieces.

After five or six years, I may be able to travel somewhere. Right now, I'm still getting so much mail, so many invitations from Viking, Vantage, University of Michigan, Carleton, and other elite colleges whose sponsored trips we went on. I will not go on these trips, as Connie's memory would make me more depressed and upset, and I might have panic attacks when I remember our trips and being together. I would remember how Connie used to be with me every minute, how we used to take the taxi, get out at the airport, and fly by ourselves when we were on the Michigan university tour, how happy we were! We would be picked up and stay in the hotel, and then go on the cruise or sometimes a land tour or both, depending upon which tour we were taking. I won't go to the places I have been with Connie. I might go to places I had not gone before, like Turkey, Egypt, Saudi Arabia, Dubai- places where we wanted to go, but somehow, we could not. People behave according to what they believe, but I hope they will understand the message I am conveying

45

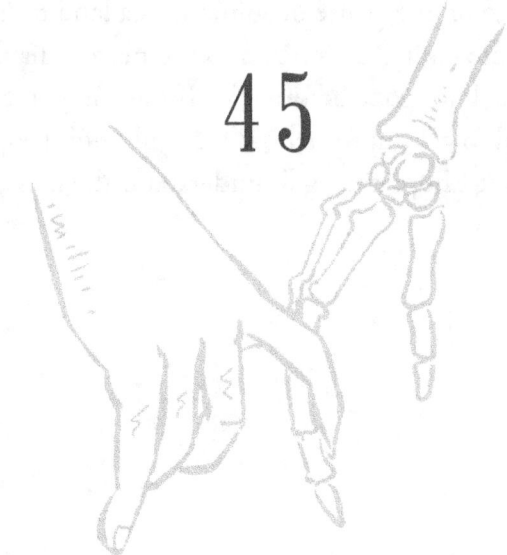

Seeing Connie Everywhere

I would like to mention the many practical things about the sadness I feel. For a long time after Connie's death, her caretakers and other people did the laundry. I didn't do it because I was doing other things. I wanted to change the sheets and wash a few clothes today, so I waited for our helper to come. But since she is not coming until next week, I decided to do it myself. So today, September 20th, 2015, I started doing laundry. I think it is one of the most emotionally difficult things I did today. It was intolerable, especially when I changed the sheets. The sheets are very clean, and the side on which Connie used to sleep hasn't been touched. It was just very painful for me to have this experience.

    I feel this kind of heartache when I see that she is not in the bedroom, her study room, the living room, the kitchen and that she no longer shops or with me or rides in the car. I remember when we had just met each other 40 years ago- she had so much stamina to take care of everything. She was full of energy. She would change the sheets 2-3 times a week, make beds, do the cleaning, do all the laundry, including my clothes, iron our clothes, and put them neatly in the cupboard. She was a perfectionist. When she got sick later on, I think in the last 2-3 years, only then did I do a lot of household chores. I was not a perfectionist like her; I would put my garments here and there and not hang them properly. So many times, she would come, and she would see the way I had arranged her clothes, and she would say to me, "Is this the way you want to put away my clothes? Haven't you seen how I would do it?" I would tell her these things were not important anymore and that we would have to change our priorities. By then, she did not have much energy and was not very argumentative. So remembering such small things are very painful for me. I must write about this experience, and right away, I started writing- it's around 2 in the night, and I decided that I had to write this so that I would not forget. I think these kinds of things are the true rhythm of pain.

Another thing has just popped up in my mind; maybe I should write another book or change the book's title to 'Living in Pain for 3 Years' or 'Living in Pain for 18 Months' to describe how suddenly our health is can deteriorate. I think the doctors ruined her body; otherwise, I would have never imagined that she would go downhill so fast.

I avoid going to her shower room, a walk-in shower that she specially built for herself. In one of our bathrooms, we had a tub, and when she couldn't use it for the last 2-3 years, she spent a lot of money and got a walk-in shower built for her to enjoy her baths. Sadly, she did not have enough time to enjoy the new shower. I just cannot believe that she could not shower herself when she got sick for about 18 months. She was on the oxygen tank, and she would sit on the walker, and I would make her comfortable to enter the shower. She was very modest and independent. She would ask me just to pass her the towel and leave the shower. I would later help with the drying after she was done with the shower.

Her legs were swollen, and I massaged her legs with cream for a few minutes every day. It used to bring tears to my eyes that she was retaining so much water. I thought her doctors were not very concerned, so I reprimanded them. I would tell them that they saw Connie only for a few minutes and were so busy, but if they were forced to see what she was going through for 24 hours a day, they would realize the damage they had done to her. I said this to the doctors so many times. One of her doctors was very good in the beginning, and when the case went out of control, he was willing to listen to anything, and he would not answer back, although I'm sure he didn't like listening to criticism. If he had argued with me then, maybe we would have had more complicated problems. I was ready to fight with him in the court of law. The most important thing for me was Connie, and I had decided that if the doctor said anything or argued with me, I was ready for a battle. I did not pursue that more because I did not want to get distracted from paying attention to Connie.

One of the other things I face every day when I go to check my mailbox, or if I am coming in from the front door, is that I imagine I can see her sitting on the balcony with her walker along with her oxygen. I remember how I would bring my car outside, help her into the car, and she would sit with me on one of our numerous trips to the hospital. I know it was the most difficult thing for her and me, but it gave me some happiness and sadness even then. I used to feel more sadness and a little bit of happiness that she was still alive and she was with me, and we were together. Even if I had to carry her wheelchair, I would be very happy, and such happiness I had never felt earlier when we were taking trips all over the world. I think this was true love.

When we were young and had a lot of fun, that was also love; but later in our lives, our love was like worshiping God. Just like you surrender yourself and become a saint like you have renounced the world, I had left the whole world, and practically my whole life was to be with Connie. Her weak body had become my place of worship. Instead of praying to God in the temple, I offer my prayers as my devotion to her while in the room. Whenever I saw her sitting, sleeping, or uncomfortable, I would pray to God that if there was good karma, please give her strength and make her better. This is the way I was worshipping her.

Even now, it is very difficult for me to take a shower in her walk-in shower. To avoid that, I go to the health club almost every day. I swim and exercise and then take a shower there. These are the lengths I go to to avoid the pain. I am not saying that this is the reaction of every human being because although everyone has gone through grief, perhaps they may have had some different experiences. I am not trying to compare myself to them, nor am I trying to say that I am the only person who has seen suffering because every individual on this planet has gone through some suffering, and everyone's suffering is different. I consider happiness and unhappiness as sisters, and my philosophy is that a candle has less light and more darkness. Only a few people can study with a candle, but there is darkness if you move away from the candle.

I cannot describe this agony. It is very difficult, and I don't want to be ungrateful to the mighty Lord, but I am certainly in many agonies. It is very easy for people to say that Connie was sick for a long time and that everyone has to pass away, but I have seen her death and suffering. I'm sure many people have seen that. I'm sure some people are all alone like me, and some people suffer by themselves. I'm not making any comparative statement, nor do I have any statistics, but I think I might have seen very few people who were alone in my life. Even in those cases, they found children, a spouse, friends, and far-away relatives to come and help. Some of the widow ladies used to volunteer with Northwestern University. I'm not sick right now, but if I ask faculty for help, students there, who have a program that helps seniors who live alone, will surely come and help. I don't want to ask for their help right now because I want to be active. I should keep on moving all the time.

The things I am describing right now are very painful, and I don't know how long it will take me to overcome the grief. People who thought they understood my pain do not even understand it 1%. It is very hard for me when they say that they are sorry that she is gone. If they had seen the kind of suffering I saw, then perhaps it would have stayed with them for their whole life. This suffering will stay with me until the day I die. Every single incident has stuck in my brain, mind, soul, and heart like a movie.

It may be a good message, or it may be a depressing message for people. I have no idea how readers will perceive it, but they will know how to preplan and be prepared so that they don't have to go through this. I have seen many people who had no plan and suffered in the end; however, there is no guarantee that things will work according to that plan even if you plan something. Look at Connie- she had planned long-term care, but look at what happened. I want to ask for forgiveness if I have offended anyone because this is my personal experience and has no relevance with anyone else.

I remember seeing a box office hit Indian movie during our teenage age, "Who Kaun Thi," meaning, "Who was she." It can be easily seen on YouTube even now, and I am sure with Netflix. It is an excellent movie and has super songs. After Connie's demise, I always have been thinking about her and keep her beautiful face everywhere I go—walking, riding in the car, picking up and dropping me at the O'Hareairport. There was a great love in that carry-on and how Connie used to pack and empty and then do the laundry and would never allow me to wear anything but Ralph Lauren or Christian Dior shirts and Nautica socks to match each outfit. I wondered how my wife is like my mother getting me up early, making sure that I dress properly and according to the year's season. How much love was involved in that, and how she must be thinking of going to Marshall Fields (now Macy's) to buy these things for me. Her clothing, ties, suits, and those carry-on suitcases are still with me, and though I may have to spend money to get it fixed, I would especially carry that carry-on along with two of her suitcases. I am talking about the suitcases she bought me 30 years ago. I have preserved them and will continue to preserve them. That is a source of Connie's memories with me. Who she was is now like two desperate, lost Souls waiting to meet each other. That is what the whole movie and beautiful songs and lyrics are about. I would try to translate the lyrics into the English language and would compose my songs. If possible, I would work hard and get an album with professional musical instruments, directions, etc., "My Tribute to My Love."

46

My Emotions and India

I must mention that Connie Darling was and would be special all my life. Our first trip to India was in July 1979, three years after our marriage. We were both thrilled to go and spent seven weeks in India. It was great for us, our family, and friends, and I was finding if I had come to a different planet. We stayed with my brother, and every day, morning 'til night, family and friends walk in, as the tradition for visiting was to walk in without calling beforehand. At that time, people in India offered true hospitality. Now, a small percentage of friends and family members call before visiting. I think I prefer that to surprise visits. Nowadays, people have less time to visit due to working and the traffic in India. In Delhi, some families live far away, and traffic has become a big problem. I don't want to travel far in the city to see people because of traffic.

Connie and I went to Kashmir, Taj, Jaipur; we sightseeing in Delhi and saw historical and ancient places. Some of the most beautiful places in Delhi are Chandni Chowk and Connaught Place. The shopping is excellent and lots of fun. You can find handicrafts and things that are exported all over the world. For lunch, we would have picnics or go to the houses of friends and relatives. We went to dinner every night with relatives. We started going to the home of my uncle, Dr. Behl, and my English Aunt Marjorie. I was extremely close to them. Connie and Marjorie became best friends, and after we returned to the USA, Uncle Behl and

Aunt Marjorie visited us in Evanston, along with their daughter Vanita, who was like a daughter to me. We had lots of good times. My uncle refused to take any time off work. He was devoted to his medical profession, writing books, attending conferences at Northwestern University and presenting his thesis, etc., and mixed his trip with vacations. Connie was also working, and we did our best to provide the hospitality.

I learned a great lesson which I have been following until now, except for later when we get comfortable life. Uncle told me, "Son, I want to stay with you to spend time with both of you and pick up the three years we spent apart, missing each other. While I am here, I would like to contribute to your bills for food, gas, telephone, electricity, etc." I told him that it wasn't necessary, as we could easily afford to house them, and I would not take a penny. He said, if you don't take my offer, I will stay in a hotel. "Son, I can very easily afford to help out, and you are both working people, and unless I contribute, I would rather stay in the hotel, and you would have to come and meet me and have lunch, dinner with us." I did not argue, and I told him that he would never stay in a hotel when I could house him. I would accept the cost of the phone calls to India, as it was three dollars per minute compared to 30 cents now. He agreed, and the consideration he showed me enlightened me. Connie and I did not stay anywhere in India except with my brother and at Dr. Behl's house. I then started getting emotional about India. I wanted to come every year to India for my vacation.

Connie also started to join me. We both were confused that it was a long flight to Australia and suggested that we stop for a week in India and take a flight from Delhi as it's not that long from Delhi to Australia, China, and Russia. However, after four annual vacations, Connie started telling me that Pradeep, can't you go every two years or 18 months as we can visit Australia, New Zealand, China, and Egypt and do a few more cruises with the University of Michigan. I never said no. I have to blame all my life and regret that she truly wanted to see Australia and New Zealand. She, later on, was not ready for China, Egypt, and Turkey, or even India due to the long flights. I only regret missing Australia and New Zealand. I know that those two she was most interested in.

I must mention that I had four Indian friends who were professional, and we had worked together in the same profession and lived in Chicago. Their wives were part of our family. I can say that four friends, their Indian wives, and Connie and Pradeep were close. All four and their spouses took two trips together and never asked us. Connie and I were very much hurt, and they made some big excuses. It hurt us very much. Connie told me Pradeep, "these four with their Indian wives only want Indians and Indians. I know that the Indians in my circle always wanted to be Indians in the USA. I told my friends and relatives bluntly that you think you are in the USA. Still, you do not have a single American friend, regardless of how intelligent or educated you are. But you all get together like a big carnival and remain Indians. Still, Indians, Indian food, Indian Songs, Indian dresses, Indian languages, and go to India for visits showing how wealthy they are. Indians in India except highly educated would be considered that he or she lives in the USA. Indians in India are very polite and ignorant about their profession, education just one word. She is, or he is from America. People like me who have lived over 42 years can make out in a second that what kind of a person he or she is. I do not mean to insult anyone. Why did they pretend that they are different or have this thinking that we live in America? Although they kept to themselves at every function and party, marriage, and in our home, we all met.

We decided that it was better for us because we have different tastes, styles, and approaches to being private. Immediately, we did a self-evaluation and got the answer that we truly did not want to go with anyone but just both of us. Later, many other friends and the same wanted to go together, but we both decided not. **This is a very important point**. We truly wanted to be by ourselves, and until Connie's demise, we two were together. I did not want or need to see anyone. Not even my own 50-60 members of my family, father's sister's children, these four and their wives went- with spouses to Australia and New Zealand. They never asked Connie and Pradeep to go with them. The fact is they called and told Connie and me that we both must see both the countries. I asked them how come they did not ask us as we would have gone together. I will always regret that Connie was not able to go to Australia and New Zealand. There is no way I would ever even think of going to these two places. There is no way as Connie's memory, love, passion, and our lovely pairs of two Parrots and that two with pure love and inseparable Connie and Pradeep now is only Pradeep. Connie is gone. This pain is a sharp edge, and there is no treatment, no compensation.

47

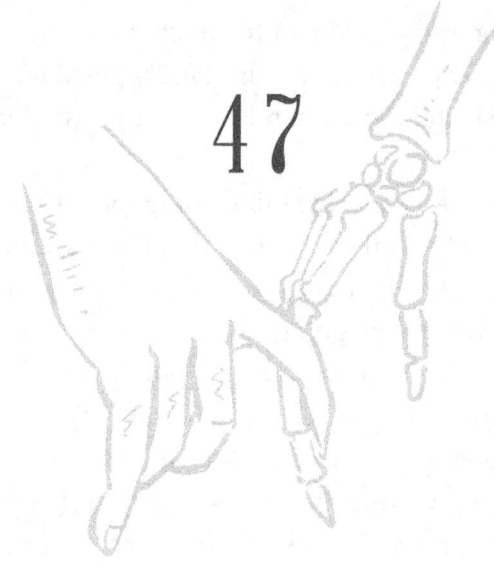

My Present Life—Pain After Connie

It is so painful for me to think of going anywhere without Connie. Sometimes, I should try to go to a restaurant and travel by myself to see how I feel. Right away, my brain and heart tell me no. This is because we always went together in our lives, except when we were working. I had to travel quite a lot, and so did Connie. I have not gone anywhere without Connie in the last 10 years. The only exception was that I used to go to India every year for two weeks, which was also difficult. Even then, I would have panic attacks at the thought of leaving Connie for two weeks. Connie used to make the decision that I might as well go. I still did not want to go because leaving her was difficult. I would go to India, but I would miss and miss her. Again, when she used to drop me at the airport, it was extremely difficult for me to decide whether I should forget about going to India and returning to Connie. Connie was strong and used to give me the power to go. Otherwise, I would regret leaving her, and after a few days, I would be on the phone booking return flights. The decision to go or to stay was difficult. In the end, I would decide to travel, but my mind was always on Connie. I would call her five or six times a day and have long talks with her. Connie used to tell me: either go or don't go, and if you go, I can keep busy cleaning the drawers and organizing my stuff. This statement, and knowing we would be in touch over the phone for hours, made my yearly trip to India to see my brother and his family possible. It was a struggle then. Now, the same struggle is still there when I leave the house alone. In reality, all these are signs of our love.

Once in a while, I think I wouldn't mind going somewhere. Still, the thought of going or even taking a flight reminds me of Connie and scares me, makes me upset, and immediately my heart tells me no. Finally, I don't even think of going---her unbearable absence stops me from going anywhere. The only place where I can go is to see my elder brother and his family in India. But even that has become upsetting- leaving our home and all the rest that I see as Connie. Even leaving the car and the garage is hard. How much pain I have to face and will always have to keep facing. Repeating this is not good writing, but it has a soothing yet painful effect on me. I never want to stop saying the same message. If someone in my situation or perhaps someone who has not fallen in love and wants true love, perhaps this book may give them some solace. At that time, you may forgive me that this book was no good but might appreciate the depth of our love. Leaving home to go to India is just unbearable. My mind tells me I should forget going anywhere. Home has become my favorite place to stay.

I had mentioned this earlier before I diverted completely into painful memories of our traveling together. Thoughts of Connie and her memory shake me. My mind then thinks of the most painful episode I went through, and I start wondering if it is true that Connie is gone? Again, I block my mind and want to believe Connie is in her study. I forgot that I prepared her cremation, chapel of peace ceremony, and the interment of her ashes in her plot next to her parents. I wonder how I could do all of that. Is it true that I was brave enough to do all that? The answer is that my love and God gave me the strength to do all that. My shock and pain were at the deepest love of pain. I had never had gone through that painful episode of losing someone, losing my wife and my world. I was upset and in deep pain; however, I could not bear the pain of knowing that Connie's body was in a funeral home. My wife was not a charity case, and I wanted her funeral and burial done immediately.

I am again repeating this episode many times. It is due to my constantly thinking about Connie. It is due to the deep love that I have lost. Even after nine months of living in pain and suffering from that, nothing has changed. The saying that time heals pain has no truth; rather, my suffering continues to increase. One common saying is that any fall, cut, or little burn incident looks fine, but its effect worsens the next day. I am giving one instance, though I have seen many painful events. One of my uncles died at a very young age. My aunt was grieving very hard. Her mother-in-law's sister said to her, "Right now, you are surrounded by lots of family members and friends. Once they go to their homes, you will have to bear this loss and pain by yourself." Connie's fall, the ambulance taking her for a check-up at the hospital, staying with the hope of coming back the same day or the next day was painful. But the happiness of coming home on February 22, 2015, was tolerable. The evening before her cardiac arrest and the delay in performing CPR, and my fight with her doctors, I was filled with anger. Her lying on the hospital bed with tubes in her mouth was unbearable. Fighting for her tubes was painful for me, and then taking the tubes out without my permission was a criminal act and shook me each minute. Her demise broke me down completely.

I don't know how I could handle all that. Her cremation and the interment of her ashes in her plot was another trauma. That trauma still haunts me after nine months. At that time of great shock and pain, I had to ensure the best cremation, select the best caskets and urns, and talk to a priest about the services. My mind was occupied, and that pain took a different direction to do many things. After all that, a different kind of pain took over as I began to do the legal work, and so many things occupied my mind and life. This pain came in different waves. I haven't had that experience before. My priorities were to ensure that she had the worlds' best funeral. I know that was done.

I am writing about Connie's demise and the whole episode again and again. It has two reasons: first, my pain, and second, that is how the human brain works and how many new brain cells open up which were not used. God has given us billions and billions of brain cells, but on average, we don't use half of them. New brain cells opened, and I now feel that I am no longer using some of my cells. This is a new segment of my life, and our relationship is making me write all these things. I still have no answer for this, and I doubt if I would ever find that answer.

Today, April 27, 2016, I was returning on the train at rush hour, when many people travel home from work. I especially wanted to observe the younger generation in their twenties and thirties- some were working, some were students. It was extremely soothing to see them with their smartphones and earplugs. All of them were busy with their phones, which is happening now in many countries, both developed and underdeveloped. I saw the same in Delhi, too, the two times I have been back since Connie's death. Honestly, it was nice, but it brings me painful memories of Connie.

In the 1970s to 1990s, traveling on the train was different, as most of the middle and senior management people were nicely dressed in suits and ties while reading papers like the Wall Street Journal, Economic Times, and New York Times. It was a half-hour of leisure for them. Offices opened at 8:15 A.M., and after reaching the office, the senior managers would have the same newspapers in the office. It was mandatory to read those papers to find out about business news and research market shares, the strategic planning of companies, and the ratings of Fortune 500 companies. It was like a Ph.D. student's workload, apart from the 50-60 hours per week that they worked. I did very well. It was a very happy life, working and sometimes spending 80% of my work traveling, staying in top hotels, and living off the company expenses.

I used to think that I was a king and happy as Connie was also a professional and had to leave by 7:15 A.M. to be at colleges and schools where she taught Spanish and French. Punctuality was a must for her. With the amount of traveling I did, if I were a few minutes late, that would be mitigated by my work. I used to work 16-17 hours a day when I traveled, and many of my juniors would say, "Pradeep, it is 5 P.M. You are leaving- leaving early- the good life- you enjoy your easy independence, no one is there to say anything to you, man. We have to work another hour. You leave early." This was a very sarcastic, planned remark, and it used to make me mad. I used to tell them, "You sit on your rear end the whole day doing nothing and take a two-hour lunch, your productivity is zero, and that is why you have to stay long hours. Why don't you work hard from 8:15 to 5 and cut your phone calls and lunches? I wish I could get rid of you, as you are a burden on the payroll and get paid for doing nothing." I hated those sarcastic comments.

Later, senior management was informed of this, as they kept track of the efficiency and productivity of their employees, and our Chairman started firing these unproductive employees. He openly told me he wanted the best employees, and five professional development courses were required to stay in that largest worldwide finance company. There was a lot of hard work but many awards and rewards in return. Our motto was "We are playing to win." That became my theme: I wanted to be a winner at any cost. Connie was a winner, as she was teaching, and at that time, there was much less political rivalry and jealousy in education. One of the reasons is that the economy was good; unemployment was very low compared to today's 10% unemployment rate. I would say that the rate is worse than that, as many people have stopped working and cannot find a job, and unemployment benefits beyond 48 weeks are not available. As such, those are not part of the census, and therefore the figure is distorted.

I would say that when Connie and I were in senior positions at work, this was the best time of our lives. We had no cell phones and no computers until 1988, although we became experts at computers and smartphones. "Necessity is the mother of invention." That was the life I had with Connie. Now, I feel lost in an unknown world without her, but I find her in our sweet home, as she is still with me. All these forgotten things have come to my new eyes and new brain after going through the whole traumatic period in April 2013. In 1998, she contracted PRP, and her family problems were at their worst. I believe the stress of these things caused her cancer. Her immune system was weak with the stress of PRP and the issues with her brother, causing her to fall ill with Stage 1 breast cancer. I am positive of this, whatever the doctors may say. The stress caused by her brother and his wife, along with Connie's mother, made her sick. The greed and cold blood of Connie's brother and his family are difficult to imagine.

48

Connie's Efficiency in Everything

Connie was so efficient in everything, whether at home, grocery shopping, taking care of the laundry, ironing, keeping our clothes properly folded, hanging clothes properly on the hangers in the appropriate closets and drawers. She was also efficient at accounting and keeping inventory of the house, including our clothing, silver, furniture, paintings, crystal, glasses, and other kitchen wares, carpets, and everything.

Connie was also very particular about cleaning the house, ensuring that the carpets were regularly cleaned, the table polished, the oven and granite counters cleaned. She kept track of our monthly food expenses with receipts, house assessments, electric bills, telephone, and the Internet. She also compared television and Internet bills for accuracy. By doing this, she saved us lots of money when the company billed us the wrong amount. She used to cut coupons from every Sunday's newspaper and other papers to save our hard-earned money. I am convinced that she must have saved over $30,000 to $50,000 in forty years due to these habits. It was not that she was miserly or cheap. She was conservative, and the money she saved was used for other shopping, travel, dining out. Her habit also made me save money when I went shopping for her, the house, and myself. Today, I can still do all of these things, but I am heartbroken and don't even shop much, nor do I care about money. Her demise has taken away all these qualities. I get lost again and again about these things, and the pain brings back memories of everything. I repeat, and perhaps will keep repeating, all of this about Connie and her qualities. I have taken her demise very hard. I don't think I will see any ray of happiness.

Our Karma reminds me of Connie's many great deeds, and mine, too.

In March 1993, my Uncle Behl told me that I should come back to India to handle his pharmaceutical companies and four charitable hospitals, provided that Connie agrees. It was absolutely a great opportunity for me; however, I was confused about it, and Connie told me that she could try living six months in India and six months in the USA to look after her mother. Although we were both ready to sacrifice for each other, it was a difficult decision. Finally, I went back to the USA and was promoted to a very senior position. I hired many employees, and they had to be trained, as they had little experience in my field. It was a great challenge, and there were times I regretted passing up my uncle's opportunity. But later, it worked out well for over 5 years. At that time, one employee didn't have the minimum experience of 15 years, but I trained him well in the most basic work in less than four years. In this way, I was able to help him, his wife, and their children.

After 3.8 years, he decided to apply for the same position but earned a few thousand dollars a year more. I advised him not to go and to spend more time learning from me. But he was sure that he knew everything. I could have given him more money, but I didn't as I had to train him again. He left his position with me for a few thousand dollars more a year, and I told him that he is not training, and a few thousand dollars might not be worth the experience he would lose. Afterward, he was always in touch with Connie and me. Connie always told me that "Pradeep, you are a very kind man and always willing to help others. That is a good thing. However, I hate interfering in your feelings, but many people take advantage of your soft touch heart. You have been hurt so many times, so think before you try to do good- these people are users and call when they need your help." I knew Connie was always right, and I was still the same. Now, after the demise of Connie, I realized all that and am extremely angry that people, friends, and relatives have betrayed me. Connie is not there anymore to see how correct and smart she was, and I didn't take her advice seriously. I must admit now that Pradeep is changed and would not allow anyone to take advantage of my soft heart or that I am always ready to please them. I would never like to see those ungrateful people and users anymore. Connie's demise has shattered me and changed my happiness and, to some degree, angry man, except my brother and his family and some unknown people. I would always be nice and helpful to outsiders.

I spent Christmas and Thanksgiving alone in 2015 for the first time in the 42 years I have lived in the USA.

49

Connie was My Destiny—Like a True Episode on the TV Program-Wanted

In memory of my Connie Darling, there was an excellent weekly TV show of one hour, "Wanted," 20 years ago. Connie and I always watched this program. The program requested the audience to inform the FBI if anyone had seen or had knowledge of these hardcore criminals. The journalist asked that you please inform the FBI on the number provided even if a viewer had a clue about them. One of the programs was very touching and applied to my life too. My entire career and its advancement are due to one person: my beautiful wife and friend of 41 years, My Connie. The program was about a successful business and a wealthy man in his late forties. When he was 10-12 years old, this man lost his way and didn't know what to do or how to survive. The same kid was weeping on the TV. He had been looking for the man who encouraged this kid to remain in the USA and gave him an American gal and one dollar to explore the USA and find his fate in the land of opportunity. The same kid was looking for the man to meet him, say thanks, and see him as his father and his family for any help and would do anything for him as he was the person who encouraged him to go to the USA. He was weeping, saying, please let me know if you recognized this picture of him. And the search was being funded by his own money. The boy wanted to thank this person, who he said was not a man but a god, for his support. Connie was amazing to my start in the USA. She was everything for me and my success. Connie was my best destiny and was instrumental to my success.

The following section includes email messages I have exchanged with friends, family, and organizations.

> From the Carleton Alumni Network, Alumni Farewells:
> Constance (Fuller) Berry
> September 4, 2015, at 2:12 am

Pradeep Berry

I don't know where to start and where to end. I can write and write, but it is no ending story of true love. Yes, I am Pradeep Berry, Husband of over 39 years of my most precious, best friend and darling wife, Mrs. Constance Berry (Connie)—Constance Fullerwhen she graduated in 1959. I had the opportunity to visit Connie at Carleton six years ago during her Alumni. I truly enjoyed it, and the food and the lectures were great. My Connie demised on February 28, 2015, which was not expected. I wish, in my opinion, she had listened to me to go to the Mayo Clinic, the best on this planet, which detected her condition in four days on November 8, 2014. However, it was too late. My life has changed since then. I don't know what I am going to do without Connie. She was everything for me.

We were two bodies and one soul. I pray to the mighty Lord that we meet again in our next lives as the same loving couple. "CONNIE AND PRADEEP." This hope is giving me the power to live and fulfill the desires of Connie, though physically, she is not with me, but the spiritual way she is with me and watching over me. I am also writing a biography for Darling Connie and would do my best to bring many parts of our lives while giving great quotes from many world scholars. I just feel like talking and talking about Connie, which gives me the most power. I could have never imagined I would go through such pain, as I know very well that we all have to go one day. God exists all the time, but human beings and animals have to go. However, when it comes to me, the loss of some special person knowledge vanishes. I am only quoting this only for myself, as each person handles things in their way. But I have to bear this no ending pain all the time. I pray Connie to give me the power to bear this loss. I can realize the pain of the king who made the seventh wonder of the world "Taj Mahal" in memory of his wife, Mumtaz Mahal, as she had asked him to build a special monument in her memory, "so that the world can remember their love." Pradeep Berry-- Loving Husband.

"My full efforts for her Justice."

This recounts my legal battle for justice after Connie's death.

This is the second voice message for honorable Mr.Please fight for justice. This is the USA and not an underdeveloped country where there's no justice and no humanity. If there is no justice for my 41 years of marriage to the most precious super education and priceless American-born darling Constance Berry, I would say we should not take pride in the USA. We then are in the same crowd of other countries. The USA should investigate the case even if these doctors have to be summoned under oath in the court's law. We need strength and courage to leave a great future for the coming generation and keep the USA on top of the world. Thanks for your help and support in looking into this.

Sincerely,
Pradeep Berry

Dear Pradeep,

I have received and reviewed your legal inquiry.

(Name Withheld) Law Offices is honored by your request that we review your potential claim. Sadly, we cannot accept all the cases we are offered and regret that we cannot represent you in connection with this claim and cannot take any action on your behalf. This does not mean that we are expressing an opinion that you do not have a viable claim; other lawyers may be very willing to undertake your case.

Also, remember that there are one or more statutes of limitations and/or statutes of repose that may apply to your case. This means that if you do not file a lawsuit within the time established by law, your claim will be barred FOREVER regardless of its merit. Therefore, if you wish to pursue your claim, you should contact another attorney without delay to discuss the appropriate time frames and to take IMMEDIATE action to preserve your claims.

To locate a lawyer that practices in this specialized area for a second opinion, you should contact the Chicago Bar Association Referral Service.

September 29, 2015

Dear Mr. (Name Withheld)

I have been reading your articles. I am writing for My Darling wife of 40 years- Mrs. Constance Ann Berry, a graduate of Carleton and University of Michigan and Masters in Spanish and French. The most diamond in my life died, in my opinion, due to the negligence of Drs. until I took her to MC, and they detected in four days- Palliative Care. I am in deep pain. She was born in Glenview in IL, American -highly intellectual and a great reader and more and more. We were two bodies and one soul. I should finish with the book in a couple of months.

Thanks.
Sincerely,
Pradeep Berry

"Many tributes For Connie from Our neighbors"

Dear (Name Withheld)

Thanks for coming to the peace ceremony of my darling wife- Connie, of over 40 years. I am absolutely at a great loss without her, and she was the most important part of my life and would remain that way. I miss and miss her all the time ---of day and night. I used to go to India for two weeks every year but didn't go since 2011. I was in a different mood then. Now, I am planning to go to see my brother and his family and other family members this weekend for two months, depending upon how I feel. I have not told any of my relatives in India or over in Chicago about her demise, as I took her death very hard. The only person I told is my real elder brother. I have been busy sorting out many things. How mighty Lord gave me the strength, I don't know. I have to find a way to cope with this never-ending loss. Connie had always thought very highly of you. She went suddenly from my life, leaving me alone. I can't believe or imagine. Thanks for your time and support.

Sincerely,
Pradeep

Dear Pradeep,

Thank you so much for this note. It was an honor to attend the service for Connie; I always had such high esteem for her. From the time I moved into this building, she was a source of good sense, good humor, infinite practicality, and kindness. This building overall would have been a much worse place were it not for her, not only in terms of her leadership for all those years but also in terms of her radiant goodwill. She was truly what the Biblical phrase calls "salt of the earth." We all were lucky to have her, but you, most of all, of course. Never having been married, I can only imagine what you're going through in terms of the loss you feel at every moment. But I do know from having watched friends and family members move through grief that you WILL get through it. Things will become easier, and you'll be able to let go of things gradually. But grief has its own schedule with every single person; there's no timetable. I am very glad you're going to India, and for such a long time. It will truly give you time and space apart to breathe, to be, to consider what life might hold for you in its very different form now. And you'll be with your brother, another thing about which I'm glad. If I may presume to say so, a person can't do all of this alone. We're put here to lean on and help each other; let your family do that. You deserve to be supported right now.

Take this time for yourself. You have spent years devoting your time to Connie, which of course, was the best and the right thing to do, but now the caregiver needs some care.

Godspeed, Pradeep. I hope that when I see you next, you will be refreshed and will have found a measure of peace.

(Name Withheld)

ELEGIAC PAEAN

From (Name Withheld)

I pray that the frustration and anger over the bad memories of Connie's care heal, Pradeep. They will only weigh you down. Connie had such a long, beautiful life, Pradeep. I've forgotten how many cancers she survived and all the suffering she experienced—yet, kept pulling her up. Surely, God was with her cancers and suffering. In each incident, God blessed her with more time—and again more time—and again more time. He prolonged her life, along with your care, far longer than other cancer patients. He could have taken her with first cancer or anyone immediately after that. Instead, He took her after this last cancer. She needed to be at peace. Her struggle was for so long. She didn't want wheelchairs, oxygen and walkers, and seclusion at home, Pradeep.

If the doctors failed—and if they lied to you—that is very tragic, Pradeep. What you will do about this, I don't know. However, it will only take away from the time you have remaining to enjoy God's blessings and what Connie left for you. Don't let an emotional cancer eat away at you,

Pradeep.
We'll talk later, Pradeep
(Name Withheld)

(Name Withheld)

Thanks for your kind words. Yes, you are right. I didn't want to be social anymore and wanted every time with Connie. I was happy if someone wanted to come and see Connie and be there for hospitality. Her one friend used to visit every two weeks. I used to serve her cookies, pastry's from Bakery, make different kinds of milkshakes, etc. All these things gave me happiness. As long as we were together, I was happy. Her two weeks in the hospital, and my anger like a tiger, on 8 doctors, including others, would be remembered by them whole their lives. They were the culprits. I told all of them when they went behind my back to take her tubes. They are inhuman; I never expected this from you all, two doctors and 4 nurses, and shame to you and your profession. You are ruining the image of doctors, whom we consider next to god to treat sickness, and Dracula's behavior. Her tubes were to be taken out on March 2nd, and they told me that I had to make a decision of what to do next. I had to decide. They took out the tubes on the 27th without my permission. However, I have lost my Kohinoor Diamond.

When I went to India in May 2015 for a little change, I, too, as an American citizen, was invited to the USA embassy to celebrate the 4th of July. The program was extremely wonderful, but I was thinking of Connie. There were over 1000 USA citizens and their families. Guard of honor, band, food, drinks, singers, dancing, fireworks, rides, and things for the kids. They don't allow other than USA citizens. I talked to the USA staff, Indians working there, and the Food preparing people for the USA citizens in their own kitchen in the USA Embassy. They don't allow any food from outside. Everyone has to pay for the entrance and food. Delhi Police and military security were there. Diplomatic people live like lords, and there were USA tourists, students on exchange programs, etc. It was nice, but with Connie" absence, I was very depressed and thinking I wish she were with me to have thousands and thousands of better times-- it would have been gold. I will tell you more about it, when I get back on the 23 July. Thanks for your kind words and phrases. Anything you want me to bring? Don't hesitate.

Pradeep

(Name Withheld)

Trust you and your family are doing well. I have been thinking about you for a while, but just didn't write it is hot and I stay mostly in the house in air conditioning. I do go to some places if my brother and his son are going. They offer me to take anywhere I want to go, but I don't think I have a great desire to do much, nor do I want to meet anyone, as I used to when Connie was alive. In fact, some of my other family and friends I don't want to meet I am happy with my brother's family, including his two boys, Mona, and the girls. I am waiting to come back to my home, knowing that Connie is not there, but her lovely decorative place still gives me both happiness and unhappiness. Also, going to her cemetery gives me the same. I have practically lost my charm of doing, going, and meeting my friends and relatives here and in Chicago. I am happy meeting people, like you, (Name Withheld) and (Name Withheld) outsiders, like in the funeral home ladies, who helped me for the cremation, and few selective. I don't think I want to see Connie's siblings. I know they want me to come and see them, but I won't. They could not find a time to see Connie. Connie was too upset with their behavior for a very long time but still wanted to see her family. I never ever said no, and we used to meet, but inside, Connie's siblings were insecure that her grown-up kids didn't come close to us, as they were crazy for both of us… I would not say anything to her siblings except hello. However, I don't want to meet as Connie's absence would pain me. Let me know if anything new.

Take care,
Pradeep

Dear Pradeep,

It would be presumptuous to say I know your pain. Only the person who is experiencing it knows its depth.

Yes, it will be difficult for you to return because you had been so very busy at the time Connie died (making arrangements, taking care of business). Then you had (Name Withheld) with you. Next, you had Mona and the girls with you. Then, you went to India. Constant movement. When you return, everything will stand still for you, and you will have to be strong. You will have to learn more than ever about your God. You already know that. Pray for direction. Pray for the right people to be presented to you in your life. Prepare first, to feel the grief here all alone. But if you ask God for direction, you will be led to the right people, places, and things to help you move forward.

Again, Pradeep, I can only say that we are alone in our grief. We can feel alone in a crowd. You will get through this. You will not "get over" it, but you will be able to live a full life with Connie at your side in a different way. You are not giving her up.

Give my love to Mona. She is such a lovely lady and such a good mother. Please don't worry about bringing anything back for me, Pradeep.

Take care of yourself.
Pradeep,

(Name Withheld)

You were and still are such an exceptional husband, Pradeep. Not too many women are given that gift. You, Pradeep, will someday have your own spring—your own Eternity. For now, all you can do is remember Connie in your heart...in your dreams. She is with you. Talk to her as if she were standing next to you. Now she is all-wise, all-knowing; she can read your mind and your heart without you ever speaking words. They know us more than they did when they were with us.

Take care,
Pradeep.

(Name Withheld)

Thanks for your kind words and phrases. I renewed Connie's account, which perhaps night had canceled as I had no desire to read, watch TV, and other magazines, and I was still paying for the TV as (Name Withheld) but billed me saying they would put a hold, but they charged the whole amount, and they are doing the same thing. Consumer Report person was very nice, and he renewed Connie and yours, and due to the circumstances, he was touched and was charging me less than the regular price. Upon Connie's wishes, he gave a great price for you also, and now I would get from January, and I think when yours is expired. So you would keep getting it, and I would get happy to read on her behalf. (Name Withheld) would still be in the picture and certificate you would have to take, I can tell you, and no matter you say no. I might leave on 20th October 2015 and, I was thinking of one month or five weeks, but then I made the reservation for December 24. This is due to the fact that I am using my miles, and they have little inventory, but I would keep on checking to come early. Please suggest to me, am I going for a long time.

Two things, I feel it is long for you to do the things. Secondly, I would be thinking of Connie's house where she is gone and home is alone while I am too missing her chairs, her computer, her room, her pictures, and her Cemetery where I come quite often. In fact, I am writing this from the Cemetery. India attractions are that I want to see my brother and his family and Grandnieces. However, I can come early if I miss Connie and her rooms and the home atmosphere. How much my life and mind has changed due to Connie? I am writing her biography and want to finish at the earliest. Time would do that. I never thought I would be so much upset and suffer pain for Connie. I do not want to see her family, nor do I want any relationship with any of them. Here, I have (Name Withheld) and few in the health club, and I just talk to people in the stores when I go shopping grocery. That is enough.

(Name Withheld)

Thanks a lot for your kind words and phrases, and I am extremely grateful to you for your kindness. Yes, I am truly going through a series of pain and suffering due to my wife of 41 years, and I will not be happy with any of my friends and relatives, though it may be a temporary diversion of my mind, after that, I will do so would be the same. I don't enjoy anything and stopped eating at the super restaurants and food and travel. I make simple food to survive, and that is all. I have no desire to travel like we were doing it. I was the happiest person who has now become totally different. I don't buy anymore that God had a different purpose, and I ask God what bad I did, or she did except helping others and attended the good and bad events of all. I would be happy when her biography is written, but sadness would be there. However, I truly admire your passion for me, and I would try to follow the suggestion.

Thanks, Pradeep.
From:" (Name Withheld)

On Sat, Sep. 19, 2015, at 9:20 AM,

Good Day Sir Pradeep K. Berry,

I am the guy you spoke with earlier over the phone. I decided to send you a message today because I am so worried about your condition, and I wanted to show my deepest sympathy for the death of your wife. I hope that you will be OK soon and be strong. Remember that God has a purpose for all the things happening in our life.

"I know for certain that we never lose the people we love, even to death. They continue to participate in every act, thought, and decision we make. Their love leaves an indelible imprint in our memories. We find comfort in knowing that our lives have been enriched by having shared their love."

—Leo Buscaglia

Return to Alumni Farewells Comments

September 2015

Mona berry,

I have no words to describe her personality. As much I knew her, she was a wonderful person, full of life, who wanted to explore the whole world, was a dedicated wife. With her farsightedness and her way of judging, no one can be like her. We all are missing you, Connie aunty. We have lost a gem of our family.

Hi Pradeep,

Again, I am very sorry for your loss, and I am happy to do everything I can to make this process easier for you. For security purposes, please attach a scanned copy of the death certificate. This will give us the authorization we need to access their account. Once I have this, I will be happy to look into your request.
    Thank you for your patience, and again, my sincerest sympathies during this difficult time.
Regards,

Supervisor
Customer Support

(Name Withheld)

Thanks for your kind words and phrases and advice about Connie. I would discuss a few more points with you when you meet me around 5.30 or whatever is okay. I would come home from my doctor's appointment tomorrow and can be available around 5.30 six whatever is Good. Otherwise, you give me the date when you can come. I have a few doctor appointments this week and one for physical therapy, but I can always adjust the time according to your convenience. Wednesday I should be home by Six, Thursday I can be home by 5.30 or six, Friday I can be home by 6.30. Nothing is happening on Saturday and Sunday. MONDAY 12 IS OK. You see your schedule and decide, and I will go at your convenience. Hope you find

(Name Withheld)
Thanks for your help. Pradeep

You are not to feel guilty for your dedication to Connie's memories, nor to continue grieving, Pradeep. It's such a tribute to Connie that your love continues.

(Name Withheld)

Thanks for your kind words and support. I would say once a week, and if it is not too much for you, you can come over, and I can show you. Also, I want you to see the collage pictures and other things I have put together. I love them, and I would like you to see the beginning of our 41 years of marriage pictures and some in between. I would like to put more later on. That gives happiness and sadness. I, therefore, live in two worlds- happy and sad. I can't take Connie out of my mind or believe that she is no longer with me. Please let me know if the plants etc., are too much due to your health. I want you to be frank as your health is first. My flight so far is on the 20th. If you want any other magazine, please let me know too. I would like you to see those pictures and a very rare thing THANKA, which Connie bought 35 years ago from India, and that was one of her favorite paintings, but she wanted to frame and find a place to hang. I got the framework done over here and asked someone to hang it along with other pictures. You could suggest to me, too, if I tried to hang TANKA somewhere else as Connie would not have allowed me to hang in the living room. So whenever you have time, come over. Please take care of your health and fitness.

Regards.
Pradeep

Thank you for all your trouble, Pradeep. It's the small things that make some people happy.

(Name Withheld)

Hope your trip arrangements are going smoothly.

Hello, Pradeep—

What a lovely idea. I think it will be a wonderful and therapeutic thing for you to write about your cherished life with dear Connie. Such a dynamic, well-rounded, thoughtful, and humane person SHOULD be memorialized in writing. And you, who knew her best of all, are the perfect person to put her into words. I'm so sorry for your pain. And I miss Connie, as I'm sure several of us in the building do. Her intelligent, benevolent presence leaves a great void.
Pradeep, but I hope this is of at least a little aid.
Please take care of yourself.

(Name Withheld)

Dear (Name Withheld)

It was in my mind for sometimes that I talked to you. I am writing a biography about Connie and bringing out our love destiny, true love, and love quotes from the world's scholars-' going back 520BC, painful end, my suffering, her education, reading, love for world travel, the house was her life, best restaurants, and food, our experience of travel, some true episode, some of her best things she always remembers, her role as a wife, best friend, sister and a mother with evidence of this written in the Indian century ago books with proof, a message from Gandhi, Dr. Nelson Mandela, Dr. Martin Luther King, Jr., our bad relationship with her family and nephews and nieces. However, she was the best aunt of their and how spoiled they were due to their rich and greedy mother. Some of their experiences with her are the Broadway shows, Las Vegas show, Mozart and Vienna and her character, her charity and belief in ethics, honest living, no lies, her contributions in exposing USA culture 41 years ago, and so many things under different headings, etc. I was wondering if you know someone who can proofread and edit the and just a second eye. I have great respect for you, and Connie was Crazy for your intelligence and personality and being a team player. So frankly, let me know. Hope you are doing well. It is 7 AM morning. People are going to work, and I am going to sleep. How life has changed for me without Connie, who meant a world for me, and I am truly living in pain and the trauma and, in my opinion, Medical malpractice and conspiracy which killed her. I will not rest until I find someone for fighting, as many attorneys have refused to take the case, and I would keep trying. I have informed the FBI and Senator. I have recorded 32 minutes of videos and 6 minutes and five videos showing negligence while alive and how much I fought with these doctors and was like a great tiger. God gave me the strength, and again a second time, they did something behind my back when I was just gone for one hour; otherwise, I was in the hospital from 20 to 28 had lived on 3 -4 hours' sleep. I don't know how I was able to do all that? More later.

Thanks.
Pradeep.

(Name Withheld)

Trust you and your family are doing well. I also hope your knee is better and better and better. I am doing well with my family and family to the market and to pass the time. I do go to the gym for one hour, as there is no indoor swimming pool. I am also getting pain in my kegs which started on May 22, and when I came from India on July 23, I saw a few doctors and went for physical therapy. How are everything in the building and our apartment? Connie always remains in my heart and soul all the time, and I can't believe that she is not more with me. I would never- never be able to forget Connie, who was my world and precious Diamond. I am writing a biography, but it has been slow, but I will spend four-five hours daily. I was writing the whole day sometimes till 6 AM in the USA. I have to proofread and edit again and again. Please be in touch.

Pradeep

Dear

Trust you are doing well. My name is Pradeep Berry, and I am the husband of my darling wife and best friend Constance Berry—(Constance Fuller before marriage), a graduate of Carleton College in Minnesota and University of Michigan, in 1960- 61. Constance and I were married for over 40 years. We were two bodies and one soul. We had been getting emails from the University of Michigan for 40 plus years and have taken many trips with the University of Michigan Alumni. To name some, Crotona and Tuscany in Italy, Ireland, Budapest to Amsterdam and Ryan. Later, we cruised with Vantage to Norwegian, and Europe, etc. It breaks my heart and soul to inform you and the university that CONNIE- my world expires unexpectedly, in my opinion, due to the negligence of the Doctors in North share health care in Evanston, Illinois, on the 28th of February, 2015. It was Mayo Clinic in Rochester, on November, 2nd 2014, that detected her case as Palliative care for my precious gold. Later, after many painful episodes and series of traumatic things She and later myself went through, I think every movement of my day.,

I lost my battle and saw my wife taking her last four breaths, and I could not do anything. I have lost my life and don't think I would do anything, including travel, dining, symphony, Broadway Shows, Oscar-winning movies, to name some. Finally, I would like to be connected with the University of Michigan. She left money for Carleton and the University of Michigan. I would like to continue sending some small donations. I had left a very high-powered senior management position in 2006 for any darling and never looked back. Connie wanted to enjoy and travel more and more. We truly enjoyed whatever Connie wanted. Having said all that, we worked and traveled to the USA, India, and Europe, Alaskan cruise and Caribbean Cruise, and other countries before. In our 40 years of marriage, we were both extremely happy. I wrote long as a part of the tribute to Connie. Thanks. Pradeep Berry.

Thank you, Mr. Berry, for the email and information. I have made progress on reviewing the records and expect to be finished by the end of the week and will reach out to you then. Please feel free to provide me with any additional information in the interim. Thanks again.

I miss all but would not go and remember that Connie is not with me physically with pain. I would put all in her biography, including the following... Seven trips to India and then our 10,000 years civilization, Lord Krishna, Chanukah in 520 BC, Egypt, mummies, many world scholars, Nelson Mandela, Gandhi, Dr. Martin Luther King, Jr., Mayo Clinic, her favorite music, our happiness- two bodies and one soul. Her clothing, her shoes, her walker, oxygen, her house, I want spotless. I am going to have a cleaning girl for here hours weekly for cleaning. I want to do things that used to make Connie happy, but happy, her plants, her commentary. I go every week or twice.

Mr.:

I want to apologize for writing again. I forgot a few things; perhaps you have already read and listened through the voice mail. Please think like a Judge or Defense Lawyer. The doctor ruined Constance's case and handed it over on November 25, at 6.30, when he left the message on our voice mail. I still have the same message saying he has been discussing the case with MC. I am going to give the case to Breast cancer and specialist Dr. in the same building, why he was trying to see if he would like to talk to me and why he was there in intensive care with 4 days before when the other doctors assured me that they would be extremely helpful to Constance with her in Palliative care and Constance Berry would be fine and after we have stabilized for 2 I day's and she would be fine. Later they all joined hands with B, who ruined Constance's case, and finally to k her tubes in my absence and without my permission? .and my wife died the most same night. Please seriously think over this point. Regards. Pradeep Berry

(Name withheld)... Thanks for your kind words of wisdom and prompt response. I wrote for 27th because Krishna's birthday is on the 26th, and she was keen. However, Mona decided that they could have a party on the 10 and she has no problem if I leave on the 12th. I have confirmed seats on the 12th and can change them for the 27th. I am not worried about Christmas, and I would not mind being alone. After all, I have to come either 12th or 27th regardless. I miss Connie's empty room and her cemetery and my home. I am not doing a lot, even if I am busy with kids and in the market.

Still, I am not in a mood. I didn't want to go to two days function of my half-brother. Connie had told me that I should not go for that marriage, as my half-brother cheated my brother and me. I would never go again to Connie Darling's wishes. Some family is upset about it that I didn't go. But I don't care, Connie Darling's words I can't compromise. That would be an extremely powerful hurting, too, Connie, if I did that. Weather, I would have to bear on the 12 or 27th. Again, I would not feel lonely during holidays. I am lonely to some extent here too. I am writing a biography, and I have to find a proofreader and edit work. I would be happy if you desire to do. I don't want to hurt you, but I definitely would like to pay for that. I mean that extremely strong about it. Please don't get me wrong, nor please feel hurt for that. I might have 200 pages. I have to edit and proofread, and then I would have to get a second person—maybe one or two months. I didn't get a whole lot chance to do here due to the other things"""" like going out with my brother and talking with my family and kids. After all, they want me to spend time with them. Thanks for your kind words and phrases, and time.

Regards.
Pradeep

(Name withheld).

It is 6 AM, and I was busy, so that I would be brief. Mary, if I come on the 27 December rather 12th December. Would there be any problem? Although I sometimes don't think I can stay longer than 12th

(Name withheld). To
Today at 9:07 AM

Thanks for your kind words of wisdom and prompt response. I wrote for 27th because Krishna's birthday is on the 26th, and she was keen. However, Mona decided that they could have a party. Your coming home on the 27th doesn't affect me. The weather here turned snowy and very cold these last two days. It's supposed to warm up for Thanksgiving.

    It's such a shock to leave warm weather and walk off the plane into drifts of snow! Perhaps you should research what the weather will be like in this area for the winter. At the same time, you will get an idea of what the weather will be like when your plane arrives here.

For no other reason, you can escape bad weather for those two extra weeks. Winter is long and depressing here.

(Name withheld).

p.s. I just realized, Pradeep, Christmas here will be very lonely for you. Even if you are not in the mood for Christmas, if you are here alone, you will feel all the gaiety and joy around you of other families and on the TV shows blasting Christmas music. I never tell people what to do, Pradeep, so, surprisingly, I'm going to say this: You should return on the 27th and remain there for the holidays. Oh, I just realized—perhaps a trip will be difficult to plan if people are coming and going on flights for Christmas the 25th and then again for New Year's Day. That's a hectic time for travel. You need to research this also.

(Name withheld).

It is 6 AM, and I was busy, so I would be brief, if I come on the 27 December rather 12th December. Would there be any problem? Although I sometimes don't think I can stay longer than the 12th, I miss Connie and the house and everything. But still, I thought if you have any questions or suggestions. In a way, 27th looks long compared to the 12th of December, and I may stick to the 12th. However, I hope you are doing well and good luck with your own home and family and your health. Thanks. Pradeep Enjoy the remainder of your stay, Pradeep. I assume you don't have any holiday in India on our Thanksgiving Day (11/26), which pertains to a part of the history of America. It must be difficult having "a foot in two countries."

Thanks for your reply and its contents. Regarding Thanksgiving, you are right; India never celebrates, nor do many people know about it. Thanksgiving was an extremely important part of my 41 years of marriage with Connie. It was so great. Connie and I always celebrated every year. It was great-but great. Practically, every year Connie used to have Thanksgiving and Easter each year with great style, silver plates, cranberry sauce, mashed potatoes, broccoli, rice, snacks of many kinds, turkey filling on the barbeque, drinks, three kinds of desserts- Banana Cream

Pie, Pumpkin pie and nutmeg pie (special only on Thanksgiving). Connie used to make everything from scratch and just perfect and absolutely selective. There used to be over 20, so evil but evil. Connie took a loan from the bank, and we were paying the mortgages. In 2002, Connie got cancer, and I am sure those evils put an evil eye on Connie. After that, we went to people, including her parents, her brother's family, and his in-laws. That was, I would say, were golden days. I used to help Connie and the whole table set up, wine, whiskey, snack food -you name, it was there. The same at Easter. It all was when we were on the fourth floor- two bedrooms- where Cindy and Tara live. I know we were happy when we moved to our current unit in 2001, we were overjoyed, and Connie did an excellent job renovating and furniture. I told Connie, bluntly, that when her brother and sister-in-law came to see the house-(Connie invited them and the family). Mary, I immediately told Connie that her brother and sister-in-law were jealous, and I hope these devils have not put evil eye as they were so evil. , They thought, how can we afford a bigger unit, and Connie's mother must have given her money. Those evil people were at her brother's house for Christmas and only two times for thanksgiving. Later, we started going out to Prairie Grass in Northbrook, and three-four times we took Sylvia. Prairie Grass has an excellent thanksgiving special- a little expensive. We were only invited for Christmas when it was a gift time and for two days in their Green Lake big house in summer. In January 2011, we bought the garage from Barbara White's brother, after she died, as he was poor and immediately agreed to sell. He had bad relations with Barbara, but, somehow, he took the power of attorney of Barbara White from Barbara's father and put his name too. It was alright for us, and we were happy to have a garage and especially for Connie. I had promised Connie, I would make sure you have a garage, and we were looking for different houses to move from 1310 to have a garage. But my words came true, and we got the garage. After returning from Sanibel in 2012 and in August 2012, we bought a new car, and a garage was there, Connie's Toyota Camry. I started renting from Phyllis. After buying the car, we went to her niece's house in Wauconda- near Libertyville and the jealousy and greed they showed—I was mad and told Connie these evils were begging for our first new Lexus- first-time (we bought in 41 years) as we preferred to travel. Her brother has so many Lexus and whatnot, but these rascals could not stand that. We bought a garage, now Lexus, and right after,

Connie started going down. Connie drove Lexus for fifteen minutes when we went to Lake Geneva to try Lexus. That upset me like hell as these rascals, Dracula's evil souls, put an evil eye on my Connie. They never came to see us, and when Connie's mother was sick, Connie went through hell, and I quit my high-paid position in 2005 to be with Connie and look after her and her mother out of town. Her siblings and family were not on talking terms, and I avoided them and encouraged Connie. I would do anything to make her happy.After Connie's mother died in August 2006, Connie and I arranged all the last rights, and Connie paid every dime. Her sibling and family did not spend a dime, nor did any of them speak at the time of her chapel of peace, except myself, and Connie was very happy that I gave wonderful tributes to her mother. But for years, she lived in pain that these siblings had nothing to say about their mother and grandmother who did so much, loved and loved them more than Connie's mother loved us. Her siblings, kids, spouses, grandkids were like wooden statues. Connie was in Pain and Pain for years. I bet it was nothing but great, and Connie and I used to work day and nights and weeks to do a perfect job. I miss Connie, Thanksgiving, and now Christmas regardless of where I am, and I would live in pain when I think of these two holidays. I would enjoy in my house alone with her pictures and candles and go to the cemetery--------- Mona gave that advice to me today. Mary, I must say that on Thanksgiving and Christmas, I was always with Connie. Last Thanksgiving, I made a good dinner for her at home. Christmas I bought some nice things and cakes etc. NO matter what it was, but being with Connie every moment in her room, movie watching reading, and just being with her -just next to her- next to her in the car, next to sit in the kitchen, taking her to the hospital, carrying her on the wheelchair, taking her wheelchair to the bathroom in the hospital, giving a shower to Connie, taking her to her room, filling her water in the morning, afternoon and at night, her green glass on the kitchen table—you can see water there and in her room, in the bedroom which I am still doing. You would keep on doing and praying her three-four times, sleeping with her pictures in my home in India in my bedroom, full of her pictures everywhere and going anywhere with her pictures in my pocket, her ashes still in our house in urns, (Though according to Hindu religion, Ashes have to disbursed, I still took from the Liz at the funeral home and got two beautiful urns, and they are in our house. I pray to them. I feel closer but live in pain but pain.

I am writing all the family episodes, hospitals, our love, our education, her qualities, her love for cooking, dining, traveling, books, magazines, charity, Sanibel, all week. I have cut down on going out, not traveling, not spending on clothes. Anything Connie wanted, I would do that but would live very simply. Now Connie is gone, and that is how I am going to go through my life. The most difficult period and painful part of my life- MY CONNIE

Thanks for your nice compliments about our marriage and, most importantly, Connie Darling. I truly can't describe Connie's beauties along with all the great qualities, knowledge, responsible in every aspect. I can't find any fault whatsoever. "People who think they knew Connie did not know Connie. People, who knew, can't describe Connie. This quote would be in my book. Thanksgiving and Christmas were extremely important in our lives, and so were Easter and many other things. Now, I would not enjoy any of these things, regardless, Mary, anyone tells me. Marriage is never going to happen, and no way I can think of that. Connie was Connie. I would marry any day if God gave me my Connie Darling, and I would be more than a king. It would end all my sorrows. But I can't have that unless God personally makes it happen. I know I am dreaming, but sometimes dreams and God's blessing seeing the devotion can happen. It may not be Connie Darling as a wife, sister, mother, and father. I would accept her in any form, as long as Her Face and voice and qualities what she had. I think my mind is that I want to be there on Christmas and would put flowers on her cemetery as I did before one day before going to India and it was pitch dark at 6.30, but I managed with darkness and cell phone battery- Flesh- You can download free from Google, and you would like it. They are great. Later, I brought the car and turned on the lights. Peace of mind and sadness, and that is what I get, but I still like to go for my happiness. Connie's brother and his whole family of 16 people have never visited Connie's parents' cemetery next to Connie Darling. Pradeep Berry is the only person Connie can visit, which I would like to do with great pleasure and happiness. I become upset if I don't go there once or twice a week. You give me great advice about getting over this most painful thing of my life, but I may not be able to treat the problem soon. I showed your email to

Sincerely,
Pradeep

ELEGIAC PAEAN

Thanks for your nice compliments about our marriage and, most importantly, Connie Darling. I truly can't describe Connie's beauties and all the great qualities, knowledge, and responsibility in every aspect. I can't find any fault whatsoever. "People, who think, they knew Connie, did not know Connie. People, who knew, can't describe Connie". This quote would be in my book. Thanksgiving and Christmas were extremely important in our lives, and so were Easter and many other things. Now, I would not enjoy any of these things, regardless, Mary, anyone tells me. Marriage is never going to happen, and no way I can think of that. Connie was Connie. If God gives me my Connie Darling, I would Mary any day, and I would be more than a king. It would end all my sorrows. But I can't have that unless God personally makes it happen. I know I am dreaming, but sometimes dreams and God's blessing seeing the devotion can happen. It may not be Connie Darling as a wife, sister, mother, and father. I would accept her in any form, as long as Her Face and voice and qualities what she had. I think my mind is that I want to be there on Christmas and would put flowers on her cemetery as I did before one day before going to India and it was pitch dark at 6.30, but I managed with darkness and cell phone battery- Flesh- You can download free from Google, and you would like it. They are great. Later, I brought the car and turned on the lights. Peace of mind and sadness, and that is what I get, but I still like to go for my happiness. Connie's brother and his whole family of 16 people have never visited Connie's parents' cemetery next to Connie Darling. Pradeep Berry is the only person Connie can visit, which I would like to do with great pleasure and happiness. I become upset if I don't go there once or twice a week. You give me great advice about getting over this most painful thing of my life, but I may not be able to treat the problem soon. I showed you your email too. Sincerely, Pradeep, Pradeep. Very few people have those types of memories. So many couples struggle with their partner and marriage. You were both so blessed, Pradeep. Such a wonderful life.

(Name Withheld)

What an awful story about Connie's family. She would tell me parts of the conflict, but I never heard the stories of what happened when they had her mother move out and all the rest. No, I don't believe in the evil eye causing harm to Pradeep, but you are entitled to believe whatever you or your spiritual beliefs teach. When I was little, my grandmother and father (both from Calabria, Italy) used to talk about the evil eye and stories from Italy. The stories would scare me because I was so little—and my mother would tell my father to stop scaring the children. We didn't have TV, so his occasional storytelling would be our entertainment. However, it would be before bedtime, and we would have bad dreams.

I envy Connie her skills. I was never a great cook or hostess, although I did have family over when the kids were being raised, and my husband was alive. It was a struggle for me—even to this day. I burn things and am a bundle of nerves. You were blessed to have Connie create such a beautiful ambiance for those times.

Please don't feel bad that you gave me much of the story at length—it is so healthy to vent and let things out, Pradeep. You painted a beautiful picture of all Connie created in your lives. Keep hope within you that when your grief lifts, good things may come to you. Don't say no because I have seen it in my own personal family's lives. I will say good night, Pradeep.

Pradeep -

Thanks again for calling last week, and it was great to hear from you. I'm so happy that you and Connie are doing well and, in particular, that you're now engaged with teaching and writing. And happy belated 70th birthday last July 29th!

I'll be happy to share my thoughts and observations regarding yourself and Connie as you requested; please also let me know more specifically what might be helpful. What I've largely observed is that you've been an exceptionally devoted and close couple. This is all the more remarkable with you being from India and not having your immediate family here, your heavy job-related travel commitments, and Connie's health issues in more recent years. But you've managed to maintain a close and enduring bond through it all for 30+ years. Altogether, your closeness as a couple is what I aspire to for myself.

I've been most recently busy working as a Credit and Portfolio Manager in Commercial Lending at a $700 million NY-based thrift headquartered in the Bronx. Historically, the bank has been principally engaged in residential and commercial mortgages but was recently expanded into commercial lending, including ABL and SBA loans. I've been pleased to continue to work in banking and advance my career here in NY, especially since I turn 60 in January, and it's getting harder as one gets older. And as I've said, as much as I miss seeing people such as yourself in Chicago to whom I was close, I've benefited on balance being where I have better opportunities.

The biggest event in my life is meeting and marrying on Saturday, November 26th, in Great Neck, NY, a special woman, Karen Ferrare. Karen is an attorney who was born in Brooklyn and grew up in Long Island. Karen is previously married with no children. This will be my third and final wedding in life and my final shot at complete happiness. We've been together for over a year and have shared an apartment on Manhattan's UES since early June. You and Connie are cordially invited, and please give me your address for an invitation. Please also feel free to visit us at any time. As you know, there's always so much to do and see in the Big Apple.

I plan on coming back to Chicago next spring but have too much otherwise going on till then. In the meantime, let's be sure to continue to stay in touch, and I hope to see you in November for my wedding.

Ed Muller—Senior VP Banking New York

Dear Ed,

I am very great full to you for your sincere compliments, and I know you mean this. I have known you since 1993, and we have been very close friends. The time we spent at ABL consulting was the one the imaging times. Connie is Connie. I truly mean that. I have never seen another person like Connie, nor do I would ever. I am writing this from the core of my heart. MY CONNIE is special. You recall going with Connie and me to Monticello, Indiana, for the(Name withheld) company in my white Toyota car in 1995 or 1994. A small town and I recall you going to the library there. How much love was developed with Victoria and how much fun was that, and the time you came to Sanibel, we took you to Captiva and had grouper fish, fresh lemon pie, the beautiful drive, and our two-bedroom Condominium. We asked you to stay with us, but you had to go to work on Monday. Those memories are good and bad, but the reality is there. People avoid good or bad past, but it is nice to remember to share with those people. I am going to thank you again, and Connie is very appreciative of what we are doing. Thanks for the nice letter. Best wishes to you and Karen. I am sure you would find yourself in the world of joy with Karen. Best wishes. For whomsoever, this note is for.

I have had the great good fortune to have maintained a close and valued friendship with Pradeep for over twenty years. During this time, he has been a loyal and devoted friend for whom anyone could wish.

I can honestly say and truthfully assert that I have never known as close and devoted a couple as Pradeep and Connie. Their abiding love and complete dedication have been abundantly evident. This is particularly noteworthy, given Connie's health issues in recent years. I'll be completely happy if I even come close to attaining this level of dedication that one can have as a couple in my impending marriage.

Ed Muller. Vice President -- Banking

In memory of Connie, I am giving my tributes to a great Piano teacher,
Mildred Honor:

"I am a former elementary school music teacher from Des Moines, Iowa. This is a true story and a beautiful and touching story of love and perseverance. Well worth reading. At the prodding of my friends, I am writing this story. My name is Mildred Honor, and I am a former elementary school music teacher from Des Moines, Iowa. I have always supplemented my income by teaching piano lessons—something I have done for over 30 years. During those years, I found that children have many levels of musical ability, and even though I have never had the pleasure of having a prodigy, I have taught some very talented students. However, I have also had my share of what I call 'musically challenged' pupils—one such pupil being Robby. Robby was 11 years old when his mother (a single mom) dropped him off for his first piano lesson. I prefer that students (especially boys) begin at an earlier age, which I explained to Robby. But Robby said that it had always been his mother's dream to hear him play the piano, so I took him as a student. Well, Robby began his piano lessons, and from the beginning, I thought it was a hopeless endeavor. As much as

Robby tried, he lacked the sense of tone and basic rhythm needed to excel. But he dutifully reviewed his scales and some elementary piano pieces that I require all my students to learn. Over the months, he tried and tried while I listened and cringed and tried to encourage him. At the end of each weekly lesson, he would always say, 'My mom's going to hear me play someday. But to me, it seemed hopeless; he just did not have any inborn ability. I only knew his mother from a distance as she dropped Robby off or waited in her aged car to pick him up. She always waved and smiled but never dropped in.

Then one day, Robby stopped coming for his lessons. I thought about calling him but assumed that he had decided to pursue something else because of his lack of ability. I was also glad that he had stopped coming—he was a bad advertisement for my teaching! Several weeks later, I mailed a flyer recital to the students' homes. To my surprise, Robby (who had received a flyer) asked me if he could be in the recital. I told him that the recital was for current pupils and did not qualify because he had dropped out. He told me that his mother had been sick and unable to take him to his piano lessons but that he had been practicing. 'Please, Miss Honor, I've just got to play,' he insisted. I don't know what led me to allow him to play in the recital—perhaps it was his insistence or something inside of me saying that it would be all right. The recital night came, and the high school gymnasium was packed with parents, relatives, and friends. I put Robby last in the program, just before I came up and thanked all the students and played a finishing piece. I thought that any damage he might do would come at the end of the program, and I could always salvage his poor performance through my 'curtain closer'. Well, the recital went off without a hitch, the students had been practicing, and it showed. Then Robby came upon the stage. His clothes were wrinkled, and his hair looked as though he had run an egg beater through it. 'Why wasn't he dressed up like the other students?' I thought. 'Why didn't his mother at least make him comb his hair for this special night?'

Robby pulled out the piano bench, and I was surprised when he announced that he had chosen to play Mozart's Concerto No. 21 in C Major. I was not prepared for what I heard next. His fingers were light on the keys; they even danced nimbly on the ivories. He went from pianissimo to fortissimo, from allegro to virtuoso; his speeded chords that Mozart demands were magnificent! Never had I heard Mozart played so well by anyone his age. After six and a half minutes, he ended in a grand crescendo, and everyone was on their feet in wild applause! Overcome, and in tears, I ran up on stage and put my arms around Robby in joy.

"I have never heard you play like that Robby, how did you do it?" Through the microphone, Robby explained: 'Well, Miss Honor... remember I told you that my mom was sick? Well, she had cancer and passed away this morning. And well...she was born deaf, so tonight was the first time she had ever heard me play, and I wanted to make it special.' There wasn't a dry eye in the house that evening. As the people from Social Services led Robby from the stage to be placed into foster care, I noticed that even their eyes were red and puffy. I thought to myself then how much richer my life had been for taking Robby as my pupil. No, I have never had a prodigy, but I became a prodigy...of Robby that night. He was the teacher, and I was the pupil, for he had taught me the meaning of perseverance and love and believing in yourself, and maybe even taking a chance on someone, and you didn't know why.

Robby was killed years later in the senseless bombing of the Alfred P. Murray Federal Building in Oklahoma City in April 1995. Connie was right. Now I am facing my choice of isolated life as I am going through the pain of Connie. But with her watching over me, going to her cemetery regularly gives me a big boost and pain. I ask at the cemetery, "Connie, please give me the strength so that I can get us justice for the medical negligence you suffered."My Connie would never have requested a DNR order and wanted full code, and she told me this by body language after her cardiac arrest. The delay before she got CPR was the worst thing I saw, and later on, the afternoon of the 27th of February, when I made the sin of leaving her room for one hour, the medical staff did what they wanted to save themselves from their negligence. I pray that I get justice, otherwise in the court of the Lord, the Supreme Power of this world God, they will be punished millions of times over until they pay their dues. It will happen. Connie's last wishes and her soul and my destroyed life and the curses from the core of my heart will never forgive them. That is how we feel. Many people have been very cruel.

A story of a writer who wanted respect and recognition of his work but later realized that he is a candle that will have to burn, giving light to others. This writer cum director, and producer was Guru Dutt in Indian history.

CONSTANCE ANN BERRY
BEST FRIEND & MOST PRECIOUS DARLING
WIFE OF 40 YEARS OF PRADEEP BERRY

I was thinking and thinking and moved around and saw several other stones which had the same color and design as other people's families, and they had a beloved son of XYZ—beloved wife and father or husband of XYZ.

I was thinking of a song by Cliff Richard, who was born in Lucknow, UP state in India. He used to come to India around I had finished high school and was sixteen years old. My brother and our very close friends who liked music listened to his concerts and saw the hit movies, "Bachelor Boy" and "Summer Holiday." These were hit movies in 1963 and 1964. I was a good singer, and my brother and I sang these songs on the stage. Here are the lyrics of those two songs:

BACHELOR BOY.

Performed by Cliff Richard
"Bachelor Boy"

When I was young, my father said,
"Son, I've got something to say."
And what he told me I'll never forget until my dying day.

[Chorus 1:]

He said, "Son, you'll be a bachelor boy
And that's the way to stay.
Son, you'll be a bachelor boy until your dying day."

When I was sixteen, I fell in love
With a girl as sweet as can be.
But I remembered just in time what my daddy said to me.

[Chorus 1]

As time goes by, I probably will meet a girl and fall in love.
Then, I'll get married, have A-wife and A-child
And they'll be my turtle dove.

[Chorus 2:]

But until then, I'll be a bachelor boy
and that's the way I'll stay-yay-yay,
Happy to be a bachelor boy until my dying day.
Yeah, I'll be a bachelor boy
and that's the way I'll stay-yay-yay,
Happy to be a bachelor boy until my dying day.

Connie always followed the great message of Gandhi, father of the nation of India, that we should be humble and contribute either money or time to teach and give free education to the unprivileged or the weaker section of the community. Connie always wanted to see the weaker section progress and devoted time for teaching and giving her research papers to students all over to read and gain knowledge to advance their careers. Her habit of reading and writing during work and after teaching and coming home to be a great housewife kept her busy most of the time. She was extremely productive every minute of her time for most of our marriage. Yes, she loved going out to social events, traveling, attending functions, marriages, birthdays, and dancing, and she was full of joy and fun. We enjoyed a few soft drinks. I was a scotch lover, and she joined me to keep me a company to have two drinks more or less daily with me. When I quit drinking 26 years ago, it was her happiness that we could enjoy our dinner around 6 P.M. and have the whole evening to work and study books, journals, and papers or watch award-winning films and intellectual shows. She chose the movies we would watch in theaters and on Netflix. I cannot even think of that anymore. All of those shows- whether on Broadway or TV- have been a thing of the past for me since February 28, 2015. I now watch the news and a few programs like 20/20 or Jimmy Fallon and Seth Meyers, but that, too, is to occupy my mind. I turn on the TV, but these programs take me back to Connie, and I am watching, but in truth, I am remembering Connie, and then I doze off in her memories and suddenly realize that if I was watching Connie's life, with me. It is a daily routine. No matter what

ELEGIAC PAEAN

I am doing, my mind is half on my work and half on Connie. Today, June 7th, it is 2:15 A.M., and I am writing, but 90% of my mind is on Connie, and I feel I want to write non-stop for 48 hours; however, I think of my sleep and health, and I have to force myself to stop writing and sleep. I wish God would give me 28 hours to a day instead of 24.

In memory of Connie, I want to share a true episode that happened over 5,000 years back in India during the time of Lord Rama, who was an incarnation of Lord Vishnu. Rama, his wife Sita, and younger brother Laxman were exiled to the jungles for fourteen years on their stepmother, who wanted her son to take the throne. However, after their exile, her son Bharat also went into exile with Rama. When Rama returned, his younger brother Shatrugan-ji handled the kingdom without sitting on Rama's throne or wearing his crown for fourteen years. This is celebrated in the greatest festival of Diwali, Deepawali, in memory of the return of Lord Rama. During that time, Lord Rama had to fight with one of the greatest scholars in Indian history, King Ravana, who had devoted his life to praying to Lord Shiva and was extremely powerful and wise, with the intelligence of ten human beings. King Ravana was destroyed and was granted that he could only be killed by an arrow in his stomach, as his wife had made him drink Amrit (an antidote) in his sleep, so he did not know if anyone could ever kill him. Ravana's wife was scared that if Ravana found out he had Amrit in his stomach, he would destroy the world. Only his wife and one of his brothers, Vibushan, knew this. His family begged Ravana not to fight with Lord Rama and not to abduct Sita. He abducted Sita to see the true power of Rama. When Ravana disregarded their pleas, his brother Vibushan, a secret follower of Rama, told Rama how Ravana could be killed. During the battle between Lord Rama and Ravana, Lord Rama shot an arrow into Ravana's stomach to bleed the Amrit out of his body, and he died.

Lord Rama asked his brother Laxman to go to the dying Ravana and request that he share his knowledge before dying. Laxman-ji went to Ravana and asked him to share his knowledge, but Ravana refused because Laxman had approached his head rather than his feet. Finally, Lord Rama went to Ravana's feet and asked, "Oh King Ravana, please do not take all of your knowledge away. Please share some knowledge before you die. You were my enemy before, but now I have killed you. You are not my enemy. Please consider me your disciple and share your knowledge." Ravana said,

"I wish I was your teacher and had not kidnapped your wife. I wish instead I would have acted as your teacher." He further narrated that humans have a tendency to do bad things first and good things later. Please do not postpone good things. Postpone bad things. We should withhold our ego and act to help humanity. Immediately after that, King Ravana died. Even today, many people in India worship King Ravana or Shanni Maharajah each Saturday, and people put coins. The devotees and some beggars come with mustard oil in a big pot and ask people to see their shadow.

This is very important in my life, especially when Connie was sick and a victim of her doctors' conspiracy. I prayed and prayed to both Rama and King Ravana to save Connie from her cardiac arrest and that someone should appear in the form of Lord Rama or King Ravana to save my Connie, and I was sure the same episode of Amrit in the form of oxygen or anything would save Connie. But the conspiracy of the doctors was so strong that my prayers and Amrit became dangerous, and Connie was gone. I was praying to both the lords, all the prayers of our ancestors, praying along with our friend's wife, and nothing happened. Connie took her last breath while I touched her hands and feet- she died in my presence. I have a video, and during her cremation I can be seen touching her feet and asking for forgiveness and kissing her forehead while she was dying- feet and head, feet and head. But I lost my battle like Ravana, as the conspiracy was stronger with three doctors and staff. I wish I had not gone that sixty minutes and only had to face one doctor than the 10 medical staff I faced. No one can win 10 against 1. That is what I saw and faced. I wish I had called many friends to be with me, but I was totally absorbed, and my mind was blocked. Now I think I wish I had called certain extremely close friends, but my innocent bad karmas were stronger than my good karmas. One dirty fish spoils the whole pool.

I pray that as long as I am alive as Connie has gone, I cannot ask anyone to bring her back. There must have been some lack of devotion some years ago which I cannot believe that the 60 minutes was my biggest mistake and that 60 minutes would become the biggest loss of my life and death by losing Connie, and I would haunt me each second of my life even if I am busy with work. 60 minutes absence and 60 Minutes was my favorite program from 6 P.M. to 7 P.M. on Sundays, which resulted from my bad karmas, and I will regret it as long as I live. People think, and friends and strangers alike tell me that I should concentrate on the good times of our 40 years of marriage and love, but I cannot accept that. Never. I keep thinking and will continue thinking as long as I live: why did I leave her with good faith on the assertion of the hospital staff that I could be gone for an hour. That absence of 60 minutes will never go away from my life; I should never have gone. Never. That 60-minute absence will haunt me throughout my life.

Her Death took away all the knowledge. I am hoping that MY CONNIE will be with me in our next life. That hope will continue to keep me positive and will keep me doing humanitarian deeds. Thanks, Connie, for all you did for me, and I have no words to thank and thank you. You are the one you are the one who made my career and my success in the USA. Please, I pray your soul rest in peace.

Loving left alone husband,
Pradeep Berry

A few more great messages in memory of MY CONNIE.

These messages are from CHANKYA NEETI (Chankya's Philosophy).

"A wise person will come to grief if he does the unwise acts of giving advice to a foolish pupil, looking after a woman of loose character and keeping the company of a sad one who has lost his fortune" quote 4, page 8.

"It is living death to stay in a house where there is an evil-natured, badmouthing woman of low morals. Or a cunning and deceitful friend, or an impolite talkative servant, or possibility of the presence of a snake" quote 5, page 9.

"If you were to choose between an evil person and a snake to keep company with, opt for the snake. Because a snake will bite only in self-defense, but an evil person can put a bite for any reason and any time or always" page 31.

"Skill is man's friend in a foreign land. A good-natured wife is the man's friend. Medicine is a sick man's friend, and charitable deeds are one's only friend after death" quote 15 page 63.

In my opinion, quote 3 is absolutely true. Quote, three represents Connie's brother's wife. That was the major factor between Connie and her brothers' artificial love inside an evil controlling power in the whole family of their four grown-up kids, their spouses and children, and grandchildren. I already mentioned that Connie's one real brother never came for Connie's sickness, death, cremation and ashes services, memorial, and till today, August 4, 2016. Neither have their grown-up children and their children. Not even a telephone call or even a card- nothing. Connie was a lovely aunt, and she left some money for her one nephew and three nieces. What a shame, the 42 years of relations we had are over. They are ruined because of one Evil, per Chankya.

Quote 4 is 100% true for Connie, who lived honestly, did good deeds, was self-made, and was the best wife I can think of her and her deeds even after death are helping many charities, students, cancer patients, blind school and her greatness to still leave a big chunk for her nephew and nieces. If they those nephew and nieces and parents and evil wife have any god in their heart and theses church-going people who are wealthy, arrogant, always treated Connie and Pradeep they are above and in our lifetime of 42 years never wanted to go for a trip—to Australia, Europe, Alaska and practically one trip to different parts of the world, in spite of personally asking that we too are travelers and sometimes go. His answer came from his sweet wife for him, but who was devious inside. He said. "Pradeep, we are busy for the next ten years," 26 years ago. In 1992, He told me at the restaurant when asked to join us for a trip. He said, "Pradeep, we are busy for the next 25 years." It was the most hurtful thing one could say to his biological sister's husband. That was the day Connie and I took the oath. I would never ask him or any of them to join us. We were only a token of the family during gifts time, Christmas and Thanksgiving. I strongly recommend and suggest "My readers never depend upon anyone." Children and brothers change once they have their own families. That childhood love is practically over, and then if there is an inheritance from the parents, family ties may become a war or maybe a civil war in the family. That is what I saw in my Berry family, which was painful.

Once again, the moment Connie and Pradeep met, my childhood tragedy vanished, and I no longer cared. The worst and the most devastating thing I saw was CONNIE's Sickness, and her death was I smashed and lost everything. Today, August 4th, 2016, I still feel it flying back to Evanston from Delhi after spending five weeks. I know Connie, and her house and her cemetery are very lonely, and I am lonely without Connie and her house. However, I get maximum happiness when I go back or stay in our home in Nirvana. However, Connie's loss has made me very bitter, as I had forgotten until now. I am happy not to even ask for my inheritance. Her Commentary visit is a peace of mind but full hidden pain in every vain of my body in all my body till today and forever.

Everything on earth lives according to the law of nature, and from that law emerges the glory and joy of liberty, but man is denied this fortune because he set a limited and earthly law of his own for the God-given soul. Man built a narrow and painful prison in which he secluded his affections and desires.

(Khalil Gibran)

My Sincere, loving, and heartfelt tributes to my WORLD -- "MY CONNIE." God- or doctors- have taken MY CONNIE, and only God can give me back "MY CONNIE" in this life or the next life. Sometimes I think that the blame is not on God but on the doctors who have taken my wife from me. Those doctors do not have the power to return her to me. Only God can do this. So who will return My Connie to me? Only God.

ALWAYS LOVING HUSBAND AND OUR TRUE LOVE FOR "MY CONNIE" FOREVER –TILL NEXT LIFE

PRADEEP KUMAR BERRY
AUGUST 16, 2016